Spelling Reference
for Business and School

Spelling Reference
for Business and School

JOHN M. DOYLE

Director,
Educational Research and Development
International Correspondence Schools

RITA GOUIN DOYLE

RESTON PUBLISHING COMPANY, INC., Reston, Virginia

A Prentice-Hall Company

Library of Congress Cataloging in Publication Data

Doyle, John M
  Spelling reference for business and school.

   1. English language—Orthography and spelling.
2. English language—Syllabication. I. Doyle, Rita
Gouin, 1931-   joint author. II. Title.
PE1146.D84   428'.1   76-2432
ISBN 0-87909-772-8

10 9 8 7 6 5 4 3 2 1

Printed in the United States of America.

To Rita's mom and dad
who are Memeré and Peperé
to twenty-eight grandchildren

Contents

Preface

Do you refer to a dictionary most often for word meaning or for the correct spelling of a word whose meaning you already know? When this question was asked of some 2,000 randomly selected students and secretaries, roughly eight out of ten replied "for correct spelling." This is our justification for the preparation of this book.

Although the idea of a spelling guide is not new, we believe you will find this one unique. How? Because it is structured both as a *teaching* text and as a reference book. Other books of this type have emphasized what they elect to call "common" words and include the many possible endings of these words, for example: *invent, inventible, invention, inventive, inventively, inventiveness, inventor;* or *entertain, entertained, entertainer, entertaining, entertainingly, entertainingness, entertainment.*

Although this approach does, indeed, provide the correct spelling of a specific form of a given word, does it improve your spelling capability or lessen your dependence on the guide? We believe not. What, then, is the purpose of including such things as spelling rules? Who will make the needed effort to apply these rules? Would you? Probably not.

We, too, have included special sections relating to such things as the basic rules of spelling and compounding. But in Section 1, "The Word List," we enter only what we consider to be the most basic or useful form of a given word. When you are unsure about which suffix to add, spell the word as you think it should be spelled and then refer to Section 2, "The ABCs of Spelling," to see how well (or how poorly) you did. Since the rules of spelling do not cover all possible cases, you may still make a few errors, but your spelling should show marked improvement within a very short period of time. Hopefully, within a matter of three months it will be unnecessary for you to refer to this or any other guide except on rare occasions.

In addition, because the book is intended for use by persons having widely diversified needs, we have included not only "common" words, but also many "uncommon" words relating to such things as medicine, music, chemistry, and biology, to name but a few.

The book may appear to be redundant in the listing of hyphenated expressions, such as *well-balanced, well-behaved, well-being*, and so forth. Since the omission of the hyphen, or the incorrect combining of words, is one of the most frequent errors noted in written correspondence, however, this relatively small amount of redundancy should prove to be beneficial. If you do not find the expression in this guide, or if the rules for compounding words in Section 7 still leave you in doubt, it is very likely that you are dealing with a non-hyphenated expression.

In some instances, we have also included two or three variations of a basic word, for example, using either the suffix *er* or *or*. Once again, the choice of when to include such words has been arbitrary and is based entirely on our own observations of common spelling errors. Remember, there are no such things as absolutely firm spelling rules to guide you in every case. By the same token, there were no firm rules to guide us in making some obviously arbitrary choices of which words to include and which to omit.

In cases where two words are pronounced the same, but have different meanings, an abbreviated definition is given in parentheses following the word. Although these definitions are not formal, they should provide enough guidance to help you select the correct spelling.

The vast majority of single-syllable words have been omitted because they are seldom misspelled; their inclusion would provide doubtful benefit and would only serve to decrease the usefulness of the guide. In those instances when the spelling is uncommon or when two homonyms are often misspelled, however, single-syllable words are included.

In addition to improving your spelling, we hope that the use of this book will also improve your punctuation, capitalization, word division, and word compounding. If it does any one or a combination of those things, our effort, and your own, will be worthwhile.

John M. Doyle

Rita G. Doyle

The
Word
List

A

a-back
a-baft
ab-a-lo-ne
a-ban-don
a-ban-doned
a-base
a-bash
a-bate
a-bate-ment
ab-at-toir
ab-ba-cy
ab-bey
ab-bot
ab-bre-vi-ate
ab-bre-vi-a-tion
ab-di-cate
ab-di-ca-tion
ab-do-men
ab-dom-i-nal
ab-duce
ab-duct
a-beam
ab-er-rant
ab-er-ra-tion
a-bet-tor
a-bey-ance
a-bey-ant
ab-hor
ab-hor-rence
ab-hor-rent
a-bid-ance
a-bide
a-bid-ing
a-bil-i-ty
ab-ject
ab-jur-ation
ab-jure
ab-lac-tate
ab-la-tion
ab-la-tive
a-blaze
a-ble
ab-le-gate

a-bloom
ab-lu-ent
ab-lu-tion
ab-ne-gate
ab-nor-mal
ab-nor-mal-i-ty
ab-nor-mi-ty
a-board
a-bode
a-bol-ish
ab-o-li-tion
a-bom-i-na-ble
a-bom-i-nate
a-bom-i-na-tion
ab-o-rig-i-nal
ab-o-rig-i-ne
a-bort
a-bor-ti-cide
a-bor-tion
a-bor-tion-ist
a-bor-tive
a-bound
a-bout
a-bove-board
a-brade
a-bra-sion
a-bra-sive
a-breast
a-bridge
a-bridg-ment
a-broad
ab-ro-gate
ab-rupt
ab-rup-tion
ab-scess
ab-scis-sa
ab-scis-sion
ab-scond
ab-sence
ab-sent
ab-sen-tee
ab-sent-ly
ab-sinthe

ab-so-lute
ab-so-lute-ly
ab-so-lu-tion
ab-so-lut-ism
ab-sol-u-to-ry
ab-solve
ab-so-nant
ab-sorb
ab-sorbed
ab-sorb-ent
ab-sorb-ing
ab-sorp-tion
ab-sorp-tiv-i-ty
ab-stain
ab-ste-mi-ous
ab-sten-tion
ab-sti-nence
ab-stract
ab-stract-ed
ab-strac-tion
ab-strac-tive
ab-struse
ab-surd
ab-surd-i-ty
a-bun-dance
a-bun-dant
a-buse
a-bu-sive
a-but
a-but-ment
a-but-ter
a-bys-mal
a-byss
a-byss-al
ac-a-dem-ic
as-a-dem-i-cal
a-cad-e-mi-cian
a-cad-e-my
a-can-thoid
a-can-thous
a-cap-pel-la
a-car-pous
ac-cede

ac-cel-er-an-do
ac-cel-er-ant
ac-cel-er-ate
ac-cel-er-a-tion
ac-cel-er-a-tive
ac-cel-er-a-tor
ac-cel-er-om-e-ter
ac-cent
ac-cen-tu-al
ac-cen-tu-ate
ac-cept
ac-cept-a-ble
ac-cept-ance
ac-cep-ta-tion
ac-cept-ed
ac-cess
ac-ces-sa-ry
ac-ces-si-ble
ac-ces-sion
ac-ces-so-ri-al
ac-ces-sory
ac-ci-dent
ac-ci-den-tal
ac-claim
ac-cla-ma-tion
ac-cli-mate
ac-cli-ma-tize
ac-cliv-i-ty
ac-co-lade
ac-com-mo-date
ac-com-mo-da-tion
ac-com-mo-da-tive
ac-com-pa-ni-ment
ac-com-pa-nist
ac-com-pa-ny
ac-com-pa-ny-ist
ac-com-plice
ac-com-plish
ac-com-plished
ac-com-plish-ment
ac-cord
ac-cord-ance
ac-cord-ant
ac-cord-ing
ac-cord-ing-ly

ac-cor-di-on
ac-cost
ac-couche-ment
ac-count
ac-count-a-ble
ac-count-an-cy
ac-count-ing
ac-cou-ple-ment
ac-cou-ter
ac-cou-ter-ments
ac-cred-it
ac-crete
ac-cre-tion
ac-cru-al
ac-crue
ac-cum-bent
ac-cu-mu-late
ac-cu-mu-la-tion
ac-cu-mu-la-tive
ac-cu-mu-la-tor
ac-cu-ra-cy
ac-cu-rate
ac-curs-ed
ac-cu-sa-tion
ac-cu-sa-ti-val
ac-cu-sa-tive
ac-cu-sa-to-ri-al
ac-cu-sa-to-ry
ac-cuse
ac-cus-tom
ac-cus-tomed
a-cen-tric
ac-er-bate
a-cer-bi-ty
ac-er-ose
a-cer-vate
a-ces-cent
ac-e-tal
ac-e-tate
a-ce-tic
a-cet-i-fy
ac-e-tone
ac-e-tous
a-ce-tum
a-cet-y-lene

ache
a-chieve
a-chieve-ment
ach-ro-mat-ic
a-chro-ma-tin
a-chro-ma-tize
a-chro-ma-tous
a-chro-mic
a-cid-ic
a-cid-i-fy
a-cid-i-ty
a-cid-u-late
a-cid-u-lous
ac-i-er-ate
ac-knowl-edge
ac-knowl-edg-ment
ac-me
ac-ne
ac-o-lyte
a-corn
a-cous-tic
a-cous-ti-cian
a-cous-tics
ac-quaint
ac-quaint-ance
ac-quaint-ed
ac-qui-esce
ac-qui-es-cence
ac-qui-es-cent
ac-quire
ac-quire-ment
ac-qui-si-tion
ac-quis-i-tive
ac-quit
ac-quit-tal
ac-quit-tance
a-cre
a-cre-age
ac-rid
ac-ri-mo-ni-ous
ac-ri-mo-ny
ac-ro-bat
ac-ro-bat-ics
ac-ro-lith
a-cron-i-cal

ac-ro-nym
ac-ro-pho-bi-a
a-cross
a-cros-tic
a-cryl-ic
act-a-ble
act-ing
ac-tin-i-um
ac-tion
ac-tion-a-ble
ac-ti-vate
ac-ti-va-tor
ac-tive
ac-tiv-ist
ac-tiv-i-ty
ac-tor
ac-tress
ac-tu-al
ac-tu-al-i-ty
ac-tu-al-ize
ac-tu-al-ly
ac-tu-ar-y
ac-tu-ate
a-cu-i-ty
a-cu-men
a-cu-mi-nate
a-cute
ad-age
a-da-gio
ad-a-mant
ad-a-man-tine
a-dapt
a-dapt-a-ble
ad-ap-ta-tion
a-dapt-er
a-dap-tive
ad-ax-i-al
ad-dend
ad-den-dum
ad-dict
ad-dict-ed
ad-dic-tion
ad-di-tion
ad-di-tion-al
ad-di-tive

ad-dle
ad-dress
ad-dress-ee
ad-dres-so-graph
ad-duce
ad-du-cent
ad-duct
ad-duc-tion
a-demp-tion
ad-e-noid
ad-e-noid-ec-to-my
ad-ept
ad-e-qua-cy
ad-e-quate
ad-here
ad-her-ence
ad-her-ent
ad-he-sion
ad-he-sive
ad-hib-it
ad-i-a-bat-ic
a-dieu
a-dios
ad-i-pose
ad-ja-cen-cy
ad-ja-cent
ad-jec-tive
ad-join
ad-join-ing
ad-journ
ad-journ-ment
ad-judge
ad-ju-di-cate
ad-ju-di-ca-tion
ad-junct
ad-junc-tive
ad-jure
ad-just
ad-just-ment
ad-ju-tant
ad-ju-vant
ad-min-is-ter
ad-min-is-trate
ad-min-is-tra-tion
ad-min-is-tra-tive

ad-mi-ra-ble
ad-mi-ral
ad-mi-ral-ty
ad-mi-ra-tion
ad-mire
ad-mis-si-ble
ad-mis-sion
ad-mis-sive
ad-mit
ad-mit-tance
ad-mit-ted-ly
ad-mix
ad-mix-ture
ad-mon-ish
ad-mo-ni-tion
ad-mon-i-tor
ad-mon-i-to-ry
a-do-be
ad-o-les-cence
ad-o-les-cent
a-dopt
a-dop-tive
a-dor-a-ble
ad-o-ra-tion
a-dore
a-dorn
a-dorn-ment
ad-re-nal
ad-ren-al-in
a-drift
a-droit
ad-script
ad-scrip-tion
ad-sorb
ad-u-late
a-dult
a-dul-ter-ant
a-dul-ter-ate
a-dul-ter-a-tion
a-dul-ter-er
a-dul-ter-ous
a-dul-ter-y
ad-um-bral
ad-um-bra-tive
ad-vance

ad-vanced
ad-vance-ment
ad-van-tage
ad-van-ta-geous
ad-vec-tion
ad-vent
ad-vent-ti-tious
ad-ven-tive
ad-ven-ture
ad-ven-ture-some
ad-ven-tur-ess
ad-ven-tur-ism
ad-ven-tur-ous
ad-verb
ad-ver-sar-y
ad-ver-sa-tive
ad-verse
ad-ver-si-ty
ad-vert
ad-vert-ent
ad-ver-tise
ad-ver-tise-ment
ad-ver-tis-ing
ad-vice
ad-vis-a-ble
ad-vise
ad-vis-ed-ly
ad-vise-ment
ad-vi-so-ry
ad-vo-ca-cy
ad-vo-cate
ad-vo-ca-tion
ad-voc-a-tory
ad-y-nam-ic
aer-ate
aer-i-al
aer-i-al-ist
aer-i-fi-ca-tion
aer-o-dy-nam-ics
aer-o-em-bo-lism
aer-og-ra-phy
aer-ol-o-gy
aer-o-me-chan-ic
aer-o-naut
aer-o-nau-tic

aer-o-pho-bi-a
aer-o-sol
aer-o-space
aes-thete
aes-thet-ic
aes-thet-ic-al
aes-thet-i-cism
af-fa-ble
af-fair
af-fect
af-fec-ta-tion
af-fect-ed
af-fec-tion
af-fec-tion-al
af-fec-tion-ate
af-fec-tive
af-fer-ent
af-fi-ance
af-fi-anced
af-fi-da-vit
af-fil-i-ate
af-fil-i-a-tion
af-fined
af-fin-i-tive
af-fin-i-ty
af-firm
af-firm-ant
af-fir-ma-tion
af-firm-a-tive
af-firm-a-to-ry
af-fix
af-fix-ture
af-fla-ted
af-fla-tus
af-flict
af-flic-tion
af-flic-tive
af-flu-ence
af-flu-ent
af-ford
af-fran-chise
af-fray
af-fright
af-front
af-fron-tive

af-fu-sion
a-field
a-fire
a-flame
a-float
a-flut-ter
a-foot
a-fore
a-fore-men-tioned
a-fore-said
a-fore-thought
a-fore-time
a-foul
a-fraid
a-fresh
af-ter
af-ter-birth
af-ter-brain
af-ter-burn-er
af-ter-deck
af-ter-ef-fect
af-ter-glow
af-ter-im-age
af-ter-math
af-ter-most
af-ter-noon
af-ter-piece
af-ter-shaft
af-ter-taste
af-ter-thought
af-ter-ward
a-gainst
a-gape
ag-ate
age-less
age-long
a-gen-cy
a-gen-da
a-gent
a-gen-tial
a-gen-tive
ag-glom-er-ate
ag-glom-er-a-tion
ag-glu-ti-nant
ag-glu-ti-nate

ag-glu-ti-na-tion
ag-glu-ti-na-tive
ag-gran-dize
ag-gra-vate
ag-gra-va-tion
ag-gre-gate
ag-gre-ga-tion
ag-gress
ag-gres-sion
ag-gres-sive
ag-gres-sor
ag-grieve
a-ghast
ag-ile
a-gil-ity
ag-i-tate
ag-i-ta-tion
ag-i-ta-tor
a-gleam
a-glim-mer
a-glit-ter
a-glow
ag-nos-tic
ag-nos-ti-cism
a-gon-ic
ag-o-nist
ag-o-nis-tic
ag-o-nize
a-gree-a-ble
a-gree-ment
ag-ri-cul-ture
ag-ri-cul-tur-ist
ag-ri-mo-ny
a-gron-o-my
a-ground
ai-grette
ai-ler-on
aim-less
air-craft
air-craft-man
air-drome
air-drop
air-field
air-flow
air-foil

air-i-ly
air-ing
air-less
air-plane
air-port
air-proof
air-ship
air-sick
air-strip
air-tight
air-way
air-wom-an
air-wor-thy
air-y
aisle
a-jar
a-kim-bo
al-a-bas-ter
a-lac-ri-ty
al-a-me-da
a-larm
a-larm-ist
al-ba-core
al-ba-tross
al-be-it
al-bes-cent
al-bi-no
al-bum
al-bu-men
al-che-mist
al-che-mize
al-che-my
al-co-hol
al-co-hol-ic
al-co-hol-ic-i-ty
al-co-hol-ism
al-cove
al-der-man
al-der-man-ic
a-lert
al-fal-fa
al-gae
al-ge-bra
al-ge-bra-ic
al-go-rithm

a-li-as
al-i-bi
al-ien
al-ien-a-ble
al-ien-a-tion
al-ien-ist
a-light
a-lign
a-lign-ment
al-i-ment
al-i-men-ta-tion
al-i-mo-ny
al-i-quot
a-live
al-ka-li
al-ka-li-fy
al-ka-line
al-ka-lize
al-ka-loid
al-lay
al-le-ga-tion
al-lege
al-leg-ed-ly
al-le-giance
al-le-giant
al-le-gor-i-cal
al-le-go-rist
al-le-go-rize
al-le-gory
al-le-gret-to
al-le-gro
al-le-lu-ia
al-ler-gen-ic
al-ler-gic
al-ler-gy
al-le-vi-ate
al-le-vi-a-tion
al-le-vi-a-tive
al-le-vi-a-tory
al-ley-way
al-li-ance
al-lied
al-li-ga-tor
al-lit-er-ate
al-lit-er-a-tion

al-lit-er-a-tive
al-lo-cate
al-lo-ca-tion
al-lo-cu-tion
al-lot-ment
all-ov-er
al-low-a-ble
al-low-ance
al-low-ed-ly
al-loy
al-lude
al-lure
al-lure-ment
al-lu-sion
al-lu-sive
al-lu-vi-al
al-ly
al-ma-nac
al-man-dine
al-might-y
al-mond
al-most
alms
a-lo-ha
a-lone
a-long
a-long-shore
a-long-side
a-loof
a-loud
al-pac-a
al-pha-bet
al-pha-bet-i-cal
al-pha-bet-ize
al-pha-nu-mer-ic
al-pine
al-read-y
al-right
al-tar
al-tar-piece
al-ter
al-ter-a-ble
al-ter-ant
al-ter-a-tion
al-ter-a-tive

al-ter-cate
al-ter-ca-tion
al-ter-nate
al-ter-nate-ly
al-ter-na-tion
al-ter-na-tive
al-ter-na-tor
al-though
al-tim-e-ter
al-tim-e-try
al-ti-tude
al-to-geth-er
al-tru-ism
al-tru-ist
al-tru-is-tic
a-lu-mi-nate
a-lu-mi-nize
a-lu-mi-nous
a-lu-mi-num
a-lum-nus
al-ways
a-lys-sum
a-mal-gam
a-mal-gam-ate
a-mal-gam-a-tion
am-a-teur
am-a-teur-ish
am-a-to-ry
a-maze
a-maze-ment
a-maz-ing
am-ba-gious
am-bas-sa-dor
am-ber
am-ber-gris
am-bi-dex-ter
am-bi-dex-ter-i-ty
am-bi-dex-trous
am-bi-ence
am-bi-ent
am-bi-gu-i-ty
am-big-u-ous
am-bi-tion
am-bi-tious
am-biv-a-lence

am-ble
am-bro-sial
am-bu-lance
am-bu-late
am-bu-la-to-ry
am-bush
a-me-ba
a-mel-io-rate
a-me-na-ble
a-mend
a-mend-a-to-ry
a-mend-ment
a-men-i-ty
am-e-thyst
a-mi-a-ble
am-i-ca-ble
a-mid
a-midst
a-mi-go
a-miss
am-i-ty
am-me-ter
am-mo-nia
am-mo-ni-ac
am-mu-ni-tion
am-ne-sia
am-nes-ty
a-moe-ba
a-mong
a-mor-al
am-o-rist
am-o-rous
a-mor-phism
a-mor-phous
am-or-ti-za-tion
am-or-tize
a-mount
a-mour
am-per-age
am-pere
am-phib-i-an
am-phi-bi-ot-ic
am-phib-i-ous
am-phi-the-a-ter
am-ple

am-pli-a-tion
am-pli-fi-ca-tion
an-plif-i-ca-to-ry
am-pli-fi-er
am-pli-fy
am-pli-tude
am-ply
am-pu-tate
am-pu-tee
am-u-let
a-muse
a-muse-ment
a-mus-ing
a-mu-sive
an-a-bi-o-sis
a-nach-ro-nism
an-a-con-da
a-nae-mi-a
an-aes-the-sia
an-a-go-ge
an-a-gram
an-a-lep-tic
an-al-ge-sic
an-a-log-i-cal
a-nal-o-gist
an-a-logue
a-nal-o-gy
a-nal-y-sis
an-a-lyst
an-a-lyt-ic
an-a-lyze
an-ar-chic
an-ar-chism
an-ar-chist
an-ar-chy
a-nath-e-ma
an-a-tom-i-cal
a-nat-o-mist
a-nat-o-mize
a-nat-o-my
an-ces-tor
an-ces-tral
an-ces-try
an-chor
an-chor-age

an-cho-vy
an-cient
an-cient-ry
an-da-lu-site
an-dan-te
and-i-ron
an-dra-dite
an-dro-gen
an-drog-y-nous
an-ec-dote
a-ne-mi-a
an-e-mom-e-ter
an-er-oid
an-es-the-sia
an-es-the-si-ol-o-gy
an-es-thet-ic
an-es-the-tist
an-es-the-tize
an-eu-rysm
an-frac-tu-ous
an-gel
an-gel-ic
an-ger
an-gi-na
an-gle
an-gler
an-gling
an-gry
an-guist
an-gu-lar
an-gu-lar-i-ty
an-gu-late
an-gu-la-tion
an-ile
an-i-line
a-nil-i-ty
an-i-mal
an-i-mate
an-i-ma-tion
an-i-ma-tor
an-i-mos-i-ty
an-ise
an-i-seed
an-i-sette
an-kle

an-klet
an-nal
an-nal-ist
an-neal
an-nex
an-nex-a-tion
an-ni-hi-la-ble
an-ni-hi-late
an-ni-ver-sa-ry
an-no-ta-tion
an-nounce
an-nounce-ment
an-nounc-er
an-noy
an-noy-ance
an-noy-ing
an-nu-al
an-nu-i-ty
an-nul
an-nu-lar
an-nu-late
an-nu-la-tion
an-nul-ment
an-nun-ci-ate
an-o-dize
an-o-dyne
a-noint
an-o-lyte
a-nom-a-ly
an-o-nym
a-non-y-mous
an-oth-er
an-swer
an-swer-a-ble
ant-ac-id
an-tag-o-nism
an-tag-o-nist
an-tag-o-nis-tic
an-tag-o-nize
ant-arc-tic
an-te
ant-eat-er
an-te-cede
an-te-ced-ence
an-te-ced-ent

an-te-ces-sor	a-or-ta	ap-pel-la-tion
an-te-date	a-part	ap-pend
an-te-fix	a-part-heid	ap-pend-age
an-te-flex-ion	a-part-ment	ap-pend-ant
an-te-lope	ap-a-tet-ic	ap-pen-dec-to-my
an-ten-na	ap-a-thet-ic	ap-pen-di-ci-tis
an-te-ri-or	ap-a-thy	ap-pen-dix
an-them	ape	ap-per-ceive
an-ther	ape-ri-tif	ap-per-cep-tion
an-the-sis	ap-er-ture	ap-per-tain
an-thol-o-gy	a-pex	ap-pe-tite
an-thra-cene	a-phon-ic	ap-pe-tiz-er
an-thra-cite	aph-o-rism	ap-pe-tiz-ing
an-thrax	aph-o-rize	ap-plaud
an-thro-poid	aph-ro-dis-i-ac	ap-plause
an-thro-pol-o-gist	a-plomb	ap-pli-ance
an-thro-pol-o-gy	a-poc-a-lypse	ap-pli-ca-ble
an-ti-bi-ot-ic	a-poc-a-lyp-tic	ap-pli-cant
an-tic	ap-o-chro-mat-ic	ap-pli-ca-tion
an-tic-i-pant	a-poc-ry-pha	ap-pli-ca-tor
an-tic-i-pate	a-pol-o-get-ics	ap-plied
an-tic-i-pa-tion	a-pol-o-gist	ap-pli-que
an-tic-i-pa-to-ry	a-pol-o-gize	ap-ply
an-ti-cli-max	ap-o-logue	ap-point
an-ti-cli-nal	a-pol-o-gy	ap-point-ment
an-ti-dote	ap-o-plex-y	ap-por-tion
an-ti-gen	a-pos-tle	ap-por-tion-ment
an-ti-his-ta-mine	a-pos-to-late	ap-po-site
an-ti-pas-to	ap-os-tol-ic	ap-prais-al
an-tip-a-thy	a-pos-tro-phe	ap-praise
an-ti-quate	a-pos-tro-phize	ap-pre-ci-a-ble
an-tique	a-poth-e-car-y	ap-pre-ci-ate
an-tiq-ui-ty	ap-pall	ap-pre-ci-a-tion
an-ti-sep-sis	ap-pall-ing	ap-pre-ci-a-tive
an-ti-sep-ti-cize	ap-pa-ra-tus	ap-pre-ci-a-to-ry
ant-ler	ap-par-el	ap-pre-hend
ant-lered	ap-par-ent	ap-pre-hen-si-ble
an-to-nym	ap-pa-ri-tion	ap-pre-hen-sion
a-nus	ap-peal	ap-pre-hen-sive
an-vil	ap-pear	ap-pren-tice
anx-i-e-ty	ap-pear-ance	ap-prise
anx-ious	ap-pease	ap-proach
an-y	ap-pel	ap-proach-a-ble
an-y-bod-y	ap-pel-lant	ap-pro-bate
an-y-where	ap-pel-late	ap-pro-ba-tion

ap-pro-pri-ate
ap-pro-pri-a-tion
ap-prov-al
ap-prove
ap-prox-i-mal
ap-prox-i-mate
ap-prox-i-ma-tion
ap-pur-te-nance
ap-pur-te-nant
a-pri-cot
a-pron
ap-ti-tude
aq-ua
aq-ua-lung
aq-ua-ma-rine
a-quar-i-um
a-quat-ic
aq-ue-duct
aq-ui-line
ar-a-besque
ar-a-ble
ar-bi-ter
ar-bi-trage
ar-bi-tral
ar-bi-trar-y
ar-bi-trate
ar-bi-tra-tion
ar-bi-tra-tor
ar-bor
ar-bo-re-al
ar-bo-re-tum
ar-cade
ar-ca-num
arch
ar-chae-o-log-i-cal
ar-chae-ol-o-gy
ar-cha-ic
ar-cha-ism
arch-di-o-cese
arched
ar-che-ol-o-gy
arch-er
arch-er-y
ar-chi-tect
ar-chi-tec-tur-al

ar-chi-tec-ture
ar-chives
arc-o-graph
arc-tic
ar-cu-ate
ar-dent
ar-dor
ar-du-ous
ar-e-a
a-re-na
ar-e-na-ceous
aren't
ar-gon
ar-go-sy
ar-got
ar-gue
ar-gu-ment
ar-gu-men-ta-tion
ar-gu-men-ta-tive
a-ri-a
ar-id
ar-i-ose
a-rio-se
ar-is-toc-ra-cy
a-ris-to-crat
a-ris-to-crat-ic
a-rith-me-tic
a-rith-me-ti-cian
ar-ma-dil-lo
ar-mor
ar-mored
ar-mor-er
ar-mo-ri-al
ar-mor-y
ar-mour
a-ro-ma
ar-o-mat-ic
a-ro-ma-ti-za-tion
a-ro-ma-tize
a-rouse
ar-raign
ar-raign-ment
ar-range
ar-range-ment
ar-rant

ar-ray
ar-ray-al
ar-rear
ar-rear-age
ar-rest
ar-rest-ing
ar-riv-al
ar-rive
ar-ro-gance
ar-ro-gant
ar-ro-gate
ar-row
ar-se-nal
ar-se-nic
ar-se-nide
ar-se-nous
ar-son
ar-te-ri-al
ar-te-ri-al-ize
ar-te-ri-o-scle-ro-sis
ar-ter-y
art-ful
ar-thri-tis
ar-ti-choke
ar-ti-cle
ar-tic-u-lar
ar-tic-u-late
ar-tic-u-la-tion
ar-ti-fact
ar-ti-fice
ar-ti-fi-cial
ar-ti-fi-ci-al-i-ty
ar-til-ler-y
ar-ti-san
art-ist
ar-tis-tic
art-ist-ry
art-less
art-y
as-bes-tos
as-cend
as-cend-an-cy
as-cend-ant
as-cend-er
as-cend-ing

as-cen-sion
as-cen-sive
as-cent
as-cer-tain
as-cet-ic
as-cet-i-cal
as-cot
as-cribe
as-crip-tion
a-sep-sis
a-sep-tic
a-sex-u-al
ash
a-shamed
ash-en
ash-es
a-side
as-i-nine
ask
a-skance
a-skew
a-slant
a-sleep
a-slope
as-par-a-gus
as-pect
as-pec-tu-al
as-pen
as-per
as-per-i-ty
as-perse
as-per-sion
as-phalt
as-phyx-i-a
as-phyx-i-ant
as-phyx-i-ate
as-pic
as-pir-ant
as-pi-rate
as-pi-ra-tion
as-pi-ra-tor
as-pir-a-to-ry
as-pire
as-pir-in
as-sail

as-sail-ant
as-sas-sin
as-sas-si-nate
as-sault
as-say
as-sem-blage
as-sem-ble
as-sem-bly
as-sent
as-sen-ta-tion
as-sen-ter
as-sert
as-ser-tion
as-ser-tive
as-sess
as-sess-ment
as-ses-sor
as-set
as-sev-er-ate
as-sev-er-a-tion
as-si-du-i-ty
as-sid-u-ous
as-sign
as-sign-a-ble
as-sign-ee
as-sign-ment
as-sim-i-late
as-sim-i-la-tion
as-sim-i-la-tive
as-sist
as-sist-ance
as-sist-ant
as-so-ci-ate
as-so-ci-a-tion
as-so-ci-a-tive
as-so-nance
as-sort
as-sort-ed
as-sort-ment
as-suage
as-sua-sive
as-sume
as-sum-ing
as-sump-tion
as-sump-tive

as-sur-ance
as-sure
as-sur-gent
a-stat-ic
as-ter-isk
as-ter-ism
a-stern
as-ter-oid
asth-ma
asth-mat-ic
a-stig-ma-tism
a-stir
as-ton-ish
as-ton-ish-ing
as-ton-ish-ment
as-tound
a-strad-dle
as-tral
a-stray
a-stride
as-trin-gent
as-trol-o-gy
as-trom-e-try
as-tro-naut
as-tron-o-mer
as-tro-nom-i-cal
as-tute
a-sun-der
a-sy-lum
a-sym-met-ric
a-sym-me-try
at-a-vism
at-el-ier
a-the-ism
a-the-ist
ath-er-o-scle-ro-sis
ath-lete
ath-let-ic
a-thwart
at-las
at-mos-phere
a-tom-ic
at-o-mic-i-ty
at-om-ism
at-om-ize

a-ton-al
a-tone-ment
a-ton-ic
a-tro-cious
a-troc-i-ty
at-ro-phied
at-ro-phy
at-tach
at-tach-ment
at-tack
at-tain
at-tain-a-ble
at-tain-der
at-tain-ment
at-tempt
at-tend
at-tend-ance
at-tend-ant
at-ten-tion
at-ten-tive
at-ten-u-ant
at-ten-u-ate
at-ten-u-a-tion
at-test
at-tes-ta-tion
at-tic
at-tire
at-ti-tude
at-ton-my
at-tor-my
at-trac-tion
at-trac-tive
at-trib-ute
at-tri-bu-tion
at-trib-u-tive
at-trite
at-tri-tion
at-tune
au-burn
auc-tion
auc-tion-eer
au-da-cious
au-dac-i-ty
au-di-ble
au-di-ence

au-di-o
au-di-phone
au-dit
au-di-tion
au-di-tive
au-di-tor
au-di-to-ri-um
au-di-to-ry
au-ger
aught
aug-ment
aug-men-ta-tion
aug-ment-a-tive
aug-ment-ed
au-gur
au-gu-ry
au-gust
aunt
au-ra
au-re-ate
au-re-o-my-cin
au-ri-cle
au-ric-u-lar
au-ric-u-late
aus-cul-ta-tion
aus-pice
aus-pi-cious
aus-tere
aus-ter-i-ty
au-then-tic
au-then-ti-cate
au-then-tic-i-ty
au-thor
au-thor-i-tar-i-an
au-thor-i-ta-tive
au-thor-i-ty
au-thor-i-za-tion
au-thor-ize
au-thor-ship
au-to-bi-og-ra-phy
au-to-clave
au-toc-ra-cy
au-to-crat
au-to-crat-ic
au-to-graph

au-to-mat
au-to-mat-ic
au-to-ma-tion
au-tom-a-tism
au-tom-a-ton
au-to-mo-bile
au-to-mo-tive
au-ton-o-mous
au-ton-o-my
au-top-sy
au-tot-o-my
au-tumn
au-tum-nal
aux-il-ia-ry
a-vail
a-vail-a-bil-i-ty
a-vail-a-ble
av-a-lanche
av-a-rice
av-a-ri-cious
a-venge
av-e-nue
av-er-age
a-verse
a-ver-sion
a-vert
a-vi-ar-y
a-vi-a-tion
a-vi-a-tor
a-vi-cul-ture
av-id
a-vid-i-ty
av-i-ga-tion
av-o-ca-do
av-o-ca-tion
a-voc-a-to-ry
a-void
a-void-ance
a-vow-al
a-vul-sion
a-vun-cu-lar
a-wak-en
awe-some
aw-ful
a-while

awk-ward

awn-ing

a-woke

ax-i-al

ax-i-om

ax-i-o-matic

ax-is

ax-le

a-zal-ea

az-ure

az-u-rite

B

bab-bitt

bab-ble

ba-boon

ba-bush-ka

ba-by-ish

bac-ca-lau-re-ate

bac-ca-rat

bac-cha-nal

bac-chant

bach-e-lor

bac-il-lar-y

bac-cil-lus

back-hand

back-ing

back-lash

back-log

back-side

back-stage

ba-con

bac-te-ria

bac-te-ri-cide

bac-te-rin

bac-te-ri-ol-o-gy

bac-te-rize

bade

badge

badg-er

bad-i-nage

bad-min-ton

baf-fle

bag-a-telle

ba-gel

bag-gage

bag-ging

bag-pipe

ba-guette

bail

bail-a-ble

bail-ee

bail-iff

bail-i-wick

bail-ment

bails-man

bait

bake

bak-er

bak-er-y

bal-a-lai-ka

bal-ance

bal-anc-er

bal-co-ny

bald

bald-head

bale

bale-ful

balky

bal-lad

bal-last

bal-le-ri-na

bal-let

bal-lis-tics

bal-loon

bal-lot

bal-lotte-ment

bal-ly-hoo

balm

balm-y

ba-lo-ney

bal-sam

bal-us-ter

bal-us-trade

bam-bi-no

bam-boo

bam-boo-zle

ba-nal

ba-nan-a

ban-dan-na

ban-deau

ban-de-role

ban-dit

ban-dit-ry

band-master

ban-do-leer

ban-dy

ban-gle

ban-ish

ban-is-ter

ban-jo

bank

bank-a-ble

bank-book

bank-er

bank-ing

bank-rupt

bank-rupt-cy

ban-ner

ban-ner-et

ban-nis-ter

banns

ban-quet

ban-quette

ban-shee

ban-tam

ban-ter

bant-ling

bap-tism

bap-tis-ter-y

bap-tis-try

bap-tize

bar-bar-i-an

bar-bar-ic

bar-ba-rism
bar-bar-i-ty
bar-ba-rize
bar-ba-rous
bar-be-cue
bar-ber
bar-bette
bar-bi-tal
bar-bi-tu-rate
bar-ca-role
bare
bar-gain
barge
bar-i-tone
bar-i-um
bar-keep-er
bark-en-tine
bark-er
bar-ley
bar-ley-corn
bar-maid
bar-na-cle
barn-storm
barn-yard
bar-o-graph
ba-rom-e-ter
ba-ron
bar-on-ess
bar-on-et
ba-roque
ba-rouche
bar-rack
bar-ra-cu-da
bar-rage
bar-ra-tor
bar-ra-try
barred
bar-rel
bar-ren
bar-rette
bar-ri-cade
bar-ri-er
bar-ring
bar-ris-ter
bar-room

bar-row
bar-tend-er
bar-ter
bar-y-tone
bas-al
ba-salt
bas-cule
base-less
base-man
base-ment
bash-ful
bas-ic
bas-i-cal-ly
bas-il
ba-sil-i-ca
ba-sin
bas-i-net
ba-sis
bas-ket
bas-ket-ball
bas-ket-ry
bass
bas-set
bas-si-net
bas-soon
bas-tard
bas-tard-ize
baste
bas-tille
bast-ing
bas-tion
batch
bate
ba-teau
bath
bathe
bath-house
ba-thom-e-ter
bath-tub
bath-y-sphere
ba-tiste
bat-man
ba-ton
bat-tal-ion
bat-ten

bat-ter
bat-ter-y
bat-ting
bat-tle
bat-tle-ment
bat-tle-ship
bat-ty
bau-ble
baux-ite
bawd
bawd-y
bawl
bay-ber-ry
bay-o-net
bay-ou
ba-zaar
ba-zoo-ka
beach
beach-head
beach-y
bea-con
bead
bead-ing
bea-dle
beads-man
bead-y
bea-gle
beak
beak-er
beam
beam-ing
beam-y
bean
bean-ie
bear
beard
bear-er
bear-ing
bear-ish
bear-skin
beast
beast-ly
beat
beat-en
beat-er

be-a-tif-ic
be-at-i-fi-ca-tion
be-at-i-fy
beat-ing
be-at-i-tude
beat-nik
beau
beau-te-ous
beau-ti-cian
beau-ti-ful
beau-ti-fy
beau-ty
beaux
beaux-arts
bea-ver
be-came
be-cause
beck-on
be-come
be-com-ing
be-daub
be-daz-zle
bed-ding
be-deck
bed-fel-low
be-dight
be-di-zen
bed-lam
bed-post
be-grag-gle
bed-rid-den
bed-room
bed-side
bed-spread
bed-spring
bed-stead
bed-straw
bed-time
beech (tree)
beech-nut
beef-eat-er
beef-steak
beef-y
bee-hive
bees-wax

beet (vegetable)
bee-tle
be-fit-ting
be-fore
be-fore-hand
be-friend
be-fud-dle
beg-gar
beg-gar-y
be-gin-ning
be-gon-ia
be-got-ten
be-grudge
be-guile
be-guine
be-hav-ior
be-hav-ior-ism
be-he-moth
be-hest
be-hold-en
be-hoove
beige
be-jew-el
be-la-bor
be-lat-ed
be-lay
belch
be-lea-guer
bel-fry
be-lie
be-lief
be-lieve
bel-la-don-na
belle (woman)
bel-li-core
bel-lig-er-ence
bel-lig-er-en-cy
bel-lig-er-ent
bel-low
bel-lows
bel-ly
belt-ing
bel-ve-dere
be-mean
be-moan

be-mused
ben-a-dryl
bench
bench-er
bend-er
be-neath
ben-e-dict
ben-e-dic-tion
ben-e-fac-tion
ben-e-fac-tor
be-nef-ic
ben-e-fice
be-nef-i-cence
be-nef-i-cent
ben-e-fi-cial
ben-e-fi-ci-ar-y
ben-e-fit
be-nev-o-lence
be-nev-o-lent
be-night-ed
be-nign
be-nig-nant
be-nig-ni-ty
ben-zene
ben-zi-dine
ben-zine
be-queath
be-quest
be-rate
ber-ceuse
be-reave
be-ret
be-rib-boned
ber-i-ber-i
ber-ry (fruit)
ber-serk
berth
ber-yl
be-ryl-li-um
be-seech
be-set-ting
be-shrew
be-side
be-siege
be-spec-ta-cled

bes-tial
bes-ti-al-i-ty
bes-tial-ize
bes-ti-ar-y
be-stow
be-strad-dle
beth-el
be-troth-al
be-trothed
bet-ter
bet-ter-ment
be-twixt
be-vel
bev-er-age
bev-y
be-ware
be-wil-der
be-witch
be-yond
bez-ant
bez-el
bi-an-gu-lar
bi-an-nu-al
bi-an-nu-late
bi-as
bi-ax-i-al
bib-li-og-ra-pher
bib-li-og-ra-phy
bib-u-lous
bi-cam-er-al
bi-car-bo-nate
bi-cen-te-nar-y
bi-cen-ten-ni-al
bi-ceps
bi-chlo-ride
bi-chro-mate
bick-er
bi-cor-po-ral
bi-cus-pid
bi-cy-cle
bi-cy-clic
bid-da-ble
bid-den
bid-ding
bi-en-ni-al

bien-ve-nue
bier
bi-fa-cial
bi-fo-cal
big-a-mist
big-a-mous
big-a-my
bight
big-ot
big-ot-ed
big-ot-ry
big-wig
bi-hour-ly
bi-jou
bi-ki-ni
bi-la-bi-al
bi-lat-er-al
bile
bilge
bi-lin-gual
bi-lin-gual-ism
bil-ious
bil-let
bill-fold
bil-liard
bil-lion
bil-lion-aire
bil-low
bil-low-y
bi-man-u-al
bi-month-ly
bi-nal
bi-na-ry
bi-nate
bin-au-ral
bind-er
binge
bin-go
bin-na-cle
bin-oc-u-lar
bi-no-mi-al
bi-o-cat-a-lyst
bi-o-chem-is-try
bi-o-dy-nam-ics
bi-o-ge-og-ra-phy

bi-og-ra-pher
bi-o-graph-i-cal
bi-og-ra-phy
bi-o-log-i-cal
bi-ol-o-gy
bi-ol-y-sis
bi-o-met-rics
bi-om-e-try
bi-o-phys-ics
bi-op-sy
bi-o-scope
bi-os-co-py
bi-par-ti-san
bi-ped
bi-plane
bi-po-lar
brick
bird-seed
bird's-eye
bi-ret-ta
birth (born)
birth-right
birth-stone
bis-cuit
bi-sect
bi-sec-tor
bi-sec-trix
bi-sex-u-al
bish-op
bish-op-ric
bis-muth
bi-son
bisque
bis-sex-tile
bis-tro
bi-sym-met-ri-cal
bitch
bit-ing
bit-ten
bit-ter
bit-tern
bit-ter-root
bit-ters
bit-ter-sweet
bi-tu-men

bi-tu-mi-nous	blight	blub-ber-y
bi-va-lent	blimp	blu-cher
bi-valve	blind	bludg-eon
biv-ou-ac	blind-er	blue-ber-ry
bi-zarre	blink	blue-bird
black-a-moor	blink-ard	blue-fish
black-board	blink-er	blue-grass
black-head	blip	blue-jack
black-jack	bliss	blue-jay
black-out	bliss-ful	blue-print
blad-der	blis-ter	blu-et
blade	blithe	bluff
blame	blithe-some	blu-ing
blame-less	blitz	blu-ish
blanch	bliz-zard	blun-der
bland	bloat	blunt
blan-dish	bloat-er	blur
blan-dish-ment	blob	blurb
blan-ket	bloc (coalition)	blurt
blan-ket-ing	block (solid mass)	blush
blank-ly	block-ade	blus-ter
blare	block-age	boar (swine)
blar-ney	block-ish	board (timber)
bla-se	bloke	boar-ish
blas-pheme	blond	boast
blas-phe-mous	blood	boast-ful
blas-phe-my	blood-hound	bob-bin
blast	blood-mobile	bob-bi-net
bla-tant	blood-red	bob-by-socks
blath-er	blood-shot	bob-by-sox-er
blaze	blood-stain	bob-cat
blaz-er	blood-sucker	bob-o-link
bla-zon	blood-test	bob-tail
bla-zon-ry	blood-y	bo-cac-cio
bleach	bloom	bode
bleach-er	bloom-er	bod-ice
bleach-er-y	blos-som	bod-i-less
bleak	blotch	bod-y-guard
blear	blot-ter	bo-gey
blear-eyed	blouse	bog-gle
bleed-er	blown	bo-gle
blem-ish	blow-torch	bo-gus
blench	blow-up	bois-ter-ous
blend	blowz-y	bold-face
blew (v)	blub-ber	bo-le-ro

bol-i-var
boll-wee-vil
bo-lo-graph
bo-lom-e-ter
bol-ster
bom-ba-ca-ceous
bom-bard
bom-bar-dier
bom-bast
bom-bas-tic
bom-ba-zine
bomb-proof
bomb-shell
bo-na fi-de
bo-nan-za
bon ap-pe-tit
bon-bon
bond-age
bonds-man
bon-fire
bon-go
bo-ni-to
bon-net
bon-ny
bo-nus
book-bind-er
book-bind-er-y
book-bind-ing
book-ie
book-keep-er
book-keep-ing
book-let
book-mo-bile
boom-er-ang
boon
boon-docks
boor (rude person)
boor-ish
boost
boost-er
boot-black
boot-ed
boot-leg
boot-less
boo-ty

booze
bo-ra-cite
bo-rax
bor-del-lo
bor-der (edge)
bor-der-land
bor-der-line
bore
bo-re-al
bore-dom
bor-er
bore-some
bo-ric
bor-ing
born (birth)
borne (*alt. pp. of*
       bear)
bo-ron
bor-ough
bor-row
borsch
bort
bos-om
bo-sun
bo-tan-i-cal
bot-a-nist
bot-a-nize
bot-a-ny
botch
both-er-a-tion
both-er-some
bot-tle-neck
bot-tom
bot-tom-less
bot-u-lin
bot-u-lism
bou-doir
bouf-fant
bough
bought
bought-en
bouil-la-baisse
bouil-lon
boul-der
boul-e-vard

bounce
bound
bound-a-ry
bound-er
bound-less
boun-ti-ous
boun-ti-ful
boun-ty
bou-quet
bour-bon
bour-geois
bour-geon
bou-tique
bou-ton-niere
bo-vine
bow-el
bow-er
bow-er-y
bow-knot
bow-ler
bow-man
box-er
box-wood
boy-cott
boy-hood
boy-ish
boy-sen-ber-ry
brace
brace-let
bra-chi-al
brack-et
brack-et-ing
brack-ish
brad-awl
brag-gart
braid
braid-ing
brail
brain
braise (cook)
brake (*n*)
brake-age
brake-man
bram-ble
bram-bling

branch
brand
bran-died
bran-dish
bran-dy
brash
brass
brass-age
bras-sard
brass-ie (golf club)
bras-siere
brass-y
brat-tle
bra-va-do
brav-er-y
bra-vo
bra-vu-ra
brawl
brawn
bray
braze (made of brass)
bra-zen
bra-zier
breach
bread
bread-stuff
breadth
break (v)
break-down
break-fast
break-ing
break-through
break-up
breast
breath
breathe
breathed
breath-er
breath-less
breath-tak-ing
bred (p.t. of breed)
breech
breech-es
breech-ing
breed

breed-er
breed-ing
breeze
breeze-way
breez-y
breth-ren
bre-vet
bre-vi-ar-y
bre-vier
brev-i-ty
brew-age
brew-er-y
brew-ing
bribe
brib-er-y
bric-a-brac
brick
brick-yard
brid-al
bride-groom
brides-maid
bridge
bridge-work
bridg-ing
bri-dle
brief
brief-ing
brief-less
bri-er
bri-er-root
bri-er-wood
bri-gade
brig-a-dier
brig-and
brig-an-tine
bright
brill
bril-liance
bril-liant
bril-lian-tine
brim-ful
brim-mer
brim-stone
brin-dle
brine

bring
brink
brin-y
bri-oche
bri-quette
brisk
bris-ket
bris-ling
bris-tle
brit-tle
broach
broad
broad-cast
broad-cloth
broad-loom
broad-mind-ed
bro-cade
broc-co-li
bro-chette
bro-chure
brock-et
brogue
broi-der
broil
broil-er
bro-kage
broke
bro-ken
bro-ken-heart-ed
bro-ker
bro-ker-age
bro-mal
bro-mate
bro-mic
bro-mide
bro-mid-ic
bro-mi-nate
bro-mine
bron-chi-a
bron-chi-al
bron-chi-tis
bron-cho-pneu-mo-nia
bron-cho-scope
bron-co (horse)
bronze

brooch	bu-col-ic	bun-ga-low
brood	bud-dy	bun-gle
brood-er	budge	bun-ion
brood-y	budg-et	bunk
brook	buff	bunk-er
broom	buf-fa-lo	bun-ny
broth	buff-er	bun-ting
broth-el	buf-fet	buoy
broth-er-hood	buf-foon	buoy-age
broth-er-in-law	bug-a-boo	buoy-an-cy
brough-am	bug-ger	buoy-ant
brought	bug-gy	bur-ble
brow	bu-gle	bur-den
brown-ie	build	bur-den-some
brown-stone	build-er	bur-dock
browse	build-ing	bu-reau
bru-in	built	bu-reau-cra-cy
bruise	built-in	bu-reau-crat
bruis-er	bulb	bu-rette
brunch	bulb-if-er-ous	bur-geon
bru-nette	bulb-ous	bur-gess
brunt	bulge	burgh-er
brush	bulk	bur-glar
brush-off	bulk-y	bur-glar-i-ous
brusque	bull-dog	bur-glar-ize
brut	bull-doze	bur-gla-ry
bru-tal	bul-let	bur-gle
bru-tal-i-ty	bul-le-tin	bur-go-mas-ter
bru-tal-ize	bull-head-ed	bur-ial
brute	bul-lion	bur-i-er
bru-ti-fy	bull-ish	burl
brut-ish	bull-ock	bur-lap
bub-ble	bull's-eye	bur-lesque
bub-bler	bul-ly	bur-ly
bu-bon-ic	bul-rush	burn-er
buc-ca-neer	bul-wark	burn-ing
buck-a-roo	bum-ble-bee	bur-nish
buck-board	bum-kin	bur-noose
buck-et	bump	burn-out
buck-le	bump-er	burn-sides
buck-ler	bump-kin	burnt
buck-ram	bump-y	burp
buck-saw	bunch	burr
buck-skin	bunch-y	bur-ro (donkey)
buck-tooth	bun-dle	bur-row (hole)

bur-sar
bur-sar-i-al
bur-sa-ry
burse
bur-si-tis
burst
bur-y (cover)
bus-boy
bush
bush-el
bush-ham-mer
bush-i-ness
bush-ing
bush-man
bush-y
bus-i-ly
busi-ness
busi-ness-like
busi-ness-man
bus-kin

bus-ses (*pl. of* bus)
bust
bus-tard
bus-tle
bu-tane
butch-er
butch-er-ly
butch-er-y
bu-tene
but-ler
but-ler-y
butt (strike)
but-ter
but-ter-fat
but-ter-fly
but-ter-milk
but-ter-nut
but-ter-scotch
but-ter-y
but-tock

but-ton
but-tress
bux-om
buy-er
buzz
buz-zard
buzz-er
buzz-saw
by-gone
by-law
by-line
by-pass
by-path
by-play
by-prod-uct
by-road
by-stand-er
by-way
by-word
By-zan-tine

C

ca-bal
cab-a-lis-tic
ca-bal-le-ro
ca-ba-na
cab-a-ret
cab-bage
cab-by
cab-i-net
cab-i-net-mak-er
ca-ble
ca-ble-gram
cab-man
ca-boo-dle
ca-boose
cab-ri-ole
cab-ri-o-let
ca-ca-o
cach-a-lot
cache
ca-chet
cach-in-nate

cack-le
ca-cog-ra-phy
ca-coph-o-ny
cac-ta-ceous
cac-tus
ca-dav-er
ca-dav-er-ous
cad-die
cade
ca-dence
ca-dent
ca-den-za
cadge
cadg-y
cad-mi-um
ca-dre
ca-du-ce-us
ca-du-ci-ty
cae-sar-e-an
ca-fe
ca-fe au lait

caf-e-te-ri-a
caf-fe-ine
caf-tan
ca-gey
ca-hoots
cais-son
cai-tiff
ca-jole
ca-jol-er-y
cal-a-bash
cal-a-boose
cal-a-man-der
cal-a-mine
cal-a-mint
cal-a-mite
ca-lam-i-tous
ca-lam-i-ty
cal-a-mus
cal-ci-fi-ca-tion
cal-ci-fy
cal-ci-mine

cal-ci-um
cal-cu-late
cal-cu-lat-ing
cal-cu-la-tion
cal-cu-la-tor
cal-cu-lus
cal-dron
cal-en-dar
cal-en-der
cal-ends
calf
calf-skin
cal-i-ber
cal-i-brate
cal-i-co
cal-i-per
ca-liph
cal-is-then-ics
calk
calk-er
call-a-ble
call-er
cal-lig-ra-phy
call-ing
cal-li-o-pe
cal-li-op-sis
cal-lis-then-ics
cal-los-i-ty
cal-lous
cal-low
cal-lus
calm
calm-ly
cal-o-mel
ca-lor-ic
cal-o-rie
cal-o-rif-ic
cal-o-rim-e-ter
cal-o-rim-e-try
cal-u-met
ca-lum-ni-ate
ca-lum-ni-a-tion
ca-lum-ni-ous
cal-um-ny
calve

cal-vi-ti-es
ca-lyx
ca-ma-ra-de-rie
cam-a-ril-la
cam-ber
cam-bi-um
cam-bric
cam-el
cam-el-eer
cam-el-hair
ca-mel-lia
cam-e-o
cam-er-a
cam-er-a-man
cam-i-on
cam-i-sole
cam-let
cam-ou-flage
cam-paign
cam-pa-ni-le
camp-fire
camp-ground
cam-phor
cam-phor-ate
cam-pi-on
cam-pus
cam-shaft
ca-nal
can-a-pe
ca-nard
ca-nar-y
ca-nas-ta
can-can
can-cel
can-cel-late
can-cel-la-tion
can-cer
can-de-la-bra
can-de-la-brum
can-dent
can-des-cent
can-did
can-di-date
can-died
can-dle

can-dle-light
can-dle-stick
can-dle-wood
can-dor
ca-nine
can-is-ter
can-ker
can-ker-ous
canned
can-ner
can-ner-y
can-ni-bal
can-ni-bal-ism
can-ni-bal-ize
can-ning
can-non
can-non-ade
can-non-eer
can-non-ry
can-not
can-ny
ca-noe
can-on
ca-non-i-cal
can-on-ist
can-on-ize
can-o-py
can-o-rous
can-ta-bi-le
can-ta-loupe
can-tan-ker-ous
can-ta-ta
can-ta-tri-ce
can-teen
can-ter
can-ti-cle
can-ti-lev-er
can-to
can-ton
can-ton-ment
can-tor
can-vas (cloth)
can-vass (debate)
can-yon
ca-pa-bil-i-ty

ca-pa-ble
ca-pa-cious
ca-pac-i-tance
ca-pac-i-tate
ca-pac-i-tive
ca-pac-i-tor
ca-pac-i-ty
cap-a-pie
ca-par-i-son
ca-per
cap-ful
cap-il-lar-i-ty
cap-il-lar-y
cap-i-tal
cap-i-tal-ism
cap-i-tal-ist
cap-i-tal-is-tic
cap-i-tal-i-za-tion
cap-i-tal-ize
cap-i-tal-ly
cap-i-tate
cap-i-ta-tion
ca-pit-u-lar
ca-pit-u-lar-y
ca-pit-u-late
ca-pit-u-la-tion
ca-pit-u-lum
ca-pon
cap-o-ral
ca-pote
cap-per
cap-puc-ci-no
ca-price
ca-pri-cious
cap-size
cap-stan
cap-stone
cap-su-late
cap-sule
cap-tain
cap-tion
cap-tious
cap-ti-vate
cap-tive
cap-tiv-i-ty

cap-tor
cap-ture
ca-put
car-a-bin
car-a-cole
car-a-cul
ca-rafe
car-a-mel
car-a-mel-ize
car-at (weight)
car-a-van
car-a-van-sa-ry
car-a-vel
car-a-way
car-bide
car-bine
car-bo-hy-drate
car-bo-lat-ed
car-bo-lize
car-bon
car-bo-na-ceous
car-bon-a-ta-tion
car-bon-ate
car-bon-a-tion
car-bon di-ox-ide
car-bon-ic
carbonic acid
car-bon-i-za-tion
car-bon-ize
carbon monoxide
car-bun-cle
car-bu-ret
car-bu-re-tion
car-bu-re-tor
car-bu-rize
car-cass
car-ci-no-ma
car-da-mom
card-board
car-di-ac
car-di-gan
car-di-nal
car-di-nal-ate
card-ing
car-di-o-gram

car-di-o-graph
car-di-oid
car-di-ol-o-gy
car-di-tis
car-doon
card-sharp
ca-reen
ca-reer
care-free
care-ful
care-less
ca-ress
car-et (mark)
care-tak-er
car-fare
car-go
car-i-bou
car-i-ca-ture
car-il-lon
ca-ri-na
car-i-ous
cark-ing
car-bine
car-load
car-min-a-tive
car-mine
car-nage
car-nal
car-nall-ite
car-na-tion
car-nel-ian
car-ni-val
car-niv-o-rous
car-ol
car-on
ca-rot-id
ca-rous-al
ca-rouse
car-ou-sel
carp
car-pen-ter
car-pet
car-pet-bag
car-pet-bag-ger
car-pet-ing

car-port
car-rack
car-riage
car-ri-er
car-ri-on
car-rot
car-rou-sel
car-ry-all
car-ry-o-ver
car-sick
cart (vehicle)
cart-age
carte (menu)
carte blanche
car-tel
car-te-lize
car-ti-lage
car-ti-lag-i-nous
cart-load
car-to-gram
car-tog-ra-phy
car-ton
car-toon
car-touche
car-tridge
cart-wheel
carve
car-vel
car-vel-built
carv-en
carv-ing
car-y-at-id
ca-sa-ba
cas-cade
cas-car-a
ca-se-a-tion
case-hard-en
case-ment
cash-book
cash-ew
cash-ier
cash-mere
cas-ing
ca-si-no
cask

cas-ket
casque
cas-se-role
cas-si-no
cas-sock
cast
cas-ta-net
cast-a-way
caste
cas-tel-lat-ed
cast-er
   (one who casts)
cas-ti-gate
cast-ing
cast-i-ron
cas-tle
cast-off
cas-tor (scent)
cas-trate
cas-u-al
cas-u-al-ty
cas-u-ist
cas-u-is-tic
cas-u-ist-ry
ca-tab-o-lism
cat-a-clysm
cat-a-clys-mic
cat-a-comb
cat-a-falque
Cat-a-lan
cat-a-lep-sy
cat-a-lin
cat-a-log
cat-a-logue
ca-tal-pa
ca-tal-y-sis
cat-a-lyst
cat-a-lyze
cat-a-ma-ran
cat-a-mount
cat-a-pult
cat-a-ract
ca-tas-ta-sis
ca-tas-tro-phe
ca-tas-tro-phism

cat-bird
cat-call
catch-all
catch-er
catch-up
catch-word
catch-y
cat-e-chism
cat-e-chist
cat-e-chu-men
cat-e-gor-i-cal
cat-e-go-ry
cat-e-nar-y
ca-ter
ca-ter-er
cat-er-pil-lar
cat-er-waul
cat-fall
cat-fish
cat-gut
ca-thar-sis
ca-thar-tic
ca-the-dral
cath-e-ter
cath-e-ter-ize
cath-ode
cathode ray
cath-o-lic
cath-o-lic-i-ty
ca-thol-i-cize
cat-nip
cat-o'-nine-tails
cat's-eye
cat's-paw
cat-sup
cat-tail
cat-tle
cat-tle-man
cat-walk
cau-cus
cau-dal
cau-dle
caught
cau-li-flow-er
caulk

caus-al
cau-sal-i-ty
cau-sa-tion
caus-a-tive
cause
cause-way
caus-tic
cau-ter-ize
cau-ter-y
cau-tion
cau-tion-a-ry
cau-tious
cav-al-cade
cav-a-lier
cav-al-ry
cav-a-ti-na
cave-in
cav-ern
cav-ern-ous
cav-i-ar
cav-il
cav-i-ty
ca-vort
cay-enne
cease-fire
cease-less
ce-dar
cede
ceil-ing
cel-a-nese
cel-e-brant
cel-e-brate
cel-e-bra-tion
ce-leb-ri-ty
cel-er-y
ce-les-tial
cel-i-ba-cy
cel-i-bate
cel-lar
cel-lar-age
cel-lar-et
cel-list
cel-lo
cel-lo-phane
cel-lu-lar

cel-lu-loid
cel-lu-lose
cel-lu-lous
Cel-si-us
(thermometer)
ce-ment
ce-men-ta-tion
cem-e-ter-y
cen-o-bite
cen-o-taph
cen-sor
cen-so-rious
cen-sor-ship
cen-sur-a-ble
cen-sure
cen-sus
cent (money)
cen-taur
cen-ta-vo
cen-te-nar-i-an
cen-te-nar-y
cen-ten-ni-al
cen-ter-piece
cen-tes-i-mal
cen-ti-grade
cen-ti-gram
cen-time
cen-ti-me-ter
cen-ti-pede
cen-tral
cen-tral-ism
cen-tral-i-ty
cen-tral-i-za-tion
cen-tral-ize
cen-trif-u-gal
cen-tri-fuge
cen-trip-e-tal
cen-trist
cen-tu-ri-al
cen-tu-ri-on
cen-tu-ry
ce-phal-ic
ceph-a-li-za-tion
ceph-a-lous
ce-ram-ic

ce-rate
ce-re-al
cer-e-bel-lum
cer-e-bral
cerebral palsy
cer-e-brate
cer-e-bra-tion
cer-e-bro-spi-nal
cer-e-brum
cer-e-mo-ni-al
cer-e-mo-ni-ous
cer-e-mo-ny
ce-rise
ce-ri-um
ce-ro-plas-tic
cer-tain-ty
cer-tif-i-cate
cer-ti-fi-ca-tion
cer-ti-fied
cer-ti-fy
cer-ti-o-ra-ri
cer-ti-tude
ce-ru-le-an
cer-vi-cal
cer-vix
Ce-sar-e-an
ce-si-um
ces-sa-tion
ces-sion
ces-sion-ar-y
cess-pool
chafe
chaff
chaf-fer
chaf-ing dish
cha-grin
chain
chair
chair-man
chaise
cha-let
chal-ice
chalk
chal-lenge
cham-ber

cham-ber-lain
cham-ber-maid
cham-bray
cha-me-le-on
cham-fer
cham-ois
champ
cham-pagne
cham-paign
cham-per-ty
cham-pi-gnon
cham-pi-on
cham-pi-on-ship
chance
chan-cel
chan-cel-ler-y
chan-cel-lor
chan-cer-y
chan-de-lier
chan-delle
chan-dler
chan-dler-y
change-a-ble
chan-nel
chant
chan-teuse
cha-os
cha-ot-ic
chap-ar-ral
cha-peau
chap-el
chap-er-on
chap-fall-en
chap-lain
chap-let
chaps
chap-ter
char-ac-ter
char-ac-ter-is-tic
char-ac-ter-is-ti-cal-ly
char-ac-ter-i-za-tion
char-ac-ter-ize
cha-rade
char-coal
chard

charge-a-ble
char-i-ly
char-i-ot
char-i-ot-eer
cha-ris-ma
char-i-ta-ble
char-i-ty
char-la-dy
char-la-tan
char-la-tan-ism
charm
char-ter
char-treuse
char-woman
chase
chasm
chas-seur
chas-sis
chaste
chas-ten
chas-tise
chas-ti-ty
chas-u-ble
cha-teau
chat-e-laine
chat-tel
chat-ter
chat-ter-box
chauf-fer (stove)
chauf-feur (driver)
chaus-sure
chau-vin-ism
cheap
 (inexpensive)
cheat
check
check-book
check-er-board
check-mate
check-off
check-up
cheek
cheep (chirp)
cheer-ful
cheer-i-o

cheer-less
cheese
cheese-cake
cheese-cloth
chef
chem-i-cal
che-mise
chem-ism
chem-ist
chem-is-try
chem-o-ther-a-peu-tics
chem-o-ther-a-py
che-nille
cher-ish
che-root
cher-ub
chess
chess-man
chest
chest-nut
chee-tah
chev-a-lier
chev-ron
chi-can-er-y
chic-co-ry
chi-chi
chick
chick-a-dee
chick-a-ree
chick-en-heart-ed
chic-le
chic-o-ry
chide
chief
chief-tain
chif-fon
chif-fo-nier
chig-ger
chi-gnon
chil-blain
child-bear-ing
child-birth
child-hood
child-like
chil-i

chill
chime
chi-me-ra
chi-mer-i-cal
chim-ney
chim-pan-zee
chi-na-ware
chin-chil-la
chink
chintz
chip-munk
chip-per
chi-rog-ra-phy
chi-rop-o-dy
chi-ro-prac-tic
chi-ro-prac-tor
chi-rop-ter
chirp
chir-rup
chis-el
chis-eled
chit-chat
chiv-al-ric
chiv-al-rous
chiv-al-ry
chive
chlo-ral
chlo-ra-mine
chlo-rate
chlo-ric
chlo-ride
chlo-rin-ate
chlo-rine
chlo-rite
chlo-ro-form
chlo-ro-phyll
chlo-ro-sis
chlo-rous
chock
chock-full
choc-o-late
choice
choir
choke
chol-er-a

chol-er-ic
cho-les-ter-ol
choose
chop-per
chop-ping
chop-stick
cho-ral
chord
chore
cho-re-a
cho-re-og-ra-pher
cho-re-og-ra-phy
cho-ric
chor-is-ter
cho-rog-ra-phy
cho-roid
chor-tle
cho-rus
chose
chow-der
chrism
chris-ten
chro-mate
chro-mat-ic
chro-ma-to-graph
chrome
chro-mic
chro-mite
chro-mi-um
chro-mo-some
chro-mo-sphere
chron-ic
chron-i-cle
chron-o-gram
chron-o-graph
chron-o-log-i-cal
chro-nol-o-gist
chro-nol-o-gy
chro-nom-e-try
chry-san-the-mum
chub-by
chuck
chuck-full
chuck-le
chud-dar

chuff
church
churl
churl-ish
churn
chute
chut-ney
chyme
ci-bo-ri-um
ci-ca-da
cic-a-trix
ci-der
ci-de-vant
ci-gar
cig-a-rette
cinch
cin-cho-na
cinc-ture
cin-der
cin-e-ma
cin-e-ma-scope
cin-e-ma-tize
cin-e-ram-a
cin-e-rar-i-um
cin-er-a-tor
ci-ne-re-ous
cin-na-bar
cin-na-mon
ci-pher
Cir-ce
cir-cle
cir-clet
cir-cuit
cir-cu-i-tous
cir-cu-i-ty
cir-cu-lar
cir-cu-lar-ize
cir-cu-late
cir-cu-la-tion
cir-cum-am-bi-ent
cir-cum-am-bu-late
cir-cum-cise
cir-cum-ci-sion
cir-cum-fer-ence
cir-cum-flex

cir-cum-flu-ent
cir-cum-flu-ous
cir-cum-fuse
cir-cum-lo-cu-tion
cir-cum-nav-i-gate
cir-cum-scribe
cir-cum-scrip-tion
cir-cum-spect
cir-cum-spec-tion
cir-cum-stance
cir-cum-stan-tial
cir-cum-stan-ti-al-i-ty
cir-cum-stan-ti-ate
cir-cum-vent
cir-cus
cirque
cir-rho-sis
cir-ro-cu-mu-lus
cir-ro-stra-tus
cist
cis-ta-ceous
cis-tern
cit-a-del
ci-ta-tion
cite (quote)
cit-ied
cit-i-fied
cit-i-zen
cit-i-zen-ship
cit-rate
cit-ron
cit-ron-el-la
cit-rus
civ-ic
civ-il
ci-vil-ian
ci-vil-i-ty
civ-i-li-za-tion
civ-i-lize
civ-il-ly
clack
claim-ant
clair-voy-ance
clair-voy-ant
clam

cla-mant
clam-ber
clam-my
clam-or
clam-or-ous
clan-des-tine
clan-gor
clank
clan-nish
clans-man
clar-et
clar-i-fy
clar-i-net
clar-i-on
clar-i-ty
clash
clas-sic
clas-si-cal
clas-si-cism
clas-si-cist
clas-si-cize
clas-si-fi-ca-tion
clas-si-fi-er
clas-si-fy
class-mate
class-room
clat-ter
clause
claus-tro-pho-bia
clav-i-cle
clav-i-er
clean
cleanse
clean-up
clear
clear-ance
clear-head-ed
cleat
cleav-a-ble
cleav-age
cleave
clef (music symbol)
cleft (a split)
clem-en-cy
clem-ent

clench
clere-sto-ry
cler-gy
cler-gy-man
cler-ic
cler-i-cal-ism
clev-er
clev-is
clew (ball of yarn)
cli-che
click (sharp sound)
cli-ent
cli-en-tele
cliff
cli-ma-tic
cli-mate
cli-max
climb
clinch
clin-ic
clin-i-cal
cli-ni-cian
clink-er
cli-nom-e-ter
clip-per
clique (small set)
cli-quish
cli-to-ris
cloak
clob-ber
cloche
clock-wise
cloi-son-ne
clois-ter
clois-tral
clos-et
close-up
cloth
clothe
clothes
clothes-pin
cloth-ier
clo-ture
cloud-less
clo-ven

clo-ver-leaf	co-co-nut	coin
clown-er-y	co-coon	coin-age
club-ba-ble	co-cotte	co-in-cide
club-foot	cod-dle	co-in-ci-dence
cluck	code	co-i-tion
clum-sy	co-deine	coke
clus-ter	co-dex	col-an-der
clutch	cod-fish	cold-blood-ed
clut-ter	codg-er	cold-heart-ed
coach-man	cod-i-cal	co-lec-to-my
co-ag-u-la-ble	cod-i-fi-ca-tion	cole-slaw
co-ag-u-lant	cod-i-fy	col-ic
co-ag-u-late	co-erce	col-i-se-um
co-a-lesce	co-er-cion	co-li-tis
co-a-li-tion	co-er-cive	col-lab-o-rate
coam-ing	co-e-val	col-lage (art form)
coarse (poor quality)	cof-fee	col-lapse
coast-al	cof-fer	col-lar
coast-er	cof-fer-dam	col-lar-bone
coast-line	cof-fin	col-lard
coax	co-gen-cy	col-lar-et
co-balt	co-gent	col-late
co-bal-tic	cog-i-tate	col-lat-er-al
cob-ble	cog-i-ta-tion	col-la-tion
cob-bler	co-gnac	col-league
cob-ble-stone	cog-nate	col-lect
cobra	cog-na-tion	col-lec-tiv-i-ty
cob-web	(relationship)	col-lec-ti-vize
co-caine	cog-ni-tion	col-lec-tor
coc-cyx	(perception)	col-leen
coch-i-neal	cog-ni-za-ble	col-lege (school)
cock-ade	cog-ni-zance	col-le-gian
cock-a-too	cog-ni-zant	col-le-giate
cock-boat	cog-nize	col-lide
cock-er-el	cog-no-men	col-lier
cock-eyed	cog-nos-ci-ble	col-lier-y
cock-le	cog-wheel	col-li-gate
cock-le-bur	co-here	col-li-mate
cock-le-shell	co-her-ence	col-li-sion
cock-ney	co-he-sion	col-lo-cate
cock-pit	co-he-sive	col-lo-ca-tion
cock-roach	co-hort	col-lo-di-on
cock-sure	coif	col-loid
cock-tail	coif-feur	col-lo-qui-al
co-coa	coif-fure	col-lo-quy

col-lude
col-lu-sion
col-lu-sive
co-logne
co-lon
colo-nel
co-lo-nial
col-o-nist
col-o-nize
col-on-nade
col-o-ny
col-o-phon
col-or-a-tion
col-o-ra-tu-ra
col-or-cast
col-or-if-ic
co-los-sal
co-los-sus
co-los-to-my
co-los-trum
col-pi-tis
col-umn
co-lum-nar
co-lum-ni-a-tion
col-umn-ist
co-ma
   (unconsciousness)
co-mate
com-a-tose
com-bat-ant
com-ba-tive
com-bi-na-tion
com-bi-na-tive
com-bine
com-bus-ti-ble
com-bus-tion
come-back
co-me-di-an
   (male joke-teller)
co-me-di-enne
   (female joke-teller)
com-e-dy
com-er
com-et
com-fit

com-fort-a-ble
com-ic
com-i-cal
com-i-ty
com-ma
   (punctuation)
com-mand
com-man-dant
com-man-deer
   (seize)
com-mand-er
   (leader)
com-mand-ment
com-man-do
com-meas-ur-a-ble
com-mem-o-rate
com-mem-o-ra-tion
com-mem-o-ra-tive
com-mence
com-mence-ment
com-mend
com-men-da-tion
com-mend-a-to-ry
com-men-sal
com-men-su-ra-ble
com-men-su-rate
com-ment
com-men-tar-y
com-men-ta-tion
com-merce
com-mer-cial
com-mi-na-tion
com-min-gle
com-mis-er-ate
com-mis-sar
com-mis-sar-y
com-mis-sion
com-mis-sion-er
com-mit-ment
com-mit-tee
com-mit-tee-man
com-mix
com-mode
com-mo-di-ous
com-mod-i-ty

com-mo-dore
com-mon
com-mon-place
com-mon-wealth
com-mo-tion
com-mu-nal
com-mu-nal-ize
com-mune
com-mu-ni-ca-ble
com-mu-ni-cant
com-mun-ni-cate
com-mu-ni-ca-to-ry
com-mun-ion
com-mu-ni-que
com-mu-nism
com-mu-nist
com-mu-ni-ty
com-mut-a-ble
com-mu-tate
com-mu-ta-tor
com-mute
co-mose
com-pact
com-pan-ion
com-pan-ion-ship
com-pan-ion-way
com-pa-ny
com-pa-ra-ble
com-pa-rat-or
com-pare
com-par-i-son
com-part-ment
com-pass
com-par-i-son
com-pat-i-ble
com-pa-tri-ot
com-peer
com-pel
com-pel-la-tion
com-pen-di-ous
com-pen-di-um
com-pen-sate
com-pen-sa-tion
com-pen-sa-to-ry
com-pete

com-pe-tence
com-pe-ten-cy
com-pe-ti-tion
com-pet-i-tive
com-pet-i-tor
com-pi-la-tion
com-pile
com-pla-cen-cy
com-pla-cent
com-plain
com-plain-ant
com-plaint
com-plai-sance
com-plai-sant
com-plet-ed
com-ple-ment
com-ple-men-tal
com-ple-men-ta-ry
com-ple-tion
com-plex
com-plex-ion
com-pli-a-ble
com-pli-ance
com-pli-ca-cy
com-pli-cate
com-pli-ca-tion
com-pli-ci-ty
com-pli-ment
com-plot
com-ply
com-po-nent
com-part
com-part-ment
com-pose
com-pos-er
com-pos-ite
com-po-si-tion
com-pos-i-tor
com-post
com-po-sure
com-pu-ta-tion
com-po-ta-tor
com-pote
com-pre-hend
com-pre-hen-si-ble

com-pre-hen-sion
com-press
com-pres-sion
com-pres-sor
com-prise
com-pro-mise
comp-tom-e-ter
com-pul-sion
com-pul-so-ry
com-punc-tion
com-punc-tious
com-pu-ta-tion
com-put-er
com-rade
co-na-tion
con-cave
con-cav-i-ty
con-ceal
con-cede
con-ceit
con-ceiv-a-ble
con-ceive
con-cent (agreement)
con-cen-trate
con-cen-tra-tion
con-cen-tric
con-cept
con-cep-tion
con-cep-tu-al
con-cern
con-cert
con-cer-ti-na
con-cert-mas-ter
con-cer-to
con-ces-sion
con-ces-sion-aire
con-ces-sion-ar-y
con-ces-sive
conch
con-ci-erge
con-cil-i-ate
con-cil-i-a-to-ry
con-cise
con-clave
con-clude

con-clu-sion
con-coc-tion
con-com-i-tant
con-cord-ance
con-cor-dat
con-course
con-crete
con-cre-tion
con-cu-bine
con-cu-pis-cence
con-cu-pis-cent
con-cur
con-cur-rence
con-cus-sion
con-demn
con-dem-na-tion
con-den-sa-ble
con-den-sate
con-dense
con-den-si-ble
con-de-scend
con-de-scen-sion
con-dign
con-di-ment
con-di-tion
con-di-tion-al
con-dole
con-do-lence
con-do-min-i-um
con-do-na-tion
con-done
con-duce
con-du-cive
con-duct
con-duc-tion
con-duc-tiv-i-ty
con-duc-tor
con-duit
con-du-pli-cate
con-fab-u-late
con-fect
con-fec-tion
con-fec-tion-ar-y
    (like a confection)
con-fec-tion-er

con-fec-tion-er-y
  (confections,
  collectively)
con-fed-er-a-cy
con-fed-er-ate
con-fer
con-fer-ee
con-fer-ence
con-fess
con-fes-sion
con-fes-sion-al
con-fes-sion-ar-y
con-fes-sor
con-fet-ti
con-fi-dant
  (trusted friend)
con-fide
con-fi-dence
con-fi-dent (sure)
con-fig-u-ra-tion
con-fine
con-firm
con-fir-ma-tion
con-fis-ca-ble
con-fis-cate
con-fis-ca-to-ry
con-fi-ture
con-fla-gra-tion
con-flict
con-flu-ence
con-flu-ent
con-form
con-for-ma-tion
con-form-i-ty
con-found
con-fra-ter-ni-ty
con-front
con-fuse
con-fu-ta-tion
con-fute
con-ge
con-geal
con-ge-la-tion
con-gen-er
con-gen-ial

con-gen-i-tal
con-gest
con-glom-er-ate
con-glu-ti-nate
con-grat-u-late
con-grat-u-la-tion
con-gre-gate
con-gre-ga-tion
con-gress
con-gres-sion-al
con-gress-man
con-gru-ent
con-gru-i-ty
con-gru-ous
con-ic
co-ni-fer
co-nif-er-ous
con-jec-ture
con-ju-gal
con-ju-gate
con-junc-tion
con-junc-ture
con-jure
con-nect
con-nec-tion
con-nip-tion
con-niv-ance
con-nive
con-nois-seur
con-no-ta-tion
con-note
con-nu-bi-al
co-noid
con-quer
con-quer-or
con-quest
con-quis-ta-dor
con-san-guin-e-ous
con-san-guin-i-ty
con-science
con-sci-en-tious
con-scious
con-script
con-scrip-tion
con-se-crate

con-se-cu-tion
con-sec-u-tive
con-sen-sus
con-sen-ta-ne-ous
con-se-quence
con-se-quen-tial
con-serv-a-ble
con-ser-va-tion
con-serv-a-tism
con-serv-a-tive
con-ser-va-toire
con-ser-va-tor
con-serv-a-to-ry
con-sid-er
con-sid-er-ate
con-sign
con-sign-ee
con-sign-ment
con-sign-or
con-sist
con-sist-en-cy
con-sist-ent
con-sis-to-ry
con-so-la-tion
con-sol-a-to-ry
con-sole
con-sol-i-date
con-som-me
con-so-nance
con-so-nant
con-sort
con-sor-ti-um
con-spec-tus
con-spic-u-ous
con-spir-a-cy
con-spire
con-sta-ble
con-stab-u-lar-y
con-stan-cy
con-stant
con-stel-late
con-ster-nate
con-sti-pate
con-stit-u-en-cy
con-sti-tute

con-sti-tu-tion-al-ist
con-strain
con-straint
con-strict
con-stric-tor
con-strin-gent
con-struct
con-struc-tion-ist
con-strue
con-sub-stan-tial
con-sul
con-su-late
con-sult
con-sult-ant
con-sult-a-tive
con-sume
con-sum-er
con-sum-mate
con-sump-tion
con-tact
con-tac-tor
con-ta-gion
con-ta-gious
con-tain-er
con-tam-i-nate
con-temn
con-tem-plate
con-tem-po-ra-ne-ous
con-tem-po-rar-y
con-tem-po-rize
con-tempt
con-tempt-i-ble
con-temp-tu-ous
con-tent-ed
con-ten-tious
con-ter-mi-nous
con-test-ant
con-tes-ta-tion
con-text
con-ti-gu-i-ty
con-tig-u-ous
con-ti-nence
con-ti-nent
con-tin-gent
con-tin-u-al

con-tin-u-a-tor
con-ti-nu-i-ty
con-tin-u-ous
con-tort
con-tor-tion-ist
con-tour
con-tra-band
con-tra-bass
con-tra-cep-tion
con-tract
con-trac-tor
con-tra-dict
con-tra-dic-tious
con-tra-dic-to-ry
con-tra-dis-tinc-tion
con-tral-to
con-trap-tion
con-tra-ri-wise
con-tra-ry
con-trast
con-tra-vene
con-tra-ven-tion
con-tre-temps
con-trib-ute
con-trib-u-tor
con-trite
con-tri-tion
con-triv-ance
con-trive
con-trol
con-trol-ler
con-tro-ver-sial
con-tro-ver-sy
con-tro-vert
con-tu-ma-cious
con-tu-ma-cy
con-tu-me-ly
con-va-lesce
con-vec-tion
con-ve-nance
con-vene
con-ven-ience
con-vent
con-ven-ti-cle
con-ven-tion-al

con-ven-tu-al
con-verge
con-ver-gence
con-vers-a-ble
con-ver-sant
con-ver-sa-tion
con-verse
con-ver-sion
con-vert
con-vert-er
con-vex
con-vey
con-vey-or
con-vict
con-vince
con-viv-i-al
con-vo-ca-tion
con-voke
con-vo-lute
con-voy
con-vulse
cook-book
coo-lie
cool-ish
coomb
coon
coop-er-age
co-op-er-ate
co-opt
co-or-di-nal
co-or-di-nate
co-pal
cope
cop-ier
co-pi-ous
cop-per
cop-per-head
cop-per-smith
cop-pice
cop-ra
cop-u-la
cop-u-late
cop-y-book
cop-y-read-er
cop-y-right

co-quet-ry
co-quette
cor-al
cor-al-line
cor-dial
cord-ite
cor-don
cor-du-roy
core
co-re-spond-ent
cork-screw
cor-mo-rant
corn-cob
cor-ne-a
cor-ner-stone
cor-ner-wise
cor-net
corn-flow-er
corn-husk
cor-nice
corn-stalk
corn-starch
cor-nu-co-pi-a
corn-y
co-rol-la
cor-ol-lar-y
co-ro-na
cor-o-nar-y
cor-o-na-tion
cor-o-ner
cor-o-net
cor-po-ral
cor-po-rate
cor-po-re-al
corps
corpse
cor-pu-lent
cor-pus
cor-pus-cle
cor-ral
cor-rect
cor-rect-i-tude
cor-re-late
cor-re-spond
cor-ri-dor

cor-ri-gi-ble
cor-rob-o-rant
cor-rob-o-rate
cor-rode
cor-ro-sion
cor-ru-gate
cor-rupt
cor-sage
cor-se-let
cor-set
cor-tege
cor-tex
cor-ti-cal
cor-ti-cate
cor-ti-sone
cor-us-cate
cor-vette
cos-met-ic
cos-mic
cos-mog-ra-phy
cos-mo-naut
cos-mo-pol-i-tan
cos-mop-o-lite
cos-set
cos-tal
cos-tume
cos-tum-er
co-te-rie
co-til-lion
cot-tage
cot-ton
couch
cou-gar
cough
council (assembly)
coun-cil-man
coun-ci-lor
coun-sel (advice)
coun-se-lor
count
coun-te-nance
coun-ter-act
coun-ter-at-tack
coun-ter-bal-ance
coun-ter-check

coun-ter-claim
coun-ter-clock-wise
coun-ter-feit
coun-ter-foil
coun-ter-in-tel-li-gence
coun-ter-mand
coun-ter-march
coun-ter-part
coun-ter-point
coun-ter-sign
coun-ter-type
count-ess
count-less
coun-tri-fied
coun-try-man
coun-try-side
coup
coupe
cou-pier
cou-plet
cou-pon
cour-age
cou-ra-geous
cour-i-er
course
    (path)
cour-te-ous
cour-te-san
cour-te-sy
court-house
cour-ti-er
court-mar-tial
court-room
court-ship
court-yard
cous-in
cou-tu-rier
cove
cov-e-nant
cov-er-all
cov-er-let
cov-ert
cov-er-ture
cov-et
cov-ey

cow-ard
cow-bell
cow-boy
cow-er
cowl
cow-lick
cox-swain
coy-o-te
co-zy
crab-bed
crack
crack-le
crack-pot
crack-up
cra-dle
craft
crafts-man
cramp
cran-ber-ry
crane
cra-ni-um
cran-kle
cran-ny
cra-vat
cra-ven
craw-fish
crawl
cray-fish
cray-on
craze
creak (sound)
cream (of milk)
crease
cre-ate
cre-a-tor
crea-ture
cre-dence
cre-den-dum
cre-den-tial
cre-den-za
cred-i-ble
cred-it-a-ble
cred-i-tor
cre-do
cre-du-li-ty

cred-u-lous
creed
creek (stream)
creel
cre-mate
cre-ma-tor
creme (liqueur)
cre-ole
cre-o-sol
crepe
crept
cre-scen-do
cres-cent
crest-fall-en
cre-tonne
crev-ice
crib-bage
crick
crick-et
cri-er
crime
crim-i-nal
crim-i-na-tive
crim-i-nol-o-gy
crimp
crim-ple
crim-son
cringe
crin-gle
crin-kle
crin-o-line
crip-ple
cri-sis
crisp
criss-cross
cri-te-ri-on
crit-ic
crit-i-cism
crit-i-cize
cri-tique
crit-ter
croak
cro-chet
crock
croc-o-dile

cro-cus
crone
cro-ny
crook
croon
crop-per
cro-quet (game)
cro-quette (meat)
cro-sier
cross-bar
cross-bred
cross-ex-am-ine
cross-wise
crotch
crotch-et
crouch
croup
crou-pi-er
crou-ton
crow-bar
crow's-foot
crow's-nest
cru-cial
cru-ci-ate
cru-ci-ble
cru-ci-fix
cru-ci-fix-ion
crude
cruise
crul-ler
crumb
crum-pet
crum-ple
crunch
crup-per
cru-sade
crush
crust
crutch
crux
cry-o-gen-ics
cry-o-lite
cry-om-e-ter
cry-o-ther-a-py
crypt

crys-tal
crys-tal-line
crys-tal-lite
crys-tal-lize
cu-bic
cu-bi-cle
cuck-old
cuck-oo
cu-cul-late
cu-cum-ber
cud-dle
cudg-el
cui-sine
cul-de-sac
cu-li-nar-y
cul-len-der
cul-mif-er-ous
cul-mi-nate
cu-lottes
cul-pa-ble
cul-prit
cul-ti-vate
cul-ti-va-tor
cul-ture
cul-vert
cum-ber
cum-ber-some
cum-brance
cum-quat
cu-mu-late
cun-ning
cup-board
cup-cake

cup-ful
cu-pid
cu-po-la
cur-a-ble
cu-ra-tor
curb-stone
curd
cur-dle
cure-all
cu-rette
cur-few
cu-ri-os-i-ty
cu-ri-ous
curl
curl-i-cue
cur-rant (raisin)
cur-ren-cy
cur-rent
    (now in progress)
cur-ric-u-lum
cur-ri-er
cur-ry
curse
cur-so-ry
cur-tail
cur-tain
cur-te-sy
cur-ti-lage
curt-sy
cur-va-ceous
cur-va-ture
cur-vi-lin-e-ar
cush-ion
cusp (point)

cus-pid (tooth)
cus-pi-dor
cus-tard
cus-to-di-al
cus-tom
cus-tom-er
cu-ta-ne-ous
cut-a-way
cut-back
cu-ti-cle
cut-lass
cut-ler-y
cut-let
cut-off
cut-out
cut-throat
cut-up
cy-an-am-ide
cy-a-nate
cy-a-nine
cy-cla-mate
cy-clic
cy-clist
cy-clo-graph
cy-cloid
cy-clone
cyl-in-der
cym-bal
cyn-i-cal
cy-press
cyst
cys-tec-to-my
cyst-ic
czar

D

dab-ber
dab-ble
dab-ster
dachs-hund
dac-tyl
dac-ty-lol-o-gy
dad-dy-long-legs

da-do
dae-dal
daf-fo-dil
daft
dag-ger
dag-gle
dahl-ia

dai-ly
dai-mon
dain-ty
dai-qui-ri
dair-y
dair-y-maid
dair-y-man

da-is
dai-sy
dale
dalles
dal-li-ance
dal-ly
dal-ton-ism
dam (barrier)
dam-age
dam-ask
dame
damn (condemn)
damp-er
dam-sel
dance
danc-er
dan-de-li-on
dan-der
dan-dle
dan-druff
dan-dy
dan-ger
dan-ger-ous
dan-gle
dank
dan-seuse
dap-per
dap-ple
dare-dev-il
dark-en
dar-kle
dark-ling
dark-ness
dark-room
dark-some
dar-ling
darned
dart
dart-er
dash-board
da-sheen
dash-er
das-tard
da-ta
date-less

da-tive
da-tum
daub
daugh-ter
daugh-ter-in-law
daunt
daunt-less
dau-phin
dav-en-port
dav-it
daw-dle
day-break
day-dream
day-light
day-time
daze
daz-zle
dea-con
de-ac-ti-vate
dead-beat
dead-eye
dead-line
deaf
deaf-mute
deal-er
dealt
dean
dean-er-y
dearth
death-less
death-like
de-ba-cle
de-bar
de-bark
de-base
de-bate
de-bauch (corrupt)
de-ben-ture
de-bil-i-tate
deb-it
deb-o-nair
de-bouch (march out)
de-bou-che
de-bouch-ment
de-brief

de-bris
debt
debt-or
de-bunk
de-but
deb-u-tante
dec-ade
dec-a-gon
de-cal-ci-fy
de-cal-co-ma-nia
de-ca-les-cence
dec-a-li-ter
dec-a-me-ter
de-camp
de-cant
de-cant-er
de-cap-i-tate
dec-are
de-car-te-lize
de-cath-lon
de-cay
de-cease
de-ce-dent
de-ceit
de-cel-er-ate
de-cen-cy
de-cen-ni-al
de-cent
de-cep-tion
dec-i-bel
de-cide
dec-i-gram
dec-ile
dec-il-lion
dec-i-mal
dec-i-mate
dec-i-me-ter
de-ci-pher
de-ci-sion
de-claim
dec-la-ma-tion
dec-la-ra-tion
de-clen-sion
dec-li-na-tion
de-clin-a-ture

de-cliv-i-ty
de-coc-tion
de-col-late
de-col-le-tage
de-com-pose
de-con-tam-i-nate
de-cor
dec-o-rate
dec-o-ra-tor
dec-o-rous
de-co-rum
de-cay
de-crease
de-cree
dec-re-ment
de-crep-it
de-cres-cent
de-cre-tive
de-cri-al
de-cry
dec-u-man
de-cum-bent
dec-u-ple
ded-i-cate
ded-i-ca-tory
de-duce
de-duct
deed
deem
deem-ster
deep
deep-dish
deep-fry
deep-sea
deep-seat-ed
deer
deer-skin
de-face
de-fal-cate
def-a-ma-tion
de-fam-a-to-ry
de-fault
de-fault-er
de-fea-sance
de-fea-si-ble

de-feat
de-feat-ism
de-fea-ture
def-e-cate
de-fect
de-fend-ant
de-fen-es-tra-tion
de-fense
de-fen-si-ble
de-fer
def-er-ence
def-er-en-tial
de-fer-ment
de-ferred
de-fi-ance
de-fi-cient
def-i-cit
de-fi-de
de-fi-er
def-i-lade
de-file
def-i-nite
def-i-na-tion
de-fin-i-tude
def-la-grate
de-flate
de-flect
def-lo-ra-tion
de-flow-er
de-flux-ion
de-fo-li-ate
de-force
de-for-ciant
de-for-est
de-form
de-fraud
de-fray
de-frock
de-frost
deft
de-func-tive
de-fy
de-gas
de-gauss-ing
de-gen-er-a-cy

de-glu-ti-nate
de-glu-ti-tion
deg-ra-da-tion
de-grade
de-gree
de-gres-sion
de-hu-man-ize
de-hu-mid-i-fy
de-hy-drate
de-hy-dro-gen-ize
de-hyp-no-tize
deic-tic
de-i-fi-ca-tion
de-i-form
de-i-fy
deign
de-ism
de-ist
de-i-ty
de-ject
de-jeu-ner
de-ju-re
de-lam-i-nate
de-late
de-lay
de-lec-ta-ble
del-e-gate
de-lete
del-e-te-ri-ous
delft
de-lib-er-ate
del-i-ca-cy
del-i-cate
del-i-ca-tes-sen
de-li-cious
de-lict
de-light
de-light-some
de-lim-i-tate
de-lin-e-ate
de-lin-e-a-tor
de-lin-quent
del-i-quesce
del-i-ques-cence
del-i-ra-tion

de-lir-i-ous
del-i-tes-cent
de-liv-er
de-lo-cal-ize
de-louse
del-phi-nine
del-phin-i-um
del-ta
de-lude
del-uge
delve
de-mag-net-ize
dem-a-gog-ic
dem-a-gogue
dem-a-gog-y
de-mand
de-mar-cate
de-ma-te-ri-al-ize
de-mean
de-mean-or
de-ment
de-men-tia
de-mer-it
dem-e-ral
de-mesne
dem-er-sal
de-mil-i-ta-rize
dem-i-mon-daine
dem-i-monde
de-mise
de-mis-sion
dem-i-tasse
de-mo-bi-lize
de-moc-ra-cy
dem-o-crat
de-moc-ra-tize
de-mod-ed
de-mod-u-late
de-mog-ra-phy
de-mol-ish
dem-o-li-tion
de-mon
de-mon-e-tize
de-mo-ni-ac
de-mon-ic

de-mon-ize
de-mon-ol-a-ter
de-mon-ol-o-gy
de-mon-stra-ble
de-mon-strant
de-mon-strate
dem-on-stra-tor
de-mor-al-ize
de-mote
demp-ster
de-mul-cent
de-mur (object)
de-mure (modest)
de-mur-rage
de-mur-ral
den-a-ry
de-na-tion-al-ize
de-nat-u-ral-ize
de-na-ture
den-dri-form
den-drite
den-drol-o-gy
den-e-ga-tion
den-gue
de-ni-al
den-i-grate
den-im
den-i-zen
de-nom-i-nate
de-nom-i-na-tion-al-ism
de-nom-i-na-tor
de-no-ta-tion
de-note
de-nounce
dense
den-si-tom-e-ter
dent
den-tal (of teeth)
den-tal-man
den-tate
den-ti-cle
den-tic-u-late
den-ti-form
den-ti-frice
den-til (small blocks)

den-ti-la-bi-al
den-ti-lin-gual
den-tin
den-ti-phone
den-tist
den-ti-tion
den-ture
de-nude
de-nun-ci-ate
de-ny
de-o-dor-ant
do-o-dor-ize
de-ox-i-dize
de-ox-y-gen-ate
de-part
de-part-ment
de-par-ture
de-pend
de-pend-ence
de-pict
dep-i-late
de-plete
de-plor-a-ble
de-plore
de-ploy
de-plume
de-po-lar-ize
de-pone
de-pop-u-late
de-port
de-por-ta-tion
de-por-tee
de-port-ment
de-pos-it
de-pos-i-tor-y
dep-o-si-tion
de-pos-i-tor
de-pot
de-prave
dep-re-cate
de-pre-ci-ate
dep-re-date
de-press
de-pres-sor
dep-ri-va-tion

de-prive
depth
dep-u-rate
dep-u-ta-tion
de-pute
dep-u-tize
de-rac-in-ate
de-raign
de-rail
de-range
der-e-lict
de-ride
de ri-gueur
de-ris-i-ble
de-ri-sive
de-rive
der-ma-ti-tis
der-mat-o-gen
der-ma-toid
der-ma-tol-o-gy
der-moid
der-ni-er
der-o-gate
der-rick
der-ring-do
der-rin-ger
des-cant
de-scend
de-scend-ant
    (descending from)
de-scend-ent
    (descending)
de-scend-i-ble
de-scen-sion
de-scribe
de-scrip-tion
de-scry
des-e-crate
de-seg-re-ga-tion
de-sen-si-tize
des-ert (dry area)
de-ser-tion
de-serve
des-ha-bille
des-ic-cate

des-ic-ca-tor
de-sid-er-ate
de-sid-er-a-tum
de-sign
des-ig-nate
de-sign-er
des-i-nence
de-sir-a-ble
de-sire
de-sir-ous
de-sist
des-o-late
de-spair
des-per-a-do
des-per-ate
des-pi-ca-ble
de-spise
de-spite
de-spoil
de-spo-li-a-tion
de-spond
de-spond-ent
des-pot
de-spu-mate
des-sert (final course)
des-sert-spoon
des-ti-na-tion
des-tine
des-ti-tute
de-stroy
de-stroy-er
de-struct-i-ble
de-struc-tor
des-ul-to-ry
de-tach
de-tail
de-tain
de-tain-er
de-tect
de-tec-tor
de-tent
de-ter
de-terge
de-ter-gent
de-te-ri-o-rate

de-ter-mi-na-ble
de-ter-mi-nate
de-ter-mine
de-ter-rent
de-ter-sive
de-test
de-test-a-ble
det-i-nue
det-o-nate
det-o-na-tor
de-tract
det-ri-ment
de-tri-tion
de-trude
de-trun-cate
de-tru-sion
deuce
deu-ter-og-a-my
de-val-ue
dev-as-tate
de-vel-op
de-vel-op-er
de-vi-ate
de-vice
dev-il
de-vi-ous
de-vis-a-ble
de-vis-al
de-vise
de-vi-sor
de-vi-tal-ize
de-vit-ri-fy
de-void
de-voir
dev-o-lu-tion
de-volve
de-vote
dev-o-tee
de-vour
de-vout
dew-ber-ry
dew-drop
dew-lap
dex-ter-i-ty
dex-ter-ous

dex-tral
dex-tro-glu-cose
dex-trose
di-a-be-tes
di-a-bet-ic
di-a-ble-rie
di-a-bol-ic
di-ab-o-lism
di-ab-o-lize
di-a-caus-tic
di-ac-id
di-ac-o-nate
di-a-crit-ic
di-ag-nose
di-ag-no-sis
di-ag-nos-ti-cian
di-ag-o-nal
di-a-gram
di-a-gram-mat-ic
di-al
di-a-lect
di-a-lec-tic
di-a-lec-ti-cian
di-al-o-gist
di-al-o-gize
di-a-logue
di-al-y-sis
di-a-lyt-ic
di-a-lyze
di-a-mag-net-ic
di-a-man-tif-er-ous
di-am-e-ter
di-a-met-ri-cal
dia-mond
di-a-per
di-aph-a-nous
di-a-pho-ret-ic
di-a-phragm
di-ar-chy
di-a-rist
di-ar-rhe-a
di-a-ry
di-a-stase
di-as-ter
di-a-ther-my

di-a-tom
di-a-tribe
di-a-zine
dib-ble
di-bro-mide
di-cast
dice
di-ceph-a-lous
di-chlo-ride
di-chot-o-my
dick-ens
dick-er
dick-ey
di-crot-ic
dic-tate
dic-ta-tor
dic-ta-to-ri-al
dic-tion
dic-tion-ar-y
dic-to-graph
dic-tum
di-dac-tic
did-dle
did-y-mous
die-hard
di-e-lec-tric
di-er-e-sis
die-sink-er
di-e-sis
die-stock
di-e-tar-y
di-e-tet-ic
di-e-ti-tian
dif-fer-ence
dif-fer-en-ti-a
dif-fi-cile
dif-fi-cult
dif-fi-dence
dif-flu-ent
dif-fract
dif-fuse
dif-fus-i-ble
dig-a-my
di-gas-tric
di-gen-e-sis

di-gest
di-gest-ant
di-gest-er
dig-it-al
dig-i-tal-in
dig-i-tal-is
dig-i-tate
dig-i-ti-form
di-glot
dig-ni-fied
dig-ni-fy
dig-ni-tar-y
di-graph
di-gress
dike
di-lac-er-ate
di-lap-i-date
di-lat-ant
di-late
di-la-tor
di-lem-ma
dil-et-tan-te
dil-i-gence
dil-ly-dal-ly
di-lute
di-lu-vi-um
di-men-sion
dim-er-ous
dim-e-ter
di-mid-i-ate
di-min-ish
di-min-u-en-do
dim-i-nu-tion
di-min-u-tive
dim-i-ty
dim-mer
dim-out
dim-ple
dim-wit
din-er
di-nette
ding-dong
din-ghy
din-gle
din-go

din-gy
dink-ey
din-ner
di-no-saur
di-oc-e-san
di-o-cese
di-ode
di-o-ram-a
di-ox-ide
di-phos-gene
diph-the-ri-a
diph-the-roid
diph-thong
di-plex
dip-lo-car-di-ac
dip-loid
di-plo-ma
di-plo-pi-a
dip-per
dip-so-ma-ni-a
dip-ter-al
dire
di-rec-tion
di-rec-tor
di-rec-to-rate
di-rec-to-ri-al
dire-ful
dirge
dir-i-gi-ble
di-ri-ge
dir-i-ment
dirk
dirn-dl
dis-a-bil-i-ty
dis-a-ble
dis-ac-cord
dis-ac-cus-tom
dis-ad-van-tage
dis-af-fect
dis-af-firm
dis-a-gree
dis-a-gree-a-ble
dis-al-low
dis-an-nul
dis-a-noint

dis-ap-pear
dis-ap-point
dis-ap-pro-ba-tion
dis-ap-prove
dis-arm
dis-ar-range
dis-ar-ray
dis-ar-tic-u-late
dis-as-sem-ble
dis-as-so-ci-ate
dis-as-ter
dis-as-trous
dis-a-vow
dis-band
dis-bar
dis-bos-om
dis-bow-el
dis-branch
dis-bur-den
dis-burse
disc
dis-cant
dis-card
dis-case
dis-cept
dis-cern
dis-cerp-ti-ble
dis-charge
dis-ci-ple
dis-ci-plin-a-ble
dis-ci-plin-al
dis-ci-pli-nar-i-an
dis-ci-pli-nar-y
dis-ci-pline
dis-dain
dis-claim-er
dis-close
dis-clo-sure
dis-cord
dis-col-or
dis-com-fit
dis-com-fi-ture
dis-com-fort
dis-com-mod-i-ty
dis-com-po-sure

dis-con-cert
dis-con-form-i-ty
dis-con-nect
dis-con-sid-er
dis-con-so-late
dis-con-tent
dis-con-tin-u-ance
dis-con-tin-ue
dis-con-ti-nu-i-ty
dis-cord
dis-cord-ant
dis-co-theque
dis-count
dis-coun-te-nance
dis-cour-age
dis-course
dis-cour-te-ous
dis-cov-er
dis-cov-er-y
dis-cred-it
dis-creet (prudent)
dis-crep-an-cy
dis-crep-ant
dis-crete (distinct)
dis-cre-tion
dis-crim-i-nate
dis-cur-sive
dis-cus (circular stone)
dis-cuss (debate)
dis-dain
dis-ease
dis-em-bark
dis-em-bod-y
dis-em-bogue
dis-em-bow-el
dis-em-broil
dis-en-chant
dis-en-cum-ber
dis-en-dow
dis-en-fran-chise
dis-en-gage
dis-en-tail
dis-en-tan-gle
dis-en-thral
dis-en-throne

dis-en-ti-tle
dis-en-tomb
dis-en-trance
dis-en-twine
dis-es-tab-lish
dis-es-teem
di-seur
dis-fav-or
dis-fea-ture
dis-fig-ure
dis-fran-chise
dis-frock
dis-gorge
dis-grace
dis-grun-tle
dis-guise
dis-gust
dis-ha-bille
dis-ha-bit-u-ate
dis-hal-low
dis-har-mo-ny
dis-heart-en
di-shev-el
dis-hon-est
dis-hon-or
dish-wa-ter
dis-il-lu-sion
dis-in-cline
dis-in-fect
dis-in-fect-ant
dis-in-gen-u-ous
dis-in-her-it
dis-in-te-grate
dis-in-ter
dis-in-ter-est
dis-ject
dis-join
dis-joint
dis-junct
dis-junc-ture
disk
dis-like
dis-lo-cate
dis-lodge
dis-loy-al

dis-mal
dis-man-tle
dis-mast
dis-may
dis-mem-ber
dis-miss
dis-mount
dis-na-ture
dis-o-be-di-ence
dis-o-bey
dis-o-blige
dis-op-er-a-tion
dis-or-der
dis-or-gan-i-za-tion
dis-or-gan-ize
dis-own
dis-par-age
dis-pa-rate
dis-par-i-ty
dis-part
dis-pas-sion
dis-patch
dis-pel
dis-pend
dis-pen-sa-ble
dis-pen-sa-ry
dis-pen-sa-tion
dis-pen-sa-tor
dis-pense
dis-per-sal
dis-perse
dis-per-sion
dis-pir-it
dis-pit-e-ous
dis-place
dis-plant
dis-play
dis-please
dis-pleas-ure
dis-plume
dis-port
dis-pose
dis-po-si-tion
dis-pos-sess
dis-po-sure

dis-proof
dis-pro-por-tion
dis-prove
dis-put-a-ble
dis-pu-tant
dis-pute
dis-qual-i-fi-ca-tion
dis-qui-et
dis-qui-e-tude
dis-qui-si-tion
dis-re-gard
dis-re-pair
dis-re-pute
dis-re-spect
dis-re-spect-a-ble
dis-robe
dis-rupt
dis-rup-ture
dis-sat-is-fac-tion
dis-sat-is-fied
dis-sect
dis-seize
dis-sem-blance
dis-sem-i-nate
dis-sen-sion
dis-sent
dis-sent-er
dis-sen-tient
dis-sen-tious
dis-ser-ta-tion
dis-serve
dis-serv-ice
dis-si-dence
dis-si-dent
dis-sil-i-ent
dis-sim-i-lar
dis-sim-i-late
   (linguistical change)
dis-si-mil-i-tude
dis-sim-u-late (disguise)
dis-si-pate
dis-so-cial
dis-so-ci-ate
dis-sol-u-ble
(can be dissolved)

dis-so-lute
dis-solve
dis-sol-vent (solvent)
dis-so-nance
dis-so-nant
dis-spread
dis-suade
dis-sua-sion
dis-sym-me-try
dis-staff
dis-tal
dis-tance
dis-tant
dis-taste
dis-tem-per
dis-tem-per-a-ture
dis-tend
dis-ten-si-ble
dis-tent
dis-tich
dis-till
dis-til-late
dis-till-er
dis-tinct
dis-tin-gue
dis-tin-guish
dis-tort
dis-tract
dis-train
dis-traint
dis-trait
dis-traught
dis-tress
dis-trib-ute
dis-trict
dis-trust
dis-turb
di-sul-fate
di-sul-fide
di-sul-fu-ric
dis-un-ion
dis-u-nite
dis-use
di-syl-la-ble
ditch

dith-er
dit-to
dit-tog-ra-phy
di-u-re-sis
di-u-ret-ic
di-ur-nal
di-va
di-va-gate
di-va-lent
di-van
di-var-i-cate
di-verge
di-ver-gen-cy
di-verse
di-ver-si-fied
di-ver-si-form
di-ver-si-fy
di-ver-sion
di-vert
di-ver-tisse-ment
di-ver-tive
di-vest
di-ves-ti-ble
di-vert-i-ture
di-vid-a-ble
di-vide
div-i-dend
di-vid-er
di-vid-u-al
div-i-na-tion
di-vine
di-vin-er
di-vin-i-ty
div-i-nize
di-vis-i-bil-i-ty
di-vis-i-ble
di-vi-sion
di-vi-sor
di-vorce
di-vor-cee
div-ot
di-vul-gate
di-vulge
di-vul-sion
diz-zy

do-a-ble
do-all
do-cent
doc-ile
dock-age
dock-er
dock-et
dock-yard
doc-tor-ate
doc-tri-naire
doc-tri-nal
doc-trine
doc-u-ment
doc-u-men-ta-ry
doc-u-men-ta-tion
dod-der
do-dec-a-gon
dodge
doe-skin
does-n't
dog-cart
dog-ear
dog-ger-el
dog-ger-y
dog-gish
dog-house
do-gie
dog-ma
dog-mat-ic
dog-ma-tism
dog-ma-tize
do-good-er
doi-ly
dol-drum
dole
dole-ful
dol-er-ite
dole-some
dol-lar
dol-man
dol-o-mite
do-lor
do-lor-ous
dol-phin
do-main

do-mes-tic
do-mes-ti-cate
do-mes-tic-i-ty
dom-i-cal
dom-i-cile
dom-i-cil-i-ar-y
dom-i-cil-i-ate
dom-i-nance
dom-i-nate
do-mi-ne
dom-i-neer
do-min-i-cal
dom-i-nie
do-min-ion
do-min-i-um
dom-i-no
do-nate
do-na-tion
don-key
don-na
don-nard
don-nish
do-nor
doo-dad
doo-dle
doo-dle-bug
dooms-day
door-bell
door-man
dorm
dor-man-cy
dor-mant
dor-mer
dor-mi-ent
dor-mi-to-ry
dor-nick
dor-sal
dos-age
do-sim-e-ter
do-sim-e-try
dos-sal
dos-ser
dos-si-er
dot-age
do-tard

dote
dou-ble-act-ing
dou-ble-breast-ed
dou-ble-cross
dou-ble-deal-ing
dou-ble-deck-er
dou-ble-head-er
dou-blet
doubt
doubt-ful
douce
dou-ceur
douche
dough
dough-boy
dough-nut
dough-ty
dour
douse
dove-cote
dove-tail
dow-a-ble
dow-a-ger
dow-dy
dow-el
dow-er-y
down-cast
down-fall
down-grade
down-heart-ed
down-stairs
down-town
down-y
dox-ol-o-gy
dox-y
doze
doz-en
drab
drab-bet
drab-ble
draft
draft-ee
drafts-man
draft-y
drag-gle

drag-gle-tailed
drag-hound
drag-net
drag-o-man
drag-on
drag-on-et
drag-on-fly
drag-on-head
drag-on-nade
dra-goon
drain-age
drain-less
drain-pipe
dram
dra-ma
dra-mat-ic
dram-a-tist
dram-a-ti-za-tion
dram-a-turge
dram-shop
dra-per-y
dras-tic
drat-ted
drave
draw-back
draw-bridge
draw-er
drawl
dray-age
dray-man
dread
dread-ful
dream
dream-land
dreamt
drear-y
dredge
drench
dress-mak-er
drib-ble
drib-let
dried
dri-er
dri-est
drift-age

drift-wood
drift-y
drill-mas-ter
drink-a-ble
drive-in
driv-el
drive-way
driz-zle
droit
droll
droll-er-y
drom-e-dar-y
drone
drool
droop
drop-si-cal
drop-sy
drought
dro-ver
drowse
drub-bing
drudge
drudg-er-y
drug-gist
dru-id-ism
drum-beat
drum-fish
drum-lin
drum-mer
drum-stick
drunk-ard
dru-pa-ceous
drupe
drupe-let
dry-as-dust
dry-clean
du-al (of two)
du-al-ism
du-al-i-ty
du-al-pur-pose
dub-bing
du-bi-e-ty
du-bi-ous
du-bi-ta-ble
du-cal

duc-at
duch-ess
duch-y
duck-bill
duck-ed
    (stooped suddenly)
duck-ling
duck-pin
duct (tube)
duc-tile
dudg-eon
du-el (combat)
du-el-lo
du-et
duf-fel
dug-out
dul-cet
dul-ci-fy
dul-ci-mer
dull-ard
dulse
dumb-bell
dumb-wait-er
dum-dum
dum-found
dum-my
dump-ish
dump-ling
dun
dunce
dun-der-head
dun-ga-ree
dun-geon
dun-nage
du-o-dec-i-mal
du-o-dec-i-mo
du-o-de-nal
du-o-den-a-ry
du-o-de-ni-tis
du-o-de-num
du-o-logue
dup-er-y
du-ple
du-plex
du-pli-cate

du-pli-ca-tor
du-plic-i-ty
du-ra-ble
du-ra-men
dur-ance
du-ra-tion
du-ress
du-ri-an
dusk-y
dust-man
dust-pan
du-te-ous
du-ti-a-ble
du-ti-ful
du-ty-free
du-um-vi-rate
dwarf-ish
dwell-ing
dwelt
dwin-dle
dy-ad
dyed-in-the-wool
dye-ing
dye-stuff
dye-wood
dy-nam-e-ter
dy-nam-ic
dy-na-mism
dy-na-mite
dy-na-mo
dy-na-mo-e-lec-tric
dy-na-mom-e-ter
dy-na-mo-tor
dy-nas-ty
dy-na-tron
dys-en-ter-y
dys-func-tion
dys-gen-ic
dys-lo-gis-tic
dys-pep-sia
dys-pep-tic
dys-pha-gi-a
dys-pho-ni-a
dys-pho-ri-a
dys-tro-phy
dys-u-ri-a

E

ea-ger
ea-gle
ea-gle-eyed
ea-glet
ear-ache
ear-drum
ear-flap
ear-ring
ear-lap
earl-dom
ear-mark
ear-mind-ed
ear-muff
ear-nest
earn-ing
ear-phone
ear-ring
ear-shot
earth-bound
earth-en-ware
earth-i-ness
earth-ling
earth-quake
ear-wax
ear-wig
ea-sel
ease-ment
eas-i-ly
east-bound
east-er-ling
east-er-ly
east-ern-most
east-north-east
east-south-east
east-ward
eas-y-go-ing
eat-a-ble
eaves
eaves-drop
eb-on-ite
eb-on-ize
e-brac-te-ate
e-bul-lience

e-bul-lient
eb-ul-li-tion
e-bur-na-tion
ec-cen-tric
ec-chy-mo-sis
ec-cle-si-a
ec-cel-si-as-tic
ec-cle-si-ol-a-try
ech-e-lon
e-cho-ic
ech-o-la-tion
e-clair
e-clat
ec-lec-tic
ec-lec-ti-cism
e-clipse
e-clip-tic
e-cole
e-col-o-gy
e-con-o-met-rics
e-co-nom-ic
e-co-nom-i-cal-ly
e-con-o-mist
e-con-o-mize
e-con-o-my
ec-sta-sy
ec-stat-ic
ec-u-men-i-cal
ec-ze-ma
e-da-cious
e-dac-i-ty
e-daph-ic
ed-dy
e-de-ma
e-den-tate
edge-wise
edg-ing
ed-i-ble
e-dict
ed-i-fi-ca-tion
ed-i-fice
ed-i-fy
e-dile

e-di-tion
ed-i-tor
ed-i-to-ri-al-ize
ed-i-to-ri-al-ly
ed-i-tor-ship
ed-u-ca-ble
ed-u-cate
ed-u-ca-tion-al
ed-u-ca-tor
ed-u-ca-to-ry
e-duce
e-duct
e-duc-tion
e-dul-co-rate
ee-rie
ef-fa-ble
ef-face
ef-fec-tive
ef-fec-tor
ef-fec-tu-al
ef-fec-tu-ate
ef-fem-i-na-cy
ef-fem-i-nate
ef-fer-ent
ef-fer-vesce
ef-fer-ves-cent
ef-fete
ef-fi-ca-cious
ef-fi-ca-cy
ef-fi-cien-cy
ef-fi-cient
ef-fi-gies
ef-fi-gy
ef-flo-resce
ef-flo-res-cence
ef-flo-res-cent
ef-flu-ence
ef-flu-ent
ef-flux
ef-fort-less
ef-fron-ter-y
ef-fulge
ef-fuse

ef-fu-sion
e-gal-i-tar-i-an
e-gal-li-te
e-gest
egg-nog
egg-plant
egg-shell
e-go-cen-tric
e-go-ism
e-go-ma-ni-a
e-go-tist
e-gre-gious
e-gress
e-gres-sion
e-gret
ei-der
ei-der-down
eight-fold
ei-ther
e-jac-u-late
e-jac-u-la-tion
e-ject
e-jec-tion
e-ject-ment
e-jec-tor
e-lab-o-rate
e-land
e-lapse
e-las-tic
e-las-tic-i-ty
e-las-tin
e-las-to-mer
e-late
el-a-ter
e-la-tion
el-bow
eld-er
el-der-ber-ry
el-dritch
e-lec-tion-eer
e-lec-tor
e-lec-tor-al
e-lec-tor-ate
e-lec-tress
e-lec-tric

electric-chair
e-lec-tric fur-nace
e-lec-tri-cian
e-lec-tric-i-ty
e-lec-tri-fy
e-lec-tro-a-nal-y-sis
e-lec-tro-car-di-o-gram
e-lec-tro-car-di-o-graph
e-lec-tro-chem-is-try
e-lec-tro-cute
e-lec-trode
e-lec-tro-de-pos-it
e-lec-tro-dy-nam-ic
e-lec-tro-dy-nam-ics
e-lec-tro-dy-na-mom-e-ter
e-lec-tro-en-
   ceph-a-lo-gram
e-lec-tro-graph
e-lec-tro-ki-net-ics
e-lec-tro-lier
e-lec-tro-lu-mi-nes-cence
e-lec-trol-y-sis
e-lec-tro-lyte
e-lec-tro-lyt-ic
e-lec-tro-lyze
e-lec-tro-mag-net
e-lec-tro-met-al-lur-gy
e-lec-trom-e-ter
e-lec-tro-mo-tive
e-lec-tron
e-lec-tro-neg-a-tive
e-lec-tron-ics
e-lec-tron-volt
e-lec-tro-phon-ic
e-lec-tro-pho-re-sis
e-lec-troph-o-rus
e-lec-tro-plate
e-lec-tro-pos-i-tive
e-lec-tro-scope
e-lec-tro-shock
e-lec-tro-stat-ics
e-lec-tro-ther-a-peu-tics
e-lec-tro-ther-a-pist
e-lec-tro-type
e-lec-trum

e-lec-tu-ar-y
el-e-gance
el-e-gant
el-e-gy
el-e-ment
el-e-men-tal
el-e-men-ta-ry
el-e-phant
el-e-phan-ti-a-sis
el-e-phan-tine
el-e-vate
el-e-va-tor
elf-in
elf-ish
e-lic-it
e-lide
el-i-gi-bil-i-ty
el-i-gi-ble
e-lim-i-nate
e-li-sion
e-lite
e-lix-ir
el-lipse
el-lip-sis
el-lip-ti-cal
el-lip-tic-i-ty
el-o-cu-tion
e-lon-gate
e-lope
el-o-quent
else-where
e-lu-ci-date
e-lude
e-lu-sion
e-lu-tri-ate
e-lu-vi-um
el-ver
elves
elv-ish
el-y-troid
el-y-tron
e-ma-ci-ate
em-a-nate
e-man-ci-pate
e-man-ci-pa-tor

e-mar-gi-nate
e-mas-cu-late
em-balm
em-bank
em-bar-go
em-bark
em-bar-ka-tion
em-bar-rass
em-bas-sa-dor
em-bas-sy
em-bat-tle
em-bay
em-bed
em-bel-lish
em-ber
em-bez-zle
em-bit-ter
em-bla-zon
em-blem
em-blem-at-ic
em-blem-a-tize
em-bel-ments
em-bod-i-ment
em-bod-y
em-bold-en
em-bo-lec-to-my
em-bol-ic
em-bos-om
em-boss
em-bou-chure
em-bow-el
em-bow-er
em-brace
em-branch-ment
em-bra-sure
em-bro-cate
em-broi-der
em-broil
em-brown
em-brute
em-bry-ec-to-my
em-bry-o
em-bry-og-e-ny
em-bry-ol-o-gy
em-bry-on-ic

em-cee
e-mend
e-men-date
em-er-ald
e-merge
e-mer-gence
e-mer-gen-cy
e-mer-gent
e-mer-i-tus
e-mersed
e-mer-sion
em-er-y
em-e-sis
e-met-ic
em-e-tine
em-i-grant
em-i-grate
e-mi-gre
em-i-nence
em-i-nent
e-mir
em-is-sar-y
e-mis-sion
e-mis-sive
em-men-a-gogue
em-met
e-mol-li-ent
e-mol-u-ment
e-mo-tion
e-mo-tion-al-ize
em-pale
em-pan-el
em-pa-thize
em-pa-thy
em-pen-nage
em-per-or
em-per-y
em-pha-sis
em-pha-size
em-phat-ic
em-phy-se-ma
em-pire
em-pir-i-cal
em-place-ment
em-ploy

em-ploy-ee
em-ploy-er
em-poi-son
em-po-ri-um
em-pov-er-ish
em-pow-er
em-press
em-pur-ple
em-py-e-ma
em-pyr-e-al
em-u-late
em-u-lous
e-mul-si-fy
e-mul-sion
e-munc-to-ry
en-a-ble
en-act
e-nam-el
e-nam-el-ware
en-am-or
en-cage
en-camp
en-camp-ment
en-car-nal-ize
en-case
en-caus-tic
en-ceinte
en-ce-phal-ic
en-ceph-a-li-ters
en-ceph-a-lo-ma
en-ceph-a-lin
en-chant
en-chant-er
en-chant-ress
en-chi-rid-i-on
en-chon-dro-ma
en-cho-ri-al
en-cir-cle
en-clave
en-clit-ic
en-close
en-clo-sure
en-co-mi-ast
en-co-mi-um
en-com-pass

en-core
en-count-er
en-cour-age
en-cri-nite
en-croach
en-crust
en-cum-ber
en-cum-brance
en-cyc-li-cal
en-cy-clo-pe-di-a
en-cy-clo-pe-dist
en-dam-age
en-dan-ger
en-dear
en-deav-or
en-dem-ic
en-der-mic
en-dive
end-less
en-do-blast
en-do-car-di-al
en-do-car-di-tis
en-do-carp
en-do-crine
en-do-cri-nol-o-gy
en-do-derm
en-dog-a-mous
en-do-gen
en-dog-e-nous
en-do-lymph
en-do-morph
en-do-par-a-site
en-do-pe-rid-i-um
en-do-phyte
en-do-plasm
en-dorse
en-do-sarc
en-do-scope
en-dos-mo-sis
en-do-sperm
en-do-spo-ri-um
en-dos-to-sis
en-do-ther-mic
en-do-tox-in
en-dow

en-due
en-dur-a-ble
en-dur-ance
en-dure
end-ways
en-e-ma
en-e-my
en-er-get-ic
en-er-gize
en-er-gy
en-er-vate
en-face
en-fee-ble
en-fet-ter
en-fi-lade
en-fin
en-fleu-rage
en-fold
en-force
en-fran-chise
en-gage
en-gar-land
en-gen-der
en-gine
en-gi-neer
en-gird
en-gir-dle
en-gla-cial
en-gorge
en-graft
en-grail
en-grain
en-gram
en-grave
en-gross
en-gulf
en-hance
en-har-mon-ic
e-nig-ma
e-nig-mat-ic
en-joy-a-ble
en-kin-dle
en-large
en-light-en
en-list

en-liv-en
en-mesh
en-mi-ty
en-ne-ad
en-no-ble
en-nui
e-nor-mi-ty
e-nor-mous
e-nough
e-nounce
en-quire
en-quir-y
en-rage
en-rap-port
en-rapt
en-rap-ture
en-reg-is-ter
en-rich
en-robe
en-roll
en-root
en-sam-ple
en-san-guine
en-sconce
en-sem-ble
en-shrine
en-shroud
en-si-form
en-sign
en-si-lage
en-sile
en-slave
en-snare
en-soul
en-sphere
en-sta-tite
en-sue
en-sure
en-swathe
en-tail
en-tan-gle
en-ta-sis
en-tente
en-ter-ic
en-ter-i-tis

en-ter-on
en-ter-os-to-my
en-ter-o-tox-e-mi-a
en-ter-prise
en-ter-tain
en-ter-tain-er
en-thet-ic
en-thrall
en-throne
en-thuse
en-thu-si-asm
en-thy-meme
en-tice
en-tice-ment
en-tire
en-tire-ty
en-ti-tle
en-ti-ty
en-tomb
en-to-mol-o-gy
en-tou-rage
en-trails
en-train
en-trance
en-trap
en-treas-ure
en-treat
en-tre-cote
en-tree
en-tre-mets
en-trench
en-tre-pre-neur
en-tre-sol
en-tro-py
en-trust
en-twine
en-twist
e-nu-cle-ate
e-nu-mer-ate
e-nun-ci-ate
en-ure
en-u-re-sis
en-vel-op
en-ve-lope
en-vel-op-ment

en-ven-om
en-vi-a-ble
en-vi-ous
en-vi-ron
en-vi-rons
en-vis-age
en-vi-sion
en-voy
en-wrap
en-wreathe
en-zo-ot-ic
en-zy-mat-ic
en-zyme
en-zy-mol-o-gy
e-o-lith
e-pact
ep-arch
ep-au-let
ep-ax-i-al
ep-en-the-sis
e-pergne
ep-ex-e-ge-sis
e-phem-er-a
e-phem-er-al
ep-i-blast
ep-i-carp
ep-i-ce-di-um
ep-i-cene
ep-i-cen-ter
ep-i-cure
ep-i-cu-re-an
ep-i-cy-cle
ep-i-cy-cloid
ep-i-dem-ic
ep-i-de-mi-ol-o-gy
ep-i-der-mis
ep-i-dic-tic
ep-i-dote
ep-i-fo-cal
ep-i-gas-tric
ep-i-gene
e-pig-e-nous
ep-i-ge-ous
ep-i-gram
ep-i-gram-mat-ic

ep-i-graph
ep-i-lep-sy
ep-i-lep-tic
e-pil-o-gist
ep-i-logue
ep-i-mor-pho-sis
ep-i-neu-ri-um
ep-i-phe-nom-e-non
e-piph-y-sis
ep-i-phyte
ep-i-rog-e-ny
e-pis-co-pa-cy
e-pis-co-pal
e-pis-co-pate
ep-i-sode
ep-i-spas-tic
e-pis-ta-sis
e-pis-te-mol-o-gy
ep-i-ster-num
e-pis-tle
ep-i-taph
e-pit-a-sis
ep-i-tha-la-mi-um
ep-i-the-li-o-ma
ep-i-thet
e-pit-o-me
e-pit-o-mize
ep-i-zo-ic
ep-och
ep-o-nym
ep-on-y-mous
ep-o-xy
ep-si-lon
eq-ua-ble
e-qual-i-tar-i-an
e-qual-i-ty
e-qual-ize
e-qua-nim-i-ty
e-quate
e-qua-tion
e-qua-tor
eq-uer-ry
e-ques-tri-an
e-ques-tri-enne
e-quil-i-brant

e-quil-i-brate
e-qui-lib-ri-um
e-quine
e-qui-noc-tial
e-qui-nox
e-quip
eq-ui-page
e-qui-poise
e-qui-pol-lent
e-qui-pon-der-ance
e-qui-po-tent
e-qui-ro-tal
eq-ui-se-tum
eq-ui-ta-ble
eq-ui-tant
eq-ui-ta-tion
eq-ui-tes
eq-ui-ty
e-quiv-a-lence
e-quiv-o-cal
eq-ui-voque
e-ra-di-a-tion
e-rad-i-ca-ble
e-ras-er
e-ras-ure
e-rec-tile
e-rec-tion
e-rec-tor
er-e-mite
er-go
er-gos-ter-ol
er-got
er-got-ism
erg-sec-ond
er-i-na-ceous
er-is-tic
er-mine
e-rode
e-rod-ent
e-rog-e-nous
e-rose
e-ro-sion
e-rot-ic
er-rand
er-rant

er-rat-ic
err-ing
er-ro-ne-ous
er-ror
er-satz
er-u-bes-cent
e-ruct
e-ruc-tate
er-u-dite
e-rum-pent
e-rupt
er-y-the-ma
es-ca-drille
es-ca-lade
es-ca-late
es-ca-la-tor
es-cal-lop
es-ca-pade
es-cape-ment
es-car-got
es-ca-role
es-carp
es-cheat-age
es-cheat-or
es-chew
es-cort
es-cri-toire
es-crow
es-cu-lent
es-cutch-eon
e-so-phag-e-al
e-soph-a-gus
es-o-ter-ic
es-pal-ier
es-pe-cial
es-per-ance
es-pi-al
es-pi-o-nage
es-pla-nade
es-pous-al
es-pouse
es-pres-so
es-prit
es-quire
es-say

es-sence
es-sen-tial
es-ta-blish
es-tate
es-teem
es-ter-i-fy
es-the-sia
es-the-sis
es-thete
es-thet-ic
es-ti-ma-ble
es-ti-mate
e-stip-u-late
es-ti-vate
es-top-page
es-top-pel
es-to-vers
es-trange
es-tray
es-treat
es-tri-al
es-tro-gen
es-trone
es-trous
es-tu-ar-y
e-su-ri-ent
etch-ing
e-ter-nal
e-ter-ni-ty
e-ter-nize
eth-ane
eth-a-nol
e-ther
e-the-re-al
e-ther-ize
eth-ic
eth-i-cize
eth-moid
eth-nar-chy
eth-nic
eth-no-cen-trism
eth-nog-e-ny
eth-nog-ra-phy
eth-nol-o-gy
e-thos

eth-yl
eth-yl-ate
eth-yl-ene
e-ti-ol-o-gy
et-i-quette
e-tude
et-y-mol-o-gize
et-y-mol-o-gy
et-y-mon
eu-ca-lyp-tus
eu-chre
eu-de-mo-ni-a
eu-di-om-e-ter
eu-gen-ic
eu-lo-gi-a
eu-lo-gist
eu-lo-gize
eu-lo-gy
eu-nuch
eu-pa-to-ri-um
eu-phe-mism
eu-phe-mize
eu-phon-ic
eu-pho-ni-ous
eu-pho-ny
eu-phor-bi-a
eu-pho-ri-a
eu-plas-tic
eu-re-ka
eu-rhyth-mic
eu-ri-pics
eu-ro-pi-um
eu-tec-tic
eu-tha-na-si-a
eu-then-ics
e-vac-u-ant
e-vac-u-ate
e-vac-u-ee
e-vade
e-vag-i-nate
e-val-u-ate
ev-a-nesce
e-van-gel-i-cal
e-van-ge-list
e-van-ge-lize

e-van-ish
e-vap-o-ra-ble
e-vap-o-rate
e-va-sion
e-vec-tion
eve-ning
e-ven-mind-ed
e-vent-ful
e-ven-tide
e-ven-tu-al
e-ven-tu-ate
ev-er-glade
ev-er-green
ev-er-last-ing
e-ver-si-ble
e-ver-sion
e-vent
ev-er-y-bod-y
ev-er-y-day
ev-er-y-one
ev-er-y-thing
ev-er-y-way
ev-er-y-where
e-vict
ev-i-dence
ev-i-den-tial
e-vil-do-er
e-vince
e-vis-cer-ate
ev-i-ta-ble
ev-o-ca-ble
ev-o-ca-tion
ev-o-ca-tor
e-voke
ev-o-lu-tion-ar-y
e-vul-sion
ew-er
ex-ac-er-bate
ex-act-i-tude
ex-ag-ger-ate
ex-al-ta-tion
ex-am-i-na-tion
ex-am-ine
ex-am-ple
ex-an-i-mate

ex-a-ni-mo
ex-an-the-ma
ex-as-per-ate
ex-cau-date
ex-ca-vate
ex-ca-va-tor
ex-ceed
ex-cel
ex-cel-lence
ex-cel-si-or
ex-cept
ex-cep-tion-a-ble
ex-cerpt
ex-cess
ex-change
ex-cheq-uer
ex-cide
ex-cip-i-ent
ex-cis-a-ble
ex-cise
ex-cise-man
ex-cit-a-bil-i-ty
ex-cit-a-ble
ex-ci-ta-tion
ex-cite
ex-cit-er
ex-claim
ex-cla-ma-tion
ex-clam-a-to-ry
ex-clave
ex-clude
ex-clu-sion
ex-cog-i-tate
ex-com-mu-ni-ca-ble
ex-com-mu-ni-cate
ex-co-ri-ate
ex-cre-ment
ex-cer-men-ti-tious
ex-cres-cence
ex-cres-cen-cy
ex-cres-cent
ex-cre-ta
ex-crete
ex-cre-to-ry
ex-cru-ci-ate

ex-cul-pate
ex-cur-sion
ex-cus-a-to-ry
ex-e-cra-ble
ex-e-crate
ex-e-cute
ex-e-cu-tion-er
ex-e-cu-tor
ex-ec-u-trix
ex-e-get-ic
ex-em-plar
ex-em-pli-fi-ca-tion
ex-empt
ex-e-qua-tur
ex-er-cise
ex-er-ci-ta-tion
ex-er-tion
ex-fo-li-ate
ex-ha-la-tion
ex-haust
ex-hib-it
ex-hi-bi-tion-er
ex-hil-a-rate
ex-hort
ex-hor-ta-tion
ex-hume
ex-i-gent
ex-i-gen-cy
ex-i-gent
ex-i-gi-ble
ex-ig-u-ous
ex-ile
ex-im-i-ous
ex-ist-ence
ex-is-ten-tial
ex-o-der-mis
ex-o-don-tia
ex-o-dus
ex-o-gen
ex-og-e-nous
ex-on-er-ate
ex-o-ra-ble
ex-or-bi-tance
ex-or-cise
ex-or-di-um

ex-os-mo-sis
ex-o-spore
ex-os-to-sis
ex-o-ter-ic
ex-o-ther-mic
ex-ot-ic
ex-ot-i-cism
ex-o-tox-ic
ex-pand
ex-panse
ex-pan-si-ble
ex-pan-sion
ex-pa-ti-ate
ex-pa-tri-ate
ex-pect-an-cy
ex-pect-ant
ex-pect-a-tive
ex-pec-to-rate
ex-pe-di-en-cy
ex-pe-di-ent
ex-pe-dite
ex-pe-di-tion-ar-y
ex-pel
ex-pel-lant
ex-pend
ex-pend-i-ture
ex-pense
ex-pe-ri-ence
ex-pe-ri-en-tial
ex-per-i-ment
ex-pert
ex-per-tise
ex-pi-a-ble
ex-pi-ate
ex-pi-ra-tion
ex-pir-a-to-ry
ex-pire
ex-pla-na-tion
ex-plan-a-to-ry
ex-plant
ex-ple-tive
ex-pli-ca-ble
ex-pli-cate
ex-plic-it
ex-plode

ex-ploit
ex-ploi-ta-tion
ex-ploit-er
ex-plo-ra-tion
ex-plor-er
ex-plo-sion
ex-po-nent
ex-po-nen-tial
ex-port
ex-por-ta-tion
ex-pose
ex-po-si-tion
ex-pos-i-tor
ex-pos-tu-late
ex-po-sure
ex-pound
ex-press
ex-press-age
ex-pres-sion-ism
ex-press-man
ex-press-way
ex-pro-pri-ate
ex-pul-sion
ex-punc-tion
ex-punge
ex-pur-gate
ex-pur-ga-to-ri-al
ex-qui-site
ex-scind
ex-sect
ex-sert
ex-sic-cate
ex-stip-u-late
ex-tant
ex-tem-po-ral
ex-tem-po-ra-ne-ous
ex-tem-po-rar-y
ex-tend
ex-ten-si-ble
ex-ten-sile
ex-ten-sim-e-ter
ex-ten-sion
ex-ten-si-ty
ex-ten-sive
ex-ten-som-e-ter

ex-ten-sor
ex-tent
ex-ten-u-ate
ex-te-ri-or
ex-ter-mi-nate
ex-ter-nal
ex-ter-ri-to-ri-al
ex-tinct
ex-tin-guish
ex-tin-guish-er
ex-tir-pate
ex-tol
ex-tort
ex-tor-tion-er
ex-tra-cel-lu-lar
ex-tract
ex-trac-tor
ex-tra-cur-ric-u-lar
ex-tra-dite
ex-tra-di-tion
ex-tra-dos

ex-tra-ju-di-cial
ex-tra-mar-i-tal
ex-tra-mu-ral
ex-tra-ne-ous
ex-tra-or-di-nar-y
ex-tra-po-late
ex-tra-sen-so-ry
ex-trav-a-gance
ex-trav-a-gan-za
ex-trav-a-sate
ex-tra-vas-cu-lar
ex-tra-ver-sion
ex-tra-vert
ex-treme
ex-trem-i-ty
ex-tri-ca-ble
ex-tri-cate
ex-trin-sic
ex-trorse
ex-tro-ver-sion
ex-tro-vert

ex-trude
ex-tru-sive
ex-u-ber-ance
ex-u-ber-ant
ex-u-ber-ate
ex-u-date
ex-ult-ant
ex-ur-bi-a
ex-u-vi-ae
eye-brow
eye-glass
eye-lash
eye-less
eye-let
eye-lid
eye-sight
eye-sore
eye-strain
eye-tooth
eye-wit-ness

F

fa-ble
fab-ric
fab-ri-ca-tion
fab-ri-koid
fab-u-list
fab-u-lous
fa-cade
face-sav-ing
fac-et
fa-ce-tious
fa-cial
fac-ile
fa-cil-i-tate
fa-cil-i-ty
fac-ing
fa-cin-o-rous
fac-sim-i-le
fact-find-ing
fac-tice
fac-tion

fac-ti-tious
fac-tor
fac-to-ri-al
fac-to-ry
fac-to-tum
fac-tu-al
fac-ture
fac-u-la
fac-ul-ta-tive
fac-ul-ty
fad-dish
fad-dist
fade-in
fade-out
fa-ga-ceous
fag-ot
fail-ing
faille
fail-safe
fail-ure

fain
fai-ne-ant
faint-heart-ed
fair-haired
fair-ish
fair-lead
fair-mind-ed
fair-way
fair-weath-er
fair-y-hood
fair-y-ism
fair-y-land
fait ac-com-pli
faith
faith-less
fak-er
fal-cate
fal-chion
fal-ci-form
fal-con

fal-con-er
fal-co-net
fal-con-i-form
fal-con-ry
fal-de-ral
fald-stool
fal-la-cious
fal-la-cy
fal-lal
fal-lal-er-y
fall-en
fall-er
fal-li-ble
fall-out
fal-low
false
false-heart-ed
false-hood
fal-set-to
fal-si-fy
fal-si-ty
fal-ter
famed
fa-mil-ial
fa-mil-iar
fa-mil-i-ar-i-ty
fa-mil-iar-ize
fam-i-ly
fam-ine
fam-ish
fa-mous
fam-u-lus
fa-nat-ic
fa-nat-i-cize
fan-cied
fan-ci-er
fan-fare
fan-gle
fan-tail
fan-tan
fan-ta-si-a
fan-tasm
fan-tas-tic
fan-ta-sy
fa-rad-ic

far-a-dism
far-a-way
farce
farce-ment
far-ci-cal
fare-well
far-fetched
far-flung
fa-ri-na
far-i-na-ceous
far-i-nose
far-kle-ber-ry
farm-er-ette
farm-house
farm-stead
farm-yard
far-ne-sol
far-o
far-off
fa-rouche
far-ra-go
far-rand
far-reach-ing
far-ri-er
far-ri-er-y
far-row
far-see-ing
far-sight-ed
far-ther
far-ther-most
far-thest
far-thing
fas-ci-a
fas-ci-cle
fas-cic-u-lar
fas-cic-u-la-tion
fas-ci-cule
fas-ci-nate
fas-ci-na-tor
fas-cine
fas-cism
fas-cist
fash-ion
fash-ion-a-ble
fash-ion-er

fas-ten
fas-tid-i-ous
fas-tig-i-ate
fast-ness
fa-tal
fa-tal-ism
fa-tal-i-ty
fa-tal-ly
fat-ed
fate-ful
fat-head
fa-ther-hood
fa-ther-in-law
fa-ther-land
fath-om
fa-tid-ic
fat-i-ga-ble
fa-tigue
fat-ling
fat-sol-u-ble
fat-ten
fa-tu-i-tous
fa-tu-i-ty
fat-u-ous
fat-wit-ted
fau-cal
fau-ces
fau-cet
fault
fault-find-er
fault-less
faun
fau-na
fa-ve-o-late
fa-vo-ni-an
fa-vor-a-ble
fa-vor-it-ism
fa-vus
fawn
fa-yal-ite
faze
fe-al-ty
fear-ful
fea-sance
fea-si-ble

feast-ful
feat
feath-er
feath-er-bed-ding
feath-er-bone
feath-er-brain
feath-er-edge
feath-er-stitch
feath-er-veined
feath-er-weight
fea-ture
feaze
fe-bric-i-ty
fe-bric-u-la
feb-ri-fa-cient
fe-brif-er-ous
fe-brif-ic
fe-brif-u-gal
feb-ri-fuge
fe-brile
fe-ces
fe-cit
fec-u-la
fec-u-lent
fe-cund
fe-cun-date
fe-cun-di-ty
fed-er-a-cy
fed-er-al
fed-er-al-ize
fed-er-a-tion
fe-do-ra
fee-ble
fee-ble-mind-ed
feed-back
feed-bag
feed-er
feel-er
feign
feigned
feint
feld-spar
fe-li-cif-ic
fe-lic-i-tate
fe-lic-i-tous

fe-lic-i-ty
fe-lid
fe-line
fell-a-ble
fel-low
fel-low-ship
fe-lo-de-se
fel-on
fe-lo-ni-ous
fel-on-ry
fel-o-ny
fel-site
fel-spar
felt-ing
fe-male
fem-i-ne-i-ty
fem-i-nie
fem-i-nin
fem-i-nine
fem-i-nin-i-ty
fem-i-nism
fem-i-nize
fem-o-ral
fe-mur
fenc-er
fen-ci-ble
fend
fend-er
fen-es-tel-la
fe-nes-tra
fe-nes-trat-ed
fen-nel
fen-ny
fe-ra-cious
fe-rac-i-ty
fe-ral
fer-de-lance
fer-e-to-ry
fe-ri-al
fe-rine
fer-i-ty
fer-ment
fer-men-ta-tion
fer-mi
fer-mi-um

fern
fern-er-y
fe-ro-cious
fe-roc-i-ty
fer-rate
fer-ret
fer-ri-age
fer-ric
fer-ri-cy-a-nide
fer-rif-er-ous
fer-rite
fer-ro-con-crete
fer-ro-cy-a-nide
fer-ro-mag-ne-sian
fer-ro-mag-net-ic
fer-ro-type
fer-rous
fer-ru-gi-nous
fer-rule
fer-ry-boat
fer-ry-man
fer-tile
fer-til-i-ty
fer-ti-li-za-tion
fer-ti-liz-er
fer-u-la
fer-u-la-ceous
fer-ule
fer-ven-cy
fer-vent
fer-vid
fer-vor
fes-cue
fess-wise
fes-ta
fes-tal
fes-ter
fes-ti-na-tion
fes-ti-val
fes-tive
fes-tiv-i-ty
fe-tal
fetch-ing
fete
fe-tial

fe-ti-cide
fet-id
fe-tish-ism
fe-tor
fet-ter
fet-ter-less
fet-tle
fe-tus
feu-ar
feud
feu-dal
feu-dal-ism
feu-da-to-ry
feuil-le-ton
fe-ver
fe-ver-ish
few-er
fez
fi-a-cre
fi-an-ce
fi-ar
fi-as-co
fi-at
fi-ber
fi-ber-board
fi-bri-form
fi-bril
fi-bril-lar
fi-brin-o-gen-ic
fi-brin-ous
fi-broid
fi-bro-in
fi-bro-ma
fi-bro-sis
fi-brous
fib-ster
fib-u-la
fick-le
fic-tile
fic-tion
fic-tion-al
fic-ti-tious
fic-tive
fid-dle
fid-dle-fad-dle

fid-dle-head
fid-dler
fid-dling
fi-del-i-ty
fidg-et
fidg-et-y
fi-du-cial
fief
field
field-er
fiend
fierce
fi-er-y
fi-es-ta
fife
fif-teen
fif-teenth
fifth
fif-ty
fig-eat-er
fight-er
fig-ment
fig-u-line
fig-ur-ate
fig-ur-a-tion
fig-ure
fig-ure-head
fig-ur-ine
fig-wort
fil-a-gree
fil-a-ment
fil-a-men-ta-ry
fi-lar
fi-lar-i-al
fil-a-ri-a-sis
fil-a-ture
fil-bert
filch
file
fi-let
fil-i-al
fil-i-a-tion
fil-i-bus-ter
fil-i-cide
fil-i-form

fil-i-gree
fil-ings
fill-er
fil-let
fil-lip
fil-lis-ter
film-strip
film-y
fil-o-plume
fi-lose
fil-ter
fil-ter-a-ble
filth
filth-y
fil-trate
fi-lum
fim-ble
fim-bri-a
fim-bri-ate
fim-bril-late
fi-na-gle
fi-nal
fi-na-le
fi-nal-i-ty
fi-na-lize
fi-nal-ly
fi-nance
fi-nan-cier
finch
find-er
fine-ly
fine-ness
fin-er-y
fi-nesse
fin-ger
fin-ger-ling
fin-ger-nail
fin-ger-print
fin-i-al
fin-i-cal
fin-ick-y
fin-ing
fi-nis
fin-ish
fi-nite

fin-i-tude	fish-worm	flam-beau
fin-let	fis-sile	flam-boy-ant
finned	fis-sion	flame
fin-ny	fis-sip-a-rous	fla-min-go
fiord	fis-sure	flam-ma-ble
fip-ple	fist-ic	flan
fire	fist-i-cuff	flange
fire-arm	fis-tu-la	flank
fire-ball	fis-tu-lous	flan-nel
fire-eat-er	fitch	flan-nel-board
fire-fly	fit-ful	flan-nel-et
fire-less	fit-ter	flan-nel-ly
fire-light	five-fin-ger	flap
fire-man	fiv-er	flap-jack
fire-place	fix-ate	flap-per
fire-plug	fix-a-tion	flare
fire-proof	fix-a-tive	flare-back
fir-er	fix-ing	flare-up
fire-side	fix-i-ty	flar-ing
fire-stone	fix-ture	flash
fire-ward-en	fiz-zle	flash-back
fire-wood	flab-ber-gast	flash-light
fire-work	flab-by	flash-o-ver
fir-ing	fla-bel-late	flask
fir-kin	fla-bel-lum	flask-et
fir-ma-ment	flac-cid	flat-boat
fir-ry	fla-con	flat-car
first	flag-el-lant	flat-foot
first-born	fla-gel-li-form	flat-foot-ed
first-class	fla-gel-lum	flat-i-ron
first-ling	flag-eo-let	flat-ling
first-ly	flag-ging	flat-ten
firth	fla-gi-tious	flat-ter-y
fis-cal	flag-man	flat-top
fish-er	flag-on	flat-u-lent
fish-er-man	flag-pole	fla-tus
fish-er-y	fla-grant	flat-ware
fish-hook	flag-ship	flaunt
fish-ing	flag-stone	flau-tist
fish-line	flail	fla-ves-cent
fish-mon-ger	flair	fla-vin
fish-plate	flak	fla-vone
fish-pond	flake	fla-vo-pro-tein
fish-tail	flak-y	fla-vor
fish-wife	flam	fla-vor-ous

flaw
flax
flax-seed
flay
flea
flea-bit-ten
fleam
fleche
fleck
flec-tion
fled
fledge
fledg-ling
fleece
fleet
flesh
flesh-ings
fletch
fletch-er
fleur-de-lis
flex-i-ble
flex-ile
flex-ion
flex-or
flex-u-os-i-ty
flex-u-ous
flex-ure
flick
fli-er
flight
flim-flam
flim-sy
flinch
flin-ders
fling
flint
flip-pant
flip-per
flirt
flir-ta-tious
flitch
flite
flit-ing
flit-ter
flit-ter-mouse

flit-ting
fliv-ver
float
float-a-ble
float-a-tion
floc-cil-la-tion
floc-cose
floc-cu-late
floc-cu-lent
floc-cu-lus
floc-cus
flock
flog
flog-ging
flood-light
floor-cloth
floor-walk-er
flop-house
flo-ra
flo-res-cence
flo-ret
flo-ri-at-ed
flo-ri-cul-ture
flor-id
flo-rif-er-ous
flor-in
flo-rist
floss
flo-tage
flo-ta-tion
flo-til-la
flot-sam
flounce
floun-der
flour
flour-ish-ing
flout
flow
flow-age
flow-er
flow-er-de-luce
flow-er-er
flow-er-et
flow-er-pot
flow-ing

flown
fluc-tu-ant
flue
flu-ent
fluff
flu-id
fluke
flume
flum-mer-y
flum-mox
flump
flung
flunk
flun-ky
flu-o-phos-phate
flu-or
flu-o-resce
flu-o-res-ce-in
flu-o-res-cence
flu-or-ic
fluor-i-date
flu-o-ride
flu-o-rine
flu-o-rite
flu-o-ro-car-bon
fluor-o-scope
flu-o-ros-co-py
flu-or-spar
flur-ry
flush
flus-ter
flus-trate
flute
flut-er
flut-ist
flut-ter
flu-vi-al
flu-vi-a-tile
flux
flux-ion
fly-a-way
fly-by-night
fly-trap
foal
foam

foam-y
fo-cal
fo-cal-ize
fo-cus
fod-der
fodg-el
foe
foe-man
fog-bound
fo-gey
fog-gage
fog-gy
fog-horn
foi-ble
foil
foin
foi-son
foist
fold-er
fo-li-a
fo-li-a-ceous
fo-li-age
fo-li-ate
fo-li-a-ture
fo-li-o
fo-li-ose
fo-li-um
folk-lore
folk-say
folk-sy
fol-li-cle
fol-lic-u-lar
fol-lic-u-lin
fol-low
fol-low-through
fol-low-up
fol-ly
fo-men-ta-tion
fond
fon-dant
fon-dle
fon-due
font
font-al
fon-ta-nel

food-stuff
fool-er-y
fool-har-dy
foot-age
foot-ball
foot-board
foot-fall
foot-ing
foot-less
foot-lights
foot-ling
foot-loose
foot-man
foot-note
foot-path
foot-print
foot-rest
foot-step
foot-wear
fop-per-y
fop-pish
for-age
fo-ra-men
fo-ram-i-nate
for-a-min-i-fer
for-as-much
for-ay
for-ay-er
for-bade
for-bear
for-bear-ance
for-bid
for-bid-dance
for-bid-den
for-borne
force
for-ceps
for-ci-ble
ford
for-done
fore-and-aft-er
fore-arm
fore-bear
fore-bode
fore-bod-ing

fore-brain
fore-cast
fore-cas-tle
fore-cit-ed
fore-close
fore-clo-sure
fore-fin-ger
fore-front
fore-gath-er
fore-go
fore-go-ing
fore-gone
fore-ground
fore-hand
fore-head
for-eign
for-eign-er
fore-knowl-edge
fore-la-dy
fore-man
fore-most
fo-ren-sic
fore-run-ner
fore-see
fore-skin
for-est
fore-stall
for-est-a-tion
for-est-er
fore-tell
fore-thought
for-ev-er
for-ev-er-more
fore-warn
fore-word
for-feit
for-fei-ture
for-fi-cate
for-gath-er
for-gave
forge
for-ger-y
for-get
for-get-me-not
for-give

for-give-ness
for-go
for-got
for-got-ten
forked
for-lorn
form
for-mal
form-al-de-hyde
for-mal-ism
for-mal-ly
for-mat
for-ma-tion
form-a-tive
for-mer
for-mi-ca
for-mi-car-i-um
for-mi-car-y
for-mi-cate
for-mi-da-ble
form-less
for-mu-la
for-mu-lar-ize
for-mu-lar-y
for-ni-cate
for-sake
for-sook
for-sooth
for-spend
for-swear
for-sworn
for-syth-i-a
fort
for-ta-bie
forte
forth
forth-com-ing
forth-right
for-ti-eth
for-ti-fi-ca-tion
for-ti-fy
for-tis-si-mo
for-ti-tude
forth-night
fort-night-ly

for-tress
for-tu-i-tism
for-tu-i-tous
for-tu-i-ty
for-tu-nate
for-tune
for-tune-tell-er
for-ty-nin-er
forty-winks
fo-rum
for-ward
for-worn
fos-sa
fosse
fos-sette
fos-sick
fos-sil
fos-sil-if-er-ous
fos-sil-ize
fos-so-ri-al
fos-ter
fos-ter-ling
fou-droy-ant
fought
foul
fou-lard
foul-mind-ed
foul-mouthed
found
foun-da-tion
foun-der-ous
found-ling
found-ry
fount
foun-tain
foun-tain-head
four-chette
four-cy-cle
four-di-men-sion-al
four-hand-ed
four-in-hand
four-o'clock
four-post-er
four-some
fourth

fou-ter
fo-ve-a
fo-ve-ate
fo-ve-o-la
fowl
fowl-ing
fox-hole
fox-hound
fox-tail
foy-er
fra-cas
frac-tion
frac-tious
frac-to-cu-mu-lus
frac-to-stra-tus
frac-ture
frag-ile
frag-ment
fra-grance
fra-grant
frail
frail-ty
fraise
fram-be-si-a
frame-up
frame-work
fran-chise
fran-ci-um
fran-gi-ble
fran-gi-pane
fran-gi-pan-i
frank
frank-furt-er
frank-in-cense
frank-lin
frank-lin-ite
frank-pledge
fran-tic
frap
fra-ter-nal
fra-ter-ni-ty
frat-er-nize
frat-ri-cide
fraud
fraud-u-lent

fraught
fraz-zle
freak
freck-le
freck-ly
freed-man
free-dom
free-lance
free-load-er
free-man
free-ma-son-ry
free-soil
free-trad-er
free-way
freeze
freeze-dry
freight
frem-i-tus
fre-net-ic
fren-u-lum
fre-num
fren-zy
fre-quen-cy
fre-quent
fres-co
fresh-en
fresh-man
fresh-wa-ter
fret-ful
fret-ted
fret-work
fri-a-ble
fri-ar
fri-ar-bird
fri-ar-y
frib-ble
fric-as-see
fric-a-tive
fric-tion
fried-cake
friend-ship
fri-er
frieze
frig-ate
fright

frig-id
frig-o-rif-ic
fri-jol
frill
fringe
frip-per-y
fri-sette
fri-seur
frisk
frisk-y
frit
frith
frit-il-lar-i-a
frit-il-lar-y
frit-ter
fri-vol-i-ty
fri-zette
friz-zle
frock
frol-ic
frol-ic-some
fro-men-ty
frond
fron-des-cence
front-age
fron-tier
fron-tiers-man
fron-tis-piece
front-let
front-page
frost-bite
frost-bit-ten
froth
frou-frou
frounce
frouz-y
frow
fro-ward
frown
frowst-y
frow-zy
froze
fruc-tif-er-ous
fruc-ti-fi-ca-tion
fruc-ti-fy

fruc-tose
fruc-tu-ous
fru-gal
fruit
fru-i-tion
fru-men-ta-ceous
fru-men-ty
frump
frus-trate
frus-tule
frus-tum
fru-tes-cent
fru-ti-cose
fry-er
fuch-sia
fud-dle
fudge
fu-el
fu-ga-cious
fu-gal
fu-gate
fu-gi-tive
fu-gle-man
ful-fill
ful-gent
ful-gu-rate
ful-gu-rite
ful-gu-rous
fu-lig-i-nous
full-faced
full-fash-ioned
full-fledged
ful-mi-nant
ful-mi-nate
ful-mi-na-tion
ful-some
ful-vous
fu-ma-role
fum-ble
fume
fu-mi-gate
fu-mi-ga-tor
fu-mi-to-ry
fum-y
fu-nam-bu-list

func-tion
func-tion-al-ism
fun-da-ment
fun-da-men-tal-ism
fun-dus
fu-ner-al
fu-ner-ar-y
fu-ne-re-al
fun-gal
fun-gi
fun-gi-ble
fun-gi-cide
fun-gi-form
fun-gold
fun-gous
fun-gus
fu-ni-cle
fu-nic-u-lar
fun-nel
fun-nies
fu-ran
fur-be-low

fur-bish
fur-cate
fur-cu-la
fur-cu-lum
fur-fu-ra-ceous
fu-ri-ous
furl
fur-long
fur-lough
fur-men-ty
fur-nace
fur-nish
fur-ni-ture
fu-ror
furred
fur-ri-er
fur-row
fur-ther
fur-ther-more
fur-ther-most
fur-thest
fur-tive

fu-run-cle
fu-ry
fu-sain
fuse
fu-se-lage
fu-si-bil-i-ty
fu-si-ble
fu-si-form
fu-sil
fu-sil-ler
fu-sil-lade
fu-sion
fuss-budg-et
fus-tic
fus-ti-gate
fu-tile
fu-til-i-tar-i-an
fu-ture
fu-ture-less
fu-tu-ri-ty
fuze
fuzz

G

gab-ar-dine
gab-ble
ga-bi-on
ga-ble
gad-a-bout
gad-fly
gadg-et
gaf-fer
gage
gag-gle
gai-e-ty
gai-ly
gain-er
gain-ful
gait
gai-ter
ga-lac-tic
ga-lac-tose

ga-lan-gal
gal-a-te-a
gal-a-vant
gal-ax-y
gal-ba-num
ga-le-ate
ga-le-i-form
ga-le-na
gal-i-ma-ti-as
gal-i-ot
gal-i-pot
gal-lant
gal-le-on
gal-ler-y
gal-ley
gal-li-mau-fry
gall-ing
gal-li-nip-per

gal-li-nule
gal-li-pot
gal-li-um
gal-li-vant
gal-lon
gal-lop
gal-lo-pade
gal-lous
gal-lows
gall-stone
gal-lus-es
ga-loot
gal-op
ga-lore
ga-losh
gal-van-ic
gal-va-nism
gal-va-nize

gal-va-nom-e-ter
gal-va-nom-e-try
gal-va-no-plas-tic
gal-va-no-plas-ty
gal-va-no-scope
gam-ba-do
gam-be-son
gam-bler
gam-bit
gam-ble
gam-bol
gam-brel
gam-ete
gam-in
gam-ma
gam-ma-di-on
gam-mer
gam-mon
gam-o-gen-e-sis
gam-o-pet-al-ous
gam-ut
gan-der
gan-gling
gan-gli-on
gang-plank
gan-grene
gang-ster
gang-way
gan-is-ter
gan-net
gant-let
gant-line
gan-try
gaol
gape
ga-rage
garb
gar-bage
gar-ble
gar-board
gar-con
gar-den
gar-de-nia
gar-get
gar-gle

gar-goyle
gar-ish
gar-land
gar-lic
gar-lick-y
gar-ment
gar-ner
gar-net
gar-ni-er-ite
gar-nish
gar-nish-ee
gar-nish-ment
gar-ni-ture
ga-rote
gar-ret
gar-ret-eer
gar-ri-son
gar-rote
gar-ru-li-ty
gar-ru-lous
gar-ter
garth
gas-con-ade
gas-e-ous
gash
gas-i-form
gas-ket
gas-light
gas-o-line
gas-om-e-ter
gasp
gas-ser
gas-trec-to-my
gas-tric
gas-trin
gas-tri-tis
gas-tro-en-ter-i-tis
gas-tro-en-ter-ol-o-gy
gas-tro-en-ter-os-to-my
gas-tro-lith
gas-trol-o-gy
gas-tro-nome
gas-tron-o-my
gas-tro-pod
gas-tro-scope

gas-tros-to-my
gas-trot-o-my
gas-tro-vas-cu-lar
gas-tru-la
gas-tru-late
ga-teau
gate-keep-er
gate-post
gate-way
gath-er
gauche
gau-che-ric
gaud-er-y
gaud-y
gauge
gaunt
gaunt-let
gaun-try
gauss
gauze
ga-vage
gav-el
gav-el-kind
ga-vi-al
ga-votte
gawk
gay-e-ty
gaze
ga-ze-bo
gaze-hound
ga-zelle
ga-zette
gaz-et-teer
ge-an-ti-cli-nal
ge-an-ti-cline
gear-ing
geese
gee-zer
gei-sha
gel-a-tin
ge-lat-i-nize
ge-lat-i-noid
ge-la-tion
geld-ing
gel-id

gem-i-nate
gem-ma
gem-mate
gem-mule
ge-mot
gen-der
gene
ge-ne-al-o-gy
gen-er-al
gen-er-al-i-za-tion
gen-er-a-tion
gen-er-a-tor
gen-er-a-trix
ge-ner-ic
gen-er-os-i-ty
gen-er-ous
gen-e-sis
gen-et
ge-net-ic
gen-ial
ge-nic-u-late
gen-i-pap
gen-i-tal
gen-i-ta-li-a
gen-i-to-u-ri-nar-y
gen-ius
gen-o-cide
gen-o-type
gen-re
gen-teel
gen-tian
gen-tia-na-ceous
gen-tile
gen-tle-man
gen-tle-man-at-arms
gen-tle-wom-an
gen-try
gen-u-flect
gen-u-ine
ge-nus
ge-o-cen-tric
ge-o-chem-is-try
ge-og-ra-pher
ge-og-ra-phy
ge-o-log-ic

ge-ol-o-gy
ge-o-mag-net-ic
ge-o-man-cer
ge-o-man-cy
ge-om-e-ter
ge-o-met-ric
ge-om-e-try
ge-o-mor-phic
ge-oph-a-gy
ge-o-phys-ics
ge-o-pol-i-tics
ge-o-ram-a
ge-o-syn-cli-nal
ge-o-syn-cline
ge-o-tax-is
ge-o-tec-ton-ic
ge-o-trop-ic
ge-ra-ni-um
ger-a-tol-o-gy
ger-bil
ger-ent
ger-i-at-rics
ger-man-der
ger-mane
ger-ma-ni-um
ger-mi-cide
ger-mi-nate
ger-on-toc-ra-cy
ger-on-tol-og-y
ger-ry-man-der
ger-und
ges-tate
ges-tic-u-late
ges-ture
get-a-way
get-up
gey-ser
ghast-ly
gher-kin
ghet-to
ghost-ly
ghoul
gi-ant
gib-ber
gib-bon

gib-bos-i-ty
gib-bous
gibe
gib-let
gid-dy
gift-ed
gift-wrap
gi-gan-te-an
gi-gan-tesque
gi-gan-tic
gi-gan-to-ma-chi-a
gig-gle
gig-o-lo
gig-ot
gil-bert
gild-er
gil-son-ite
gilt-edged
gim-bals
gim-crack
gim-let
gim-mick
gin-ger
ginger-bread
gin-ger-snap
ging-ham
gin-gi-val
gin-gi-vi-tis
gi-raffe
gir-an-dale
gir-a-sol
gird-er
gir-dle
girl-hood
girth
gi-sarme
gist
give-a-way
giz-zard
gla-bel-la
gla-brate
gla-cial
gla-cier
glad-den
glade

glad-i-a-tor
glad-i-o-la
glair-y
glam-o-rize
glance
gland
glan-du-lar
glare
glass-ful
glass-house
glass-work-er
glau-co-ma
glau-co-nite
glau-cous
glaze
glean-ing
glebe
glee-ful
gleet
glen
glen-gar-y
glide
glim-mer
glimpse
glint
glis-ten
glit-ter
gloam-ing
gloat
glo-bal
globe-trot-ter
glo-bin
glo-boid
glo-bose
glob-ule
glob-u-lin
glom-er-ate
gloom
glo-ri-fi-ca-tion
glo-ri-ole
glo-ry
glos-sal
glos-sa-tor
glos-sec-to-my
glot-tal

glove
glow-er
glow-worm
glu-ci-num
glu-co-pro-te-in
glu-cose
glu-co-side
glum
glu-ma-ceous
glu-ta-mine
glu-te-nous
glu-te-us
glu-ti-nous
glu-tose
glut-ton
gly-cer-ic
glyc-er-in
glyc-er-ol
glyc-er-yl
gly-cine
gly-co-gen
gly-col
gly-co-pro-tein
glyp-tic
glyp-tog-ra-phy
gnarled
gnash
gnat
gnaw
gnome
gnos-tic
goad
goal-ie
goat-ee
gob-ble
go-be-tween
gob-let
go-cart
god-father
god-less
god-like
god-moth-er
god-par-ent
god-send
gof-fer

go-get-ter
gog-gle-eyed
gog-let
goi-ter
goi-trous
gold-en-rod
gold-fish
gold-i-locks
gol-iard
gol-iar-der-y
go-losh
gom-pho-sic
gon-ad
gon-do-lier
gone-ness
gon-fa-lon
go-ni-om-e-ter
go-ni-on
gon-o-coc-cus
gon-or-rhea
good-bye
good-heart-ed
goose
go-pher
go-ral
gor-cock
gore
gorge
gor-ger-in
go-ril-la
gor-mand
gos-ling
gos-pel
gos-sa-mer
gos-sip
gouache
gouge
gou-lash
gourd
gour-mand
gour-met
gout-y
gou-ver-nante
gov-ern
gov-er-nor

gowns-man
grab-ble
grace-ful
gra-cious
grack-le
gra-date
gra-di-ent
gra-din
grad-u-al
graft-age
gra-ham
grail
gral-la-to-ri-al
gra-mer-cy
gra-min-e-ous
gram-mar
gram-o-phone
gram-pus
gran-a-dil-la
gran-a-ry
grand-child
grand-daugh-ter
gran-deur
grand-fa-ther
gran-dil-o-quence
gran-di-ose
grand-moth-er
grand-par-ent
grand-son
grang-er
gran-ite
gran-ite-ware
gran-it-ize
gra-niv-o-rous
gran-o-phyre
gran-tee
grant-or
gran-u-lar
gran-ule
gran-u-lose
grape-fruit
grape-vine
graphic
graph-ite
graph-ol-o-gy

graph-o-ma-ni-a
graph-o-mo-tor
grap-nel
grap-ple
grasp
grass-y
grate-ful
grat-i-fi-ca-tion
gra-ti-fy-ing
gra-tin
grat-ing
gra-tis
grat-i-tude
grat-toir
gra-tu-i-tion
grat-u-late
grau-pel
gra-va-men
grav-el
grav-el-blind
grav-en
grav-i-met-ric
gra-vim-e-try
grav-i-tate
gra-vure
graze
gra-zier
grease
great-aunt
great-grand-child
greave
grebe
greed-y
green-er-y
greet-ing
gre-gar-i-ous
grei-sen
grem-lin
gre-nade
gren-a-dier
gres-so-ri-al
grey-hound
grib-ble
grid-dle
gride

grid-i-ron
grief-strick-en
griev-ance
griffe
grif-fen
grift-er
grill (fry)
grille (mesh)
grill-room
gri-mace
grime
grind
grin-de-li-a
grind-stone
grin-go
gripe (complain)
grippe (cold)
grip-sack
gri-saille
gris-e-ous
gri-sette
grist
grit-ty
griv-et
griz-zle
groan
groats
gro-cer
grog-ger-y
grog-ram
grog-shop
groin
grom-met
grom-well
groom
grooms-man
groove
grope
gros-grain
gross
gros-su-lar-ite
gro-tesque
grot-to
grouch-y
ground-less

group-er
grouse
grout
grove
grov-el
grower
growl
grown-up
growth
grub-by
grudge
gru-el
grue-some
gruff
grum-ble
grum-met
gru-mous
grun-ion
grunt-er
guan-i-dine
gua-nine
guar-an-tee
guar-an-tor
guard-i-an
guards-man
gua-va
gu-ber-na-to-ri-al
guer-don
guer-ril-la
guess
guest

guf-faw
guid-ance
gui-don
guild
guil-der
guile
guil-lo-tine
guilt
gui-pure
guise
gui-tar
gui-tar-fish
gulch
gul-den
gulf
gul-let
gul-li-ble
gulp
gum-bo
gum-ma
gum-mite
gump-tion
gun-nel
gun-ner
gun-shot
gup-py
gur-gi-ta-tion
gur-gle
gur-nard
gush-er
gus-set

gus-ta-to-ry
gus-to
gut-ta
gut-ta-per-cha
gut-ter
gut-ter-snipe
gut-tur-al
guz-zle
gym-kha-na
gym-na-si-a
gym-nast
gym-no-sperm
gy-nan-drous
gy-nar-chy
gy-ne-ci-um
gy-ne-col-o-gy
gy-ne-pho-bia
gy-ni-at-rics
gy-no-gen-ic
gyp-sum
gy-rate
gy-ro
gy-ro-com-pass
gy-ro-plane
gy-ro-scope
gy-ro-sta-bi-liz-er
gy-ro-stat
gy-ro-stat-ic
gy-ro-stat-ics
gy-rus

H

hab-er-dash-er
hab-ile
ha-bil-i-tate
hab-it-a-ble
hab-i-tat
ha-bit-u-al
hab-i-tude
ha-chure
ha-ci-en-da
hack-le

hack-ney
hack-saw
had-dock
hade
haft
hag-fish
hag-gard
hag-gish
hag-gle
hag-i-oc-ra-cy

hag-i-og-ra-pher
hag-rid-den
hail-storm
hair-brush
hair-cut
hair-do
hair-dress-er
hair-pin
hair-rais-ing
hair-split-ter

hake
ha-la-tion
hal-berd
hal-berd-ier
hal-cy-on
hale
half-back
half-blood-ed
half-breed
half-broth-er
half-caste
half-heart-ed
half-hour-ly
half-mast
half-way
half-wit-ted
hal-i-but
hal-ide
hal-ite
hal-i-to-sis
hal-i-tus
hal-le-lu-jah
hal-liard
hall-mark
hal-lowed
hal-lu-ci-nate
hal-lu-ci-no-sis
hal-lux
hall-way
ha-lo
hal-o-gen
hal-oid
hal-o-phyte
hal-ter
halves
hal-yard
ham-a-dry-ad
ha-mate
ham-burg-er
ham-let
ham-mer
ham-mer-head
ham-mock
ham-per
ham-ster

ham-string
ham-u-lus
han-a-per
hance
hand-bag
hand-cuff
hand-ful
hand-i-cap
hand-i-craft
hand-i-work
hand-ker-chief
han-dler
hand-made
hand-maid-en
    (servant)
hand-me-down
hand-out
hand-pick
hand-rail
hand-set
hand-some
hand-writ-ing
hang-ar (shed)
hang-er (support)
hang-er-on
hang-nail
hang-out
hang-o-ver
han-ker
han-ky
han-som (vehicle)
hap-haz-ard
hap-less
hap-lite
hap-loid
hap-lol-o-gy
hap-lo-sis
hap-pen
hap-pi-ness
ha-ra-ki-ri
ha-rangue
har-ass
har-bin-ger
har-bor
hard-bit-ten

hard-boiled
hard-en
hard-head
hard-heart-ed
har-di-ness
hard-ness
hard-ship
hard-top
hard-wood
hare-bell
hare-brained
hare-lip
har-em
har-i-cot
hark
hark-en
har-le-quin-ade
har-lot
har-mat-tan
harm-ful
har-mon-ic
har-mon-i-ca
har-mon-ics
har-mo-ni-ous
har-mo-nist
har-mo-nize
har-mo-ny
har-ness
harp-ist
har-poon
harp-si-chord
har-que-bus
har-que-bus-ier
har-ri-dan
har-ri-er
har-row
har-ry
harsh
hart
har-te-beest
har-um-scar-um
har-vest
har-vest-er
has-been
hash-ish

has-let
hasp
has-sle
has-sock
has-tate
has-ten
hat-a-ble
hat-band
hat-box
hatch-er-y
hatch-et
hatch-ment
hatch-way
hate-a-ble
hate-ful
ha-tred
hat-ter
hau-berk
haugh-ty
haul-age
haunch
haunt
hau-teur
have-lock
ha-ven
hav-er-sack
hav-oc
hawk-er
hawk-eyed
hawk-nose
hawk's-eye
haw-ser
haw-ser-laid
hay-cock
hay-rack
hay-seed
hay-stack
hay-wire
haz-ard
haze
ha-zle-nut
head-ache
head-band
head-first
head-gear

head-light
head-line
head-mas-ter
head-on
head-piece
head-quar-ters
head-rest
head-set
head-strong
head-way
heal-er (mender)
heal-ing
health
heap
hear-ing
heark-en
hear-say
hearse
heart-ache
heart-beat
heart-break
heart-burn
heart-felt
heart-free
hearth
heart-rend-ing
heart-shaped
heart-sick
heart-strick-en
heart-throb
hea-then
heath-er
heat-stroke
heave
heav-en
heav-y-du-ty
heav-y-hand-ed
heav-y-heart-ed
heav-y-weight
he-be-phre-ni-a
heb-e-tate
he-bet-ic
heck-le
hec-tare
hec-tic

hec-to-gram
hec-to-graph
hec-to-li-ter
hec-to-me-ter
hed-dle
hedge-hog
hedg-er
he-don-ic
herd-ful
heel-er (one who heels)
heft-y
he-gem-o-ny
he-gu-men
heif-er
heigh
heigh-ho
height
hei-nous
heir-dom
heir-ess
heir-loom
he-li-a-cal
he-li-an-thus
hel-i-cal
hel-i-ces (*pl. of* helix)
hel-i-coid
hel-i-cop-ter
he-li-o-cen-tric
he-li-o-gram
he-li-o-graph
he-li-o-stat
he-li-o-tax-is
he-li-o-ther-a-py
he-li-o-trope
he-li-o-type
he-li-o-zo-an
hel-i-port
he-li-um
he-lix
hell-fire
hell-hound
hel-lion
helm
hel-met
hel-min-thi-a-sis

hel-min-thol-o-gy
helms-man
hel-ot-ism
hel-ot-ry
help-mate
hel-ter-skel-ter
he-ma-chrome
he-mal
he-mat-ic
hem-a-tin
hem-a-to-gen-e-sis
hem-a-tog-e-nous
he-ma-tol-o-gy
he-ma-to-ma
hem-a-to-poi-e-sis
he-ma-to-sis
hem-a-to-ther-mal
he-ma-tox-y-lin
hem-a-to-zo-on
hem-el-y-tron
hem-er-a-lo-pi-a
hem-i-al-gi-a
hem-i-cel-lu-lose
hem-i-cra-ni-a
hem-i-cy-cle
hem-i-he-dral
hem-i-hy-drate
hem-i-mor-phic
hem-i-mor-phite
he-min
hem-i-ple-gi-a
he-mip-ter-ous
hem-i-sphere
hem-i-spher-oid
hem-i-stitch
hem-i-ter-pene
hem-i-trope
hem-lock
hem-mer
he-mo-glo-bin
he-moid
he-mo-leu-co-cyte
he-mo-ly-sin
he-mol-y-sis
he-mo-phil-i-a

he-mop-ty-sis
hem-or-rhage
hem-or-rhoid
hem-or-rhoid-ec-to-my
he-mo-stat
hemp-seed
hem-stitch
hen-bit
hence-forth
hench-man
hen-dec-a-gon
hen-dec-a-syl-la-ble
hen-di-a-dys
hen-e-quen
hen-na
hen-ner-y
hen-o-the-ism
hen-peck
hen-ry
hep-a-rin
he-pat-ic
hep-a-ti-tis
hep-a-tize
hep-cat
hep-tad
hep-ta-gon
hep-ta-he-dron
hep-tam-e-ter
hep-tane
hep-tan-gu-lar
hep-tar-chy
hep-ta-stick
her-ald
her-ba-ceous
herb-age
her-bar-i-um
her-biv-o-rous
her-cu-le-an
herd-er
herds-man
here-a-bout
here-af-ter
here-at
here-by
he-red-i-ta-ble

her-e-dit-a-ment
he-red-i-tar-y
he-red-i-ty
here-in
here-in-af-ter
here-in-to
here-of
here-on
her-e-sy
her-e-tic
here-to
here-to-fore
here-un-der
here-up-on
here-with
her-i-ot
her-it-age
her-i-tor
her-ma
her-maph-ro-dite
her-me-neu-tic
her-mit
her-ni-a
her-ni-or-rha-phy
he-ro-ic
her-o-in (drug)
her-o-ine (female hero)
her-on
her-pes
her-ring
her-ring-bone
her-self
hertz
hes-i-tate
hes-per-i-din
hes-so-nite
he-tae-ra
het-er-o-cer-cal
het-er-o-chro-mat-ic
het-er-o-chro-mo-some
het-er-o-clite
het-er-o-cy-clic
het-er-o-dox
het-er-o-dyne
het-er-o-ga-mete

het-er-og-a-mous
het-er-og-a-my
het-er-o-ge-ne-i-ty
het-er-o-ge-ne-ous
het-er-og-e-nous
het-er-og-o-nous
het-er-og-o-ny
het-er-og-ra-phy
het-er-og-y-nous
het-er-ol-o-gy
het-er-ol-y-sis
het-er-o-mor-phic
het-er-on-o-mous
het-er-o-nym
het-er-o-plas-ty
het-er-op-ter-ous
het-er-o-sex-u-al
het-er-o-sis
het-er-os-po-rous
het-er-o-typ-ic
heu-ris-tic
hew (cut)
hex-a-chord
hex-ad
hex-a-gon
hex-ag-o-nal
hex-a-gram
hex-a-he-dron
hex-am-er-ous
hex-am-e-ter
hex-an-gu-lar
hex-a-pod
hex-ap-o-dy
hex-a-stick
hex-one
hex-ose
hey-day
hi-a-tus
hi-ba-chi
hi-ber-nac-u-lum
hi-ber-nate
hi-bis-cus
hic-cup
hick-o-ry
hi-dal-go

hid-den
hide-and-seek
hid-e-ous
hide-out
hi-dro-sis
hi-er-arch
hi-er-ar-chi-cal
hi-er-at-ic
hi-er-oc-ra-cy
hi-er-o-glyph-ic
hi-er-ol-o-gy
hi-er-o-phant
hi-fa-lu-tin
hi-fi
hig-gler
high-ball
high-brow
high-er-up
high-fa-lu-tin
high-fi-del-i-ty
high-mind-ed
hi-jack
hi-lar-i-ous
hill-bil-ly
hilt
hi-lum
hi-mat-i-on
hind-brain
hin-drance
hinge
hin-ter-land
hip-bone
hip-po-cam-pus
hip-po-cras
hip-po-drome
hip-po-griff
hip-po-pot-a-mus
hip-shot
hir-cine
hire-ling
hir-sute
hi-run-dine
his-pid
his-ta-mine
his-ti-dine

his-to-gen
his-to-gram
his-toid
his-tol-o-gy
his-tol-y-sis
his-tone
his-to-ri-an
his-to-ri-og-ra-pher
his-to-ry
his-tri-on-ic
hitch-hike
hith-er
hives
heard
hoarse
hoar-y
hoax
hob-ble
hob-ble-bush
hob-by-horse
hob-gob-lin
hob-nail
hob-nob
hock-ey
hock-shop
ho-cus
ho-cus-po-cus
hodge-podge
hod-man
hoe-cake
ho-gan
hog-gish
hog-tie
hog-wash
hoicks
hoi-den
hoi-pol-loi
hoist
hoi-ty-toi-ty
ho-key-po-key
ho-kum
hold-o-ver
hold-up
hol-i-day
ho-li-ness

ho-lism
hol-ler
hol-lo
hol-low
hol-low-eyed
hol-ly
hol-ly-hock
hol-mi-um
hol-o-blas-tic
hol-o-caine
hol-o-caust
hol-o-cene
hol-o-graph
hol-o-he-dral
hol-o-phote
hol-o-phras-tic
hol-o-thu-ri-an
hol-ster
hom-age
hom-bre
hom-burg
home-bred
home-brew
home-land
home-made
home-mak-er
ho-me-o-mor-phism
ho-me-o-path-ic
ho-me-op-a-thy
ho-me-o-stat-ic
home-work
home-y
hom-i-cide
hom-i-let-ic
hom-i-let-ics
hom-i-ly
hom-i-ny
ho-mo-cer-cal
ho-mo-chro-mat-ic
ho-mo-chro-mous
ho-mo-mor-phism
ho-moe-op-a-thy
ho-mog-a-my
ho-mo-ge-ne-i-ty
ho-mo-ge-ne-ous (alike)

ho-mog-e-nize
ho-mog-e-nous
ho-mog-e-ny
ho-mog-o-nous
(of flowers)
hom-o-graph
ho-mol-o-gate
ho-mo-log-i-cal
ho-mol-o-gous
hom-o-logue
ho-mo-mor-phism
hom-o-nym
ho-mon-y-my
hom-o-phone
ho-moph-o-nous
ho-mop-ter-ous
ho-mo-sex-u-al-i-ty
ho-mos-po-rous
ho-mos-po-ry
ho-mo-tox-ic
ho-mo-thal-lic
hone
hon-est
hon-ey-bee
hon-ey-comb
hon-ey-dew
hon-ey-moon
hon-ey-suck-er
hon-ey-suck-le
honk-y-tonk
hon-or
hon-o-rar-i-um
hon-or-if-ic
hooch
hood-lum
hoo-ey
hoof-bound
hoof-er
hooked
hook-up
hoo-li-gan
hoop
hoo-ray
hooves
hope-ful

hop-ple
hop-scotch
ho-ral
ho-ra-ry
horde
hore-hound
hor-i-zon-tal
hor-mone
horn-swog-gle
hor-o-loge
hor-o-scope
hor-ren-dous
hor-ri-ble
hor-rid
hor-rif-ic
hor-rip-i-la-tion
hor-ror
horse-back
horse-man
horse-shoe
horse-tail
hor-ta-tive
hor-ti-cul-ture
ho-san-na
ho-sier
hos-pice
hos-pi-ta-ble
hos-pi-tal
hos-pi-tal-i-ty
hos-pi-tal-man
hos-tage
hos-tel
host-ess
hos-tile
hos-tler
hot-spur
hour-glass
house-keep-er
house-moth-er
house-work
hous-ton-ni-a
hov-el
hov-er
how-be-it
how-itz-er

howl-er
how-so-ev-er
hua-ra-che
hub-bub
hu-bris
huck-a-back
huck-le-ber-ry
huck-ster
hud-dle
hue (tint)
huff-ish
hug-ger-mug-ger
hug-me-tight
hu-la-hu-la
hulk-ing
hul-la-ba-loo
hu-man
hu-mane
hu-man-i-tar-i-an
hu-man-kind
hum-ble
hum-bug
hum-bug-ger-y
hum-ding-er
hum-drum
hu-mer-al
hu-mer-us
hu-mid
hu-mi-dor
hu-mil-i-ty
hum-mock
hu-mor
hu-mor-esque
humph
hump-y
hunch-back
hun-dred-fold
hun-dred-per-cen-ter
hun-dredth
hun-dred-weight
hun-ger
hunt-er
hunt-ress
hunts-man
hur-dle

hur-dy-gur-dy
hurl-y-burl-y
hur-rah
hur-ri-cane
hurry
hur-ry-scur-ry
hur-tle
hus-band
husk
hus-sy
hus-tle
hutch
hut-ment
huz-za
hy-a-cinth
hy-ae-na
hy-a-line
hy-a-lite
hy-a-loid
hy-a-lo-plasm
hy-brid
hy-brid-ism
hy-brid-ize
hy-dan-to-in
hy-da-tid
hyd-no-car-pate
hy-drac-id
hy-dran-ge-a
hy-drant
hy-dranth
hy-drar-gy-ri-a-sis
hy-dras-tine
hy-dras-tic
hy-drate
hy-drat-ed
hy-drau-lic
hy-dra-zine
hy-dra-zo-ic
hy-dride
hy-dro-air-plane
hy-dro-car-bon
hy-dro-ceph-a-lus
hy-dro-chlo-ride
hy-dro-dy-nam-ic
hy-dro-e-lec-tric

hy-dro-foil
hy-dro-gen
hy-dro-gen-ate
hy-dro-gen-ize
hy-drog-e-nous
hy-drog-ra-phy
hy-droid
hy-dro-ki-net-ic
hy-dro-ki-net-ics
hy-drol-o-gy
hy-drol-y-sis
hy-dro-lyt-ic
hy-dro-lyze
hy-dro-man-cy
hy-dro-me-chan-ics
hy-dro-me-du-sa
hy-dro-mel
hy-dro-met-al-lur-gy
hy-dro-me-te-or
hy-drom-e-ter
hy-drop-a-thy
hy-dro-phane
hy-dro-pho-bi-a
hy-dro-phone
hy-dro-phyl-la-ceous
hy-dro-phyte
hy-drop-ic
hy-dro-plane
hy-dro-scope
hy-dro-sol
hy-dro-some
hy-dro-sphere
hy-dro-stat
hy-dro-stat-ic
hy-dro-sul-fide
hy-dro-ther-a-peu-tics
hy-dro-ther-a-py
hy-dro-ther-mal
hy-dro-trop-ic
hy-drous
hy-drox-ide
hy-e-na
hy-giene
hy-gro-graph
hy-grom-e-ter

hy-gro-scope
hy-lo-zo-ism
hy-men
hy-me-ne-al
hymn
hym-no-dy
hym-nol-o-gy
hy-oid
hyp-a-byss-al
hy-per-a-cid-i-ty
hy-per-a-cu-sis
hy-per-ae-mi-a
hy-per-al-ge-si-a
hy-per-bo-la
hy-per-crit-i-cal
hy-per-e-mi-a
hy-per-es-the-sia
hy-per-ir-ri-ta-bil-i-ty
hy-per-ki-ne-sia
hy-per-me-ter
hy-per-me-trop-ic
hy-per-os-to-sis
hy-per-phys-i-cal
hy-per-pi-tu-i-ta-rism
hy-per-py-rex-i-a

hy-per-sen-si-tive
hy-per-son-ic
hy-per-ten-sion
hy-per-thy-roid-ism
hy-per-ton-ic
hy-per-tro-phy
hy-pe-thral
hy-phen
hyp-no-a-nal-y-sis
hyp-noi-dal
hyp-nol-o-gy
hyp-no-sis
hyp-no-ther-a-py
hy-po-a-cid-i-ty
hy-po-blast
hyp-o-caust
hy-po-chon-dri-ac
hy-poc-ri-sy
hyp-o-crite
hy-po-derm
hy-po-eu-tec-tic
hy-po-gas-tric
hy-po-gas-tri-um
hy-po-ge-al

hyp-o-gene
hy-pog-e-nous
hy-po-glos-sal
hy-pog-y-nous
hy-po-nas-ty
hy-po-phos-phite
hy-poph-y-sis
hy-po-pi-tu-i-ta-rism
hy-po-pla-sia
hy-pos-ta-sis
hyp-o-style
hy-po-sul-fite
hy-po-tox-ic
hy-poth-e-cate
hy-po-ther-mi-a
hy-poth-e-sis
hy-po-thet-i-cal
hy-po-ton-ic
hyp-som-e-try
hys-ter-ec-to-my
hys-ter-e-sis
hys-ter-i-cal
hys-ter-oid
hys-ter-ot-o-my
hy-zone

I

i-am-bic
i-bex
i-bis
ice-berg
ice-break-er
ice-cap
ice-cold
ice-man
ich-nog-ra-phy
i-ci-cle
i-con
i-con-o-clasm
i-con-o-scope
i-de-al
i-de-ate
i-den-ti-cal

i-den-ti-fi-ca-tion
i-den-ti-ty
id-e-o-graph
i-de-o-log-ic
id-i-o-blast
id-i-o-cy
id-i-o-graph-ic
id-i-om
id-i-o-mor-phic
id-i-op-a-thy
id-i-o-phone
id-i-o-plasm
id-i-o-syn-cra-sy
id-i-ot
i-do-crase
i-dol-a-ter

i-dol-a-trize
i-dyl
i-dyl-lic
ig-loo
ig-ne-ous
ig-nes-cent
ig-nite
ig-ni-tron
ig-no-ble
ig-no-min-i-ous
ig-no-min-y
ig-no-ra-mus
ig-no-rance
i-gua-na
il-e-os-to-my
il-e-um

ill-ad-vised	im-brute	im-par-i-ty
ill-at-ease	im-bue	im-park
il-la-tion	im-ide	im-part
il-laud-a-ble	im-i-ta-ble	im-par-tial
ill-bred	im-i-tate	im-part-i-ble
il-le-gal	im-mac-u-late	im-pass-a-ble
il-leg-i-ble	im-ma-nent	im-passe
il-le-git-i-mate	im-ma-te-ri-al	im-pas-sion
ill-fat-ed	im-ma-ture	im-pas-to
ill-fa-vored	im-meas-ur-a-ble	im-pa-tience
ill-found-ed	im-me-di-a-cy	im-pav-id
ill-got-ten	im-me-di-ate	im-pawn
il-lib-er-al	im-med-i-ca-ble	im-peach
il-lic-it	im-me-mo-ri-al	im-pearl
il-lim-it-a-ble	im-mense	im-pec-ca-ble
il-lit-er-ate	im-men-su-ra-ble	im-pe-cu-ni-ous
ill-judged	im-merge	im-ped-ance
ill-look-ing	im-merse	im-pede
ill-man-nered	im-mesh	im-ped-i-tive
ill-na-tured	im-me-thod-i-cal	im-pel-ler
il-log-i-cal	im-mi-grate	im-pend
ill-o-mened	im-mi-nent	im-pen-e-tra-ble
ill-starred	im-min-gle	im-pen-i-tent
ill-timed	im-mis-ci-ble	im-pen-nate
ill-treat	im-mit-i-ga-ble	im-per-a-tive
il-lu-mi-nate	im-mix	im-pe-ra-tor
il-lu-mi-na-tor	im-mo-bile	im-per-cep-ti-ble
il-lu-mine	im-mod-er-ate	im-per-fect
il-lu-sion	im-mo-late	im-per-fo-rate
il-lus-trate	im-mor-al	im-pe-ri-al
il-lus-tra-tor	im-mor-tal	im-per-il
il-lus-tri-ous	im-mo-tile	im-pe-ri-ous
il-men-ite	im-mov-a-ble	im-per-ish-a-ble
im-age	im-mune	im-pe-ri-um
im-ag-ine	im-mu-nol-o-gy	im-per-ma-nent
i-ma-go	im-mure	im-per-me-a-ble
im-bal-ance	im-mu-si-cal	im-per-son-al
im-balm	im-mu-ta-ble	im-per-ti-nence
im-be-cile	im-pact	im-per-turb-a-ble
im-bed	im-pair	im-per-vi-ous
im-bibe	im-pale	im-pe-ti-go
im-bi-bi-tion	im-pal-pa-ble	im-pe-trate
im-bri-cate	im-pa-na-tion	im-pet-u-os-i-ty
im-bro-glio	im-pan-el	im-pet-u-ous
im-brue	im-par-a-dise	im-pe-tus

im-pi-e-ty
im-pinge
im-pi-ous
im-pla-ca-ble
im-pla-cen-tal
im-plant
im-plau-si-ble
im-plead
im-ple-ment
im-ple-tion
im-pli-cate
im-plic-it
im-plied
im-plode
im-plore
im-pol-i-cy
im-po-lite
im-pon-der-a-ble
im-port
im-por-tune
im-pose
im-po-si-tion
in-pos-si-bil-i-ty
im-post
im-pos-tor
im-pos-ture
im-po-sure
im-po-tence
im-pound
im-pov-er-ish
in-prac-ti-ca-ble
im-prac-ti-cal
im-pre-cate
im-pre-cise
im-preg-nate
in-pre-sa-ri-o
im-pre-scrip-ti-ble
im-press
im-pres-sion-a-ble
im-pri-ma-tur
im-pri-mis
im-print
im-pris-on
im-prob-a-ble
im-pro-bi-ty

im-promp-tu
im-prop-er
im-pro-pri-ate
im-pro-pri-e-ty
im-prove
im-prov-i-dent
im-prov-i-sa-tor
im-pro-vise
im-pru-dent
im-pu-dent
im-pu-dic-i-ty
im-pugn
im-pu-is-sant
im-pulse
im-pu-ni-ty
im-pure
im-pute
in-a-bil-i-ty
in-ab-sen-ti-a
in-ac-ces-si-ble
in-ac-cu-rate
in-ac-tion
in-ac-tive
in-a-dapt-a-ble
in-ad-e-quate
in-ad-mis-si-ble
in-ad-vert-ence
in-ad-vis-a-ble
in-al-ien-a-ble
in-al-ter-a-ble
in-am-o-ra-ta (mistress)
in-am-o-ra-to
    (male lover)
in-ane
in-an-i-mate
in-an-i-ty
in-ap-peas-a-ble
in-ap-pe-tence
in-ap-pli-ca-ble
in-ap-po-site
in-ap-pre-ci-a-ble
in-ap-pre-hen-si-ble
in-ap-proach-a-ble
in-ap-pro-pri-ate
in-apt

in-apt-i-tude
in-arch
in-arm
in-ar-tic-u-late
in-ar-ti-fi-cial
in-ar-tis-tic
in-as-much
in-at-ten-tive
in-au-di-ble
in-au-gu-rate
in-aus-pi-cious
in-be-ing
in-board
in-born
in-bound
in-breathe
in-bred
in-breed
in-burst
in-cage
in-cal-cu-la-ble
in-ca-les-cent
in-can-desce
in-can-ta-tion
in-ca-pa-ble
in-ca-pa-cious
in-ca-pac-i-tate
in-car-cer-ate
in-car-di-nate
in-car-na-dine
in-car-nate
in-case
in-cau-tion
in-cen-di-ar-y
in-cense
in-cen-tive
in-cept
in-cer-ti-tude
in-ces-sant
in-cest
in-cho-ate
inch-worm
in-ci-dent
in-cin-er-ate
in-cin-er-a-tor

in-cip-i-ent
in-ci-pit
in-ci-sive
in-ci-sor
in-cite
in-ci-vil-i-ty
in-clasp
in-clem-ent
in-clin-a-ble
in-cline
in-cli-nom-e-ter
in-close
in-clude
in-clu-sion
in-co-er-ci-ble
in-cog-i-ta-ble
in-cog-ni-to
in-cog-ni-zant
in-co-her-ent
in-com-bus-ti-ble
in-come
in-com-men-su-rate
in-com-mode
in-com-mu-ni-ca-ble
in-com-mu-ni-ca-do
in-com-mut-a-ble
in-com-part
in-com-pa-ra-ble
in-com-pat-i-ble
in-com-pe-tent
in-com-plete
in-com-pli-ant
in-com-pre-hen-sive
in-com-press-i-ble
in-com-put-a-ble
in-con-clu-sive
in-con-den-sa-ble
in-con-dite
in-con-form-i-ty
in-con-gru-ent
in-con-sec-u-tive
in-con-se-quen-tial
in-con-sid-er-ate
in-con-sist-ent
in-con-sol-a-ble

in-con-so-nant
in-con-spic-u-ous
in-con-stant
in-con-sum-a-ble
in-con-test-a-ble
in-con-ti-nent
in-con-trol-la-ble
in-con-tro-vert-i-ble
in-con-ven-ience
in-con-vert-i-ble
in-con-vin-ci-ble
in-co-or-di-nate
in-cor-po-rate
in-cor-po-re-al
in-cor-po-re-i-ty
in-cor-rect
in-cor-ri-gi-ble
in-cor-rupt
in-cras-sate
in-crease
in-cre-ate
in-cred-i-ble
in-cre-ment
in-cres-cent
in-cre-tion
in-crim-i-nate
in-crust
in-cu-ba-tor
in-cul-cate
in-cul-pa-ble
in-cul-pate
in-cult
in-cum-bent
in-cu-nab-u-la
in-cur
in-cur-a-ble
in-cu-ri-ous
in-cur-rence
in-cur-sion
in-debt
in-de-cen-cy
in-de-cid-u-ate
in-de-ci-pher-a-ble
in-de-ci-sion
in-de-clin-a-ble

in-de-com-pos-a-ble
in-dec-o-rous
in-deed
in-de-fat-i-ga-ble
in-de-fea-si-ble
in-de-fect-i-ble
in-de-fec-tive
in-de-fen-si-ble
in-de-fin-a-ble
in-def-i-nite
in-de-his-cent
in-del-i-ble
in-del-i-ca-cy
in-dem-ni-fy
in-dem-ni-ty
in-de-mon-stra-ble
in-den-ture
in-de-pend-ence
in-de-scrib-a-ble
in-de-struct-i-ble
in-de-ter-mi-nate
in-dex
in-di-cant
in-di-cate
in-dic-a-tive
in-di-ca-tor
in-dict
in-dif-fer-ent
in-di-gence
in-di-gest-i-ble
in-dig-nant
in-di-go
in-di-rect
in-dis-cern-i-ble
in-dis-cerp-ti-ble
in-dis-cov-er-a-ble
in-dis-creet
in-dis-cre-tion
in-dis-crim-i-nate
in-dis-pen-sa-ble
in-dis-pose
in-dis-put-a-ble
in-dis-sol-u-ble
in-dis-tinct
in-dis-tin-guish-a-ble

in-dite

in-di-um

in-di-vert-i-ble

in-di-vid-u-al

in-di-vis-i-ble

in-doc-ile

in-doc-tri-nate

in-do-lent

in-dom-i-ta-ble

in-door

in-draft

in-drawn

in-du-bi-ta-ble

in-duce

in-duct

in-dulge

in-du-line

in-du-pli-cate

in-du-rate

in-dus-tri-al

in-earth

in-e-bri-ate

in-ed-i-ble

in-ed-it-ed

in-ef-fa-ble

in-ef-face-a-ble

in-ef-fec-tive

in-ef-fi-ca-cy

in-ef-fi-cien-cy

in-e-las-tic

in-el-e-gant

in-el-i-gi-ble

in-el-o-quent

in-e-luc-ta-ble

in-e-lud-i-ble

in-ept

in-e-qual-i-ty

in-e-qui-lat-er-al

in-eq-ui-ty

in-e-rad-i-ca-ble

in-e-ras-a-ble

in-er-ra-ble

in-er-rant

in-er-rat-ic

in-er-tia

in-es-cap-a-ble

in-es-sen-tial

in-es-ti-ma-ble

in-ev-i-ta-ble

in-ex-act

in-ex-cus-a-ble

in-ex-e-cu-tion

in-ex-er-tion

in-ex-haust-i-ble

in-ex-ist-ent

in-ex-o-ra-ble

in-ex-pe-di-ent

in-ex-pen-sive

in-ex-pe-ri-ence

in-ex-pert

in-ex-pi-a-ble

in-ex-plain-a-ble

in-ex-plic-it

in-ex-press-i-ble

in-ex-pug-na-ble

in-ex-ten-si-ble

in-ex-tin-guish-a-ble

in-ex-tir-pa-ble

in ex-tre-mis

in-ex-tri-ca-ble

in-fal-li-ble

in-fa-mous

in-fan-cy

in-fan-ti-cide

in-fan-try

in-fan-try-man

in-farct

in-fat-u-ate

in-fea-si-ble

in-fect

in-fec-tious

in-fe-cund

in-fe-bi-i-tous

in-felt

in-fer

in-fer-en-tial

in-fe-ri-or

in-fer-nal

in-fer-tile

in-fest

in-feu-da-tion

in-fi-del

in-field

in-fil-trate

in-fi-nite

in-fin-i-tes-i-mal

in-fin-i-ti-val

in-firm

in-fir-ma-ry

in-flam-ma-ble

in-flate

in-fla-tion-ar-y

in-flect

in-flex-i-ble

in-flict

in-flo-res-cence

in-flow

in-flu-ence

in-flu-en-tial

in-flu-en-za

in-flux

in-fold

in-for-mal

in-form-ant

in-for-tune

in-fra-cos-tal

in-fract

in-fran-gi-ble

in-fra-red

in-fra-son-ic

in-fre-quent

in-fringe

in-fu-ri-ate

in-fus-cate

in-fu-sion

in-fu-so-ri-al

in fu-tu-ro

in-gath-er

in gem-i-nate

in-gen-er-ate

in-ge-nu-i-ty

in-gest

in-gle-nook

in-gle-side

in-glo-ri-ous

in-go-ing
in-graft
in-grain
in-grate
in-gra-ti-ate
in-grat-i-tude
in-gra-ves-cent
in-gre-di-ent
in-gress
in-grown
in-growth
in-gulf
in-gur-gi-tate
in-hab-it
in-ha-la-tion
in-har-mo-ni-ous
in-haul
in-her-ent
in-her-it
in-her-i-tor
in-he-sion
in-hib-it
in-hib-i-tor
in-hos-pi-ta-ble
in-hu-mane
in-hume
in-im-i-cal
in-im-i-ta-ble
in-eq-ui-ty
in-i-tial
in-i-ti-ate
in-ject
in-jec-tor
in-ju-di-cious
in-junc-tion
in-jus-tice
ink-ling
ink-stand
ink-well
in-laid
in-land
in-law
in-lay
in-let
in-li-er

in-mate
in-me-mo-ri-am
in-mesh
in-most
in-nate
in-ner-di-rect-ed
in-ner-most
in-ner-vate
in-so-much
in-sou-ci-ant
in-soul
in-span
in-spect
in-sphere
in-spi-ra-tion-al
in-spir-it
in-spis-sate
in-sta-ble
in-stall
in-stance
in-stant
in-stan-ta-ne-ous
in-star
in-state
in-stau-ra-tion
in-stead
in-step
in-sti-gate
in-still
in-stinct
in-sti-tute
in-struct
in-stru-ment
in-sub-or-di-nate
in-sub-stan-tial
in-suf-fer-a-ble
in-suf-flate
in-su-lar
in-su-late
in-su-lin
in-sult
in-su-per-a-ble
in-sup-port-a-ble
in-sup-press-i-ble
in-sure

in-sur-gent
in-sur-mount-a-ble
in-sur-rec-tion-ar-y
in-sus-cep-ti-ble
in-swathe
in-swept
in-tact
in-take
in-tan-gi-ble
in-te-ger
in-te-gral
in-te-grate
in-teg-ri-ty
in-teg-u-ment
in-tel-lect
in-tel-li-gence
in-tel-li-gent-si-a
in-tel-li-gi-bil-i-ty
in-tem-per-ate
in-tem-per-ance
in-tend
in-ten-er-ate
in-tense
in-tent
in-ter
in-ter-act
in-ter-blend
in-ter-bor-ough
in-ter-brain
in-ter-breed
in-ter-ca-lar-y
in-ter-ca-late
in-ter-cede
in-ter-cel-lu-lar
in-ter-cep-tor
in-ter-ces-sor
in-ter-change
in-ter-change-a-ble
in-ter-clav-i-cle
in-ter-col-le-gi-ate
in-ter-co-lo-ni-al
in-ter-co-lum-ni-a-tion
in-ter-com
in-ter-com-mon
in-ter-com-mu-ni-cate

in-ter-con-nect
in-ter-con-ti-nen-tal
in-ter-cos-tal
in-ter-course
in-ter-crop
in-ter-cross
in-ter-cur-rent
in-ter-de-nom-
   i-na-tion-al
in-ter-den-tal
in-ter-de-pend-ent
in-ter-dict
in-ter-est
in-ter-face
in-ter-fere
in-ter-fe-ren-tial
in-ter-fer-om-e-ter
in-ter-file
in-ter-flow
in-ter-flu-ent
in-ter-fluve
in-ter-fold
in-ter-fuse
in-ter-gla-cial
in-ter-grade
in-ter-growth
in-ter-im
in-te-ri-or
in-ter-ject
in-ter-knit
in-ter-lace
in-ter-lam-i-nate
in-ter-laid
in-ter-lay
in-ter-leaf
in-ter-leave
in-ter-lin-e-ar
in-ter-link
in-ter-lock
in-ter-lo-cu-tion
in-ter-lope
in-ter-lude
in-ter-lu-nar
in-ter-mar-ry
in-ter-max-il-lar-y

in-ter-med-dle
in-ter-me-di-ate
in-ter-ment
in-ter-mez-zo
in-ter-mi-gra-tion
in-ter-mi-na-ble
in-ter-min-gle
in-ter-mis-sive
in-ter-mit-tent
in-ter-mix-ture
in-ter-mo-lec-u-lar
in-term
in-ter-na-tion-al
in-ter-ne-cive
in-ter-node
in-ter-nun-cial
in-ter-o-ce-an-ic
in-ter-o-cep-tor
in-ter-os-cu-late
in-ter-pen-e-trate
in-ter-phone
in-ter-plan-e-tar-y
in-ter-play
in-ter-plead
in-ter-po-late
in-ter-pose
in-ter-pret
in-ter-ra-cial
in-ter-ra-di-al
in-ter-re-late
in-ter-ro-gate
in-ter-rupt
in-ter-scho-las-tic
in-ter-sec-tion
in-ter-sep-tal
in-ter-sex
in-ter-space
in-ter-sperse
in-ter-state
in-ter-stice
in-ter-sti-tial
in-ter-tex-ture
in-ter-trib-al
in-ter-trop-i-cal
in-ter-twine

in-ter-ur-ban
in-ter-val
in-ter-vale
in-ter-vene
in-ter-ven-tion-ist
in-ter-view
in-ter-valve
in-ter-weave
in-tes-tate
in-tes-tine
in-thrall
in-throne
in-ti-mate
in-tim-i-date
in-ti-tle
in-tol-er-ance
in-tomb
in-to-nate
in-tor-sion
in-tort
in-tox-i-cate
in-tra-car-di-ac
in-tra-cel-lu-lar
in-tra-cra-ni-al
in-trac-ta-ble
in-tra-mo-lec-u-lar
in-tra-mu-ral
in-tra-mus-cu-lar
in-tran-si-gent
in-trant
in-tra-state
in-tra-ve-nous
in-treat
in-trench
in-trep-id
in-tri-ca-cy
in-trigue
in-trin-sic
in-tro-duce
in-tro-it
in-tro-jec-tion
in-tro-mit
in-tro-spect
in-tro-vert
in-trude

in-trust
in-tu-bate
in-tu-i-tion
in-tu-i-tiv-ism
in-tu-mes-cence
in-turn
in-tus-sus-cept
in-twine
in-unc-tion
in-un-date
in-ur-bane
in-ure
in-u-tile
in-vade
in-vag-i-nate
in-va-lid
in-val-u-a-ble
in-var-i-a-ble
in-va-sion
in-vec-tive
in-veigh
in-ven-tor
in-ven-to-ry
in-ve-rac-i-ty
in-verse
in-ver-te-brate
in-vest
in-ves-ti-gate
in-vest-ment
in-vet-er-ate
in-vid-i-ous
in-vig-i-late
in-vig-or-ate
in-vin-ci-ble
in-vi-o-late
in-vis-i-ble
in-vi-ta-tion
in-vo-cate
in-voice
in-voke
in-vol-un-tar-y
in-vo-lute
in-volve
in-vul-ner-a-ble
in-ward

in-weave
in-wrought
i-o-dine
i-on-ize
i-o-ta
ip-e-cac
i-ra-cund
i-ras-ci-ble
i-rate
ire-ful
i-ren-ic
ir-i-des-cent
i-ris
i-ri-tis
irk-some
i-ron-bound
i-ron-clad
i-ron-i-cal
i-ron-mon-ger
i-ron-side
i-ron-stone
i-ron-ware
i-ron-wood
i-ron-work
ir-ra-di-ate
ir-ra-tion-al
ir-re-claim-a-ble
ir-rec-on-cil-a-ble
ir-re-cov-er-a-ble
ir-re-cu-sa-ble
ir-re-deem-a-ble
ir-re-den-tist
ir-re-duc-i-ble
ir-ref-ra-ga-ble
ir-re-fran-gi-ble
ir-ref-u-ta-ble
ir-re-gard-less
ir-reg-u-lar
ir-rel-e-vant
ir-re-liev-a-ble
ir-re-li-gion
ir-re-me-di-a-ble
ir-re-mis-si-ble
ir-re-mov-a-ble
ir-rep-a-ra-ble

ir-re-peal-a-ble
ir-re-place-a-ble
ir-re-plev-i-a-ble
ir-re-press-i-ble
ir-re-proach-a-ble
ir-re-sist-i-ble
ir-res-o-lute
ir-re-solv-a-ble
ir-re-spec-tive
ir-re-spir-a-ble
ir-re-spon-si-ble
ir-re-ten-tive
ir-re-trace-a-ble
ir-re-triev-a-ble
ir-rev-er-ence
ir-re-vers-i-ble
ir-rev-o-ca-ble
ir-ri-gate
ir-ri-tate
ir-rup-tion
i-sal-lo-bar
i-sin-glass
is-land
i-so-lar
i-so-cheim
i-so-chor
i-so-chro-mat-ic
i-soch-ro-nal
i-so-cline
i-soc-ra-cy
i-so-dy-nam-ic
i-so-gram
i-so-hel
i-so-late
i-so-mag-net-ic
i-so-met-ric
i-son-o-my
i-so-seis-mic
i-so-stat-ic
i-so-there
is-sue
isth-mus
i-tal-ic
i-tem-ize
it-er-ate

i-tin-er-ant	it-self	i-vo-ry
i-tin-er-ate	i-vied	iz-zard

J

jab-ber	jay-walk	job-ber
ja-bot	jazz	jock-ey
jac-a-mar	jeal-ous	jock-strap
ja-cinth	jean	joc-u-lar
jack-al	jeep	joc-und
jack-a-napes	jeer	jodh-purs
jack-ass	je-june	jog-gle
jack-boat	jel-ly	john-ny-cake
jack-et	jel-ly-fish	join-der
jack-in-the-box	jen-net	join-er
jack-knife	jen-ny	joint
jack-of-all-trades	jeop-ard-y	joist
jack-o'-lan-tern	jer-e-mi-ad	joke
jac-ta-tion	jer-kin	jok-er
jac-ti-ta-tion	jerk-wa-ter	jol-ly
jade	jes-sa-mine	jolt
jade-green	jes-sant	jon-quil
jag-ged	jest-er	josh
jag-uar	jet-lin-er	jos-tle
jail	jet-ti-son	jot-ting
jail-bird	jet-ton	joule
ja-lop-y	jet-ty	jounce
jal-ou-sie	jew-el	jour-nal
jamb	jew-el-fish	jour-ney
jam-beau	jew-el-weed	jour-ney-man
jam-bo-ree	jibe	joist
jan-gle	jif-fy	jo-vi-al
jan-i-tor	jig-ger	jowl
jape	jig-gle	joy-ful
jar-di-niere	jilt	ju-ba
jar-gon	jim-my	ju-be
jar-o-site	jin-gal	ju-bi-lant
jas-mine	jin-gle	ju-bi-lee
jas-per	jin-go	judge
jaun-dice	jinx	judg-ment
jaunt	jit-ney	ju-di-ca-tor
jav-e-lin	jit-ter	ju-di-cious
jaw-bone	jit-ter-bug	ju-do
jaw-break-er	jive	ju-gal

ju-gate

jug-gle

jug-u-lar

ju-gu-late

juice

ju-jit-su

ju-lep

ju-li-enne

jum-ble

jum-bo

jump-er

jun-co

junc-tion

jun-gle

jun-ior

ju-ni-per

jun-ket

jun-to

ju-pon

ju-ral

ju-rat

ju-rid-i-cal

ju-ris-con-sult

ju-ris-pru-dence

ju-rist

jus-sive

jus-tice

jus-tice-ship

jus-ti-ci-ar-y

jus-ti-fy

just-ly

jute

ju-ve-nes-cent

ju-ve-nile

jux-ta-pose

K

ka-bob

kaf-tan

kale

ka-lei-do-scope

kan-ga-roo

ka-put

ka-ra-te

kay-ak

keat

keck

kedge

keel-boat

keel-haul

keep-sake

ke-loid

kelp

ken-nel

ken-ning

ke-no

ker-a-tog-e-nous

ker-a-toid

ker-a-to-plas-ty

ker-chief

ker-nel

kern-ite

ker-o-sene

ker-ry

ker-sey

ketch

ke-tone

ke-tose

ke-to-sis

ket-tle

key-board

key-stone

kha-ki

khan

kib-butz

kib-itz

kib-lah

ki-bosh

kick-back

kick-off

kick-shaw

kid-nap

kid-ney

kier

kil-der-kin

kil-lick

kill-joy

kiln-dry

kil-o-gram

kil-o-li-ter

kil-o-me-ter

kil-o-ton

kil-o-volt

kil-o-watt

kil-o-watt-hour

kilt-ed

ki-mo-no

kin-aes-the-sia

kin-der-gar-ten

kind-heart-ed

kin-dle

kind-ness

kin-dred

kin-e-mat-ics

kin-e-scope

kin-es-the-sia

ki-net-ic

kin-folks

king-dom

king-pin

king-ship

king-size

kin-ka-jou

kins-folk

kin-ship

kins-man

ki-osk

kip-per

kis-met

kitch-en

kitch-en-ette

kitsch

kit-ten-ish

kit-ti-wake

klep-to-ma-ni-a
klys-tron
knack
knag-gy
knap-scak
knap-weed
knar
knave
knead
knee-cap
kneel
knell
knick-ers
knick-knack
knife
knight

knight-hood
knit-ting
knives
knob-by
knock-a-bout
knock-down
knock-out
knoll
knot-ted
knout
know-how
knowl-edge
know-noth-ing
knuck-le
knurl
knurl-y

ko-a-la
ko-bold
ko-lin-sky
kook-a-bur-ra
ko-sher
kow-tow
kraft
krem-lin
krieg-spiel
krul-ler
kryp-ton
ku-chen
ku-dos
kum-mel
kum-quat
ky-mo-graph
ky-pho-sis

L

lab-e-fac-tion
la-bel
la-bel-lum
la-bi-ate
la-bile
la-bi-o-den-tal
la-bi-o-ve-lar
la-bi-um
la-bor
lab-o-ra-to-ry
lab-ra-dor-ite
lab-roid
la-brum
la-bur-num
lab-y-rinth
lac-co-lith
lac-er-ate
lac-er-til-i-an
lach-es
lach-ry-mal
lack-a-dai-si-cal
lack-ey
lack-lus-ter
la-con-ic

lac-quer
la-crosse
lac-tose
lac-tate
lac-tic
lac-tom-e-ter
lac-tose
la-cu-na
la-cu-nar
la-cu-nose
la-cus-trine
lad-der
lad-die
la-dle
lady-like
lag-an
la-ger
lag-gard
lag-ger
la-gniap-pe
la-goon
la-ic
lair
la-i-ty

lam-baste
lam-bent
lam-bert
lamb-kin
lam-bre-quin
lamb-skin
la-me
la-ment
la-mi-a-ceous
lam-i-na
lam-i-na-ble
lam-i-nar
lam-i-nate
lam-pi-on
lamp-light
lam-poon
lamp-post
lam-prey
la-nate
lance-lot
lan-ce-o-late
lan-cet
lan-ci-nate
lan-dau

land-lord
land-mark
land-own-er
land-scape
land-slide
lan-grage
lan-guage
lan-guet
lan-guid
lan-guish
lan-guor
lan-i-tal
lank-y
lan-ner
lan-o-lin
lan-tern
lan-tha-nide
la-nu-go
lan-yard
la-pel
lap-ful
lap-i-date
la-pid-i-fy
la-pil-li
lap-in
lap-is
lap-pet
lapse
lar-ce-ny
lar-da-ceous
lard-er
lar-don
large-ly
lar-gess
larg-ish
lar-go
lar-i-at
lar-ine
lark-spur
lar-ri-kin
lar-rup
lar-va
lar-vi-cide
lar-yn-gi-tis
la-ryn-go-scope

lar-ynx
las-civ-i-ous
la-ser
lash-ing
las-si-tude
las-so
latch-et
latch-key
la-teen
la-ten-cy
la-tent
lat-er-al
lat-er-ite
la-tes-cent
la-tex
lath
lathe
lath-er-y
lat-i-cif-er-ous
lat-ish
lat-i-tude
lat-i-tu-di-nar-i-an
la-trine
lat-ten
lat-ter
lat-ter-day
lat-ter-most
lat-tice
lat-tice-work
lau-da-num
laud-a-to-ry
laugh-ter
launch
laun-der
laun-dry
laun-dry-man
laun-dry-wom-an
lau-ra-ceous
lau-re-ate
lau-rel
la-va
la-va-bo
lav-age
lav-a-liere
la-va-tion

lav-a-to-ry
lav-en-der
law-a-bid-ing
law-break-er
law-mak-er
lawn
law-suit
law-yer
lax-a-tion
lax-a-tive
lax-i-ty
lay-er-age
lay-ette
lay-man
lay-off
lay-out
lay-o-ver
laze
leach
lead-en
lead-er
lead-er-ship
leads-man
leaf-less
leaf-let
league
leak-age
lean-to
leapt
learn
lease
lease-hold-er
leash
least
least-wise
leath-er
leath-er-back
leath-er-neck
leav-en
leave-tak-ing
lech-er
lec-tern
lec-tion
lec-tor
lec-ture

ledg-er
lee-board
leech
leek
leer
leet
lee-ward
lee-way
left-hand
left-o-ver
left-ward
leg-a-cy
le-gal
leg-ate
leg-a-tee
le-ga-to
le-ga-tor
leg-end
leg-ged
leg-i-ble
le-gion
le-gion-naire
leg-is-late
leg-is-la-tor
le-git-i-mate
leg-u-me
le-gu-mi-nous
leis-ter
lei-sure
leit-mo-tif
lem-ma
lem-on
le-mur
length
le-ni-ent
len-ta-men-te
len-til
len-tis-si-mo
len-to
le-o-nine
leop-ard
le-o-tard
lep-er
lep-i-dop-ter-ous
lep-re-chaun

lep-ro-sar-i-um
lep-ro-sy
lep-rous
le-sion
les-see
les-sor
let-down
le-thal
leth-ar-gy
let-ter
let-tuce
let-up
leu-cite
leu-ke-mi-a
le-va-tor
lev-ee (embankment)
lev-el-head-ed
lev-er-age
le-vi-a-than
lev-i-gate
lev-in
lev-i-rate
lev-i-tate
lev-i-ty
lev-y (impose a tax)
lewd
lex-i-cal
lex-i-cog-ra-phy
lex-i-con
li-a-ble
li-ai-son
li-a-na
li-ba-tion
li-bel
lib-er-al
lib-er-ate
lib-er-tar-i-an
lib-er-tine
lib-er-ty
li-bid-i-nous
li-bi-do
li-bra
li-brar-y
li-bra-to-ry
li-bret-to

li-cense
li-cen-ti-ate
li-chen
lic-o-rice
lid-less
lie-der-kranz
lien
lieu
lieu-ten-ant
life-less
life-sav-er
life-size
life-time
lift-off
lig-a-ment
li-gate
light-er-age
light-ning
lig-ne-ous
lik-a-ble
like-li-hood
like-mind-ed
li-lac
li-la-ceous
lil-y
lim-ber
lim-bo
lime-light
li-men
lim-er-ick
lim-it-less
li-mo-nite
lim-ou-sine
lim-pid
lim-u-loid
lin-age
lin-den
lin-e-age
lin-e-ar
lin-en
lin-e-o-late
lin-er
lines-man
line-up
lin-ger

lin-ge-rie
lin-go
lin-gua
lin-guist
lin-gu-late
lin-i-ment
lin-ing
link-age
lin-net
li-no-le-um
lin-seed
lin-tel
li-on-ess
li-on-heart-ed
lip-ec-to-my
lip-id
li-poid
li-pol-y-sis
lip-stick
li-quate
liq-ue-fy
li-queur
liq-uid
liq-ui-da-tor
liq-uor
lisle
lisp
lis-some
lis-ten
list-er
list-less
lit-a-ny
lit-er-a-cy
lit-er-ate
lit-er-a-ture
lith-arge
lithe
lith-ic
lith-i-um
lith-o-graph
li-thol-o-gy
lith-o-sphere
lith-o-trite
lit-i-gate
lit-mus

lit-ter
lit-to-ral
lit-ur-gy
liv-a-ble
live-li-hood
liv-er
liv-er-wurst
liv-er-y
live-stock
liv-id
lix-iv-i-ate
liz-ard
lla-ma
loath (averse)
loathe (hate)
loaves
lo-bate
lob-by
lo-bot-o-my
lob-ster
lo-cale
lo-cate
lo-ca-tor
lock-age
lock-et
lock-out
lock-smith
lock-up
lo-co-mo-tive
lo-co-mo-tor
loc-u-lar
loc-u-lus (cavity)
lo-cus (place)
lo-cust (grasshopper)
lo-cu-tion
lodge
loft-y
lo-gan-ber-ry
log-a-rithm
log-book
loge
log-ger-head
log-gia
log-ic
log-i-on

lo-gis-tic
log-o-gram
log-o-griph
lo-gom-a-chy
log-o-type
log-roll
log-wood
loin-cloth
loi-ter
lol-li-pop
lo-ment
lone-some
lon-gev-i-ty
long-hand
long-horn
lon-gi-corn
lon-gi-tude
lon-gi-tu-di-nal
long-stand-ing
long-wind-ed
look-er-on
looking-glass
look-out
loop-hole
loos-en
lop-eared
lop-sid-ed
lo-qua-cious
lord-ship
lor-gnette
lo-ri-ca
lor-ry
lo-tion
lot-ter-y
lot-to
lo-tus
lo-tus-eat-er
loud-speak-er
lounge
loup (leap)
loupe (jeweler's glass)
louse
lou-ver
love-a-ble
love-bird

love-lock
love-lorn
low-bred
low-brow
low-down
low-land
low-volt-age
lox-o-drom-ic
loy-al
loz-enge
lub-ber
lu-bri-cate
lu-bri-cious
lu-cent
lu-cid
lu-cif-er-ous
luck-less
lu-cra-tive
lu-cre
lu-cu-brate
lu-cu-lent
lu-di-crous
lug-gage
lug-sail

lu-gu-bri-ous
luke-warm
lull-a-by
lum-ba-go
lum-bar
lum-ber-jack
lum-ber-man
lum-ber-yard
lum-bri-cal
lum-bri-coid
lu-men
lu-mi-nar-y
lu-mi-nesce
lu-mi-nif-er-ous
lu-mi-nos-i-ty
lum-mox
lump-ish
lu-na-cy
lu-nar
lu-nate
lu-na-tic
lunch-eon
lunch-room
lune
lu-nette

lung (organ)
lunge (a thrust)
lu-ni-so-lar
lu-ni-tid-al
lunk-head
lu-nu-lar
lurch
lu-rid
lurk
lus-cious
lus-ter
lus-tral
lus-trate
lu-te-ous
lux-u-ry
ly-can-thrope
ly-ce-um
lymph
lymph-ad-e-ni-tis
lym-phan-gi-al
lym-phat-ic
lynch
lynx
lyric

M

ma-ca-bre
mac-ad-am
mac-a-ron-i
mac-a-roon
ma-caw
mace
mac-er-ate
ma-che-te
ma-chic-o-lat-ed
mach-i-nate
ma-chine gun
   (automatic gun)
ma-chin-er-y
mack-er-el
mack-i-naw
mack-in-tosh

mack-le
mac-ro-cosm
mac-ro-cept
mac-ro-cyte
mac-ro-graph
ma-cron
mac-ro-phys-ics
mac-ro-scop-ic
mac-ro-spore
man-u-la
mad-am
mad-cap
mad-den
mad-e-moi-selle
made-up
mad-man

ma-dras
ma-dre
mad-re-pore
mad-ri-gal
mad-wom-an
maes-tro
mag-a-zine
ma-gen-ta
mag-got
ma-gi-cian
mag-is-te-ri-al
mag-is-trate
mag-ma
mag-na-cum-lau-de
mag-na-nim-i-ty
mag-nan-i-mous

mag-nate
mag-ne-si-um
mag-net-ic
mag-ne-to
mag-ne-to-e-lec-tric
mag-ne-to-gen-er-a-tor
mag-ne-tom-e-ter
mag-ne-to-mo-tive
mag-ne-ton
mag-ne-tron
mag-nif-i-cent
mag-ni-fy
mag-nil-o-quent
mag-ni-tude
mag-no-li-a
mag-num
mag-pie
ma-ha-ra-jah
mah-jongg
ma-hog-a-ny
maid-en-head
maid-en-hood
mai-gree
mail-box
mail-man
main-land
main-mast
main-sail
main-sheet
main-spring
main-tain
main-te-nance
maize (cereal plant)
maj-es-ty
ma-jol-i-ca
ma-jor
ma-jus-cule
make-be-lieve
make-shift
make-up
ma-la-ceous
mal-ad-jus-ted
mal-ad-min-is-ter
mal-a-droit
mal-a-dy

ma-laise
mal-a-pert
mal-a-prop-ism
mal-ap-ro-pos
ma-lar-i-a
mal-as-sim-i-la-tion
mal-con-tent
mal-e-dic-tion
mal-e-fac-tor
ma-lef-ic
ma-lev-o-lent
mal-fea-sance
mal-for-ma-tion
mal-func-tion
mal-ice
ma-lign
ma-lin-ger
mall (shaded walk)
mal-lard
mal-le-a-ble
mal-le-muck
mal-let
mal-nu-tri-tion
mal-oc-clu-sion
mal-o-dor
mal-po-si-tion
mal-prac-tice
mal-tha
malt-ose
mal-treat
malt-ster
mal-ver-sa-tion
mam-mal
mam-mif-er-ous
mam-moth
man-a-cle
man-age-a-ble
man-a-ge-ri-al
man-a-kin
man-ci-ple
man-da-mus
man-da-rin
man-date
man-da-tor
man-di-ble

man-do-lin
man-drel (axle)
man-drill (baboon)
man-du-cate
man-eat-er
ma-nege
ma-neu-ver
man-ga-nate
man-ger
man-gle
man-go
man-grove
man-gy
man-han-dle
man-hole
man-hood
ma-ni-a
man-ic-de-pres-sive
man-i-cure
man-i-fest
man-i-fold
man-i-kin (dwarf)
ma-nil-la
man-i-ple
ma-nip-u-late
man-kind
man-like
man-ne-quin (model)
man-ner-less
man-nish
ma-nom-e-ter
man-or
manse
man-serv-ant
man-sion
man-slaugh-ter
man-slay-er
man-tel (shelf
     around a fireplace)
man-tic
man-til-la
man-tis
man-tle (loose cloak)
man-tu-a
man-u-al

man-u-fac-ture
man-u-mit
ma-nure
man-u-script
man-y-sid-ed
ma-ple
mar-a-schi-no
ma-ras-mus
mar-a-thon
ma-raud
mar-ble
mar-cel
mar-ga-rine
mar-gin
mar-grave
mar-gra-vine
mar-gue-rite
mar-i-gold
ma-ri-jua-na
ma-rim-ba
mar-i-nade
ma-rine
mar-i-ner
mar-i-o-nette
mar-ish
mar-i-tal
mar-i-time
mark-down
mar-ket-a-ble
marks-man
mark-up
mar-lin
mar-ma-lade
mar-mot
ma-roon (isolate)
marque (reprisal)
mar-quee (awning)
mar-que-try
mar-riage
mar-ron (chestnut)
mar-row
mar-row-fat
mar-shal
marsh-mal-low
mar-ten

mar-tial
mar-tin (bird)
mar-ti-net
   (disciplinarian)
mar-tin-gale
mar-ti-ni
mar-tyr
mar-tyr-dom
mar-vel
mar-zi-pan
mas-car-a
mas-cot
mas-cu-line
mas-sa-cre
mas-sage
mas-se-ter
mas-seur
mas-so-ther-a-py
mas-sive
mas-tec-to-my
mas-ter-mind
mas-ter-piece
mast-head
mas-ti-cate
mas-tiff
mas-ti-tis
mas-toid
mas-tur-bate
mat-a-dor
match-mak-er
ma-te-ri-al
ma-ter-nal
ma-ter-ni-ty
math-e-mat-ics
mat-in
mat-i-nee
ma-tri-arch
ma-tri-cide
ma-tric-u-lant
ma-tric-u-late
mat-ri-mo-ny
ma-trix
ma-tron
mat-ted
mat-ter-of-course

mat-ter-of-fact
mat-tock
mat-toid
mat-tress
ma-ture
ma-tu-ti-nal
mat-zo
maud-lin
maul (a hammer)
maun-der
maun-dy
mau-so-le-um
mauve
mav-er-ick
mawk-ish
max-il-la
max-i-mal
max-im-ite
max-i-mum
may-hem
may-on-naise
may-or-al-ty
maze (confusing)
maz-zard
mead-ow
mea-ger
meal-y-mouthed
me-an-der
mean-ing-ful
mean-time
mea-sles
meas-ure
me-a-tus
me-chan-ic
mech-a-nize
med-al-ist
me-dal-lion
med-dle-some
me-di-a-cy
me-di-al
me-di-an
me-di-ate
me-di-a-tor
med-i-cal
me-dic-a-ment

med-i-cine
me-di-e-val
me-di-o-cre
med-i-tate
me-di-um
med-lar
med-ley
me-dul-la
meg-a-cy-cle
meg-a-lith
meg-a-lo-ma-ni-ac
meg-a-lo-pol-i-tan
meg-a-phone
meg-a-spore
meg-a-ton
meg-ohm
mel-an-cho-li-ac
me-lange
mel-a-nin
mel-a-no-sis
meld
me-lee
me-li-a-ceous
me-lic
mel-i-nite
mel-ior-i-ty
mel-lif-er-ous
mel-lif-lu-ent
me-lo-de-on
me-lo-di-a
mel-o-dra-ma
mel-o-dy
mel-on
melt-age
mel-ton
mem-ber-ship
mem-brane
me-men-to
mem-oir
mem-o-ra-bil-i-a
mem-o-ra-ble
mem-o-ran-dum
me-mo-ri-al
mem-o-ry
men-ace

me-nage
me-nag-er-ie
men-dac-i-ty
men-di-cant
me-ni-al
men-in-gi-tis
me-nis-cus
me-nol-o-gy
men-o-pause
men-sal
men-stru-ate
men-su-ral
men-tal-i-ty
men-tha-ceous
men-thene
men-thol
men-tion
me-phi-tis
mer-can-tile
mer-ce-nar-y
mer-cer-ize
mer-chan-dise
mer-chant-a-ble
mer-chant-man
mer-ci-ful
mer-cu-rate
mer-cu-ri-al
mer-cu-ro-chrome
mer-cu-ry
mer-cy
mer-e-tri-cious
merg-er
me-rid-i-an
me-rid-i-o-nal
me-ringue
me-ri-no
mer-i-to-ri-ous
mer-lin (falcon)
mer-lon
     (part of battlement)
mer-maid
mer-man
me-rog-o-ny
mer-o-zo-ite
mer-ri-ment

mer-ry-go-round
mer-ry-mak-er
mer-ry-thought
me-sa
me-sal-li-ance
mes-ca-line
mes-en-ceph-a-lon
mes-en-ter-y
me-sit-y-lene
mes-mer-ize
mes-o-blast
mes-o-carp
mes-o-ce-phal-ic
mes-o-cra-nic
mes-o-crat-ic
mes-o-derm
mes-o-gas-tri-um
me-son
mes-o-phyte
mes-quite
mes-sage
mes-sa-line
mes-sen-ger
mes-suage (dwelling)
mes-ti-zo
me-tab-o-lism
met-a-car-pus
met-a-cen-ter
met-a-chro-ma-tism
met-a-gal-ax-y
met-age
met-al-ize
me-tal-lic
met-al-lif-er-ous
met-al-line
met-al-log-ra-phy
met-al-loid
me-tal-lo-ther-a-py
met-al-lur-gy
met-al-work-ing
met-a-mor-phose
met-a-phase
met-a-phor
met-a-phrase
met-a-phys-i-cal

met-a-phy-si-cian
met-a-plasm
met-a-pro-te-in
met-a-so-ma-tism
me-tas-ta-ses
met-em-pir-i-cal
me-te-or
me-te-or-ol-o-gy
me-ter
meth-ac-ry-late
meth-ane
me-the-na-mine
meth-od
meth-yl-ate
meth-yl-ene
me-tic-u-lous
Me-tol
met-o-nym
met-ric
me-tri-tis
me-trol-o-gy
met-ro-nome
me-tro-nym-ic
met-ro-pol-i-tan
met-tle-some
mez-za-nine
mez-zo
mi-os-ma
mi-ca-ceous
mi-cri-fy
mi-cro-a-nal-y-sis
mi-cro-bar-o-graph
mi-crobe
mi-cro-bi-ol-o-gy
mi-cro-ce-phal-ic
mi-cro-chem-is-try
mi-cro-cli-ma-tol-o-gy
mi-cro-cline
mi-cro-cop-y
mi-cro-crys-tal-line
mi-cro-film
mi-cro-gram
mi-cro-graph
mi-crog-ra-phy
mi-cro-inch

mi-crom-e-ter
mi-cro-mo-tion
mi-cron
mi-cro-or-gan-ism
mi-cro-phone
mi-cro-pho-to-graph
mi-cro-print
mi-cro-scope
mi-cro-sec-ond
mi-cro-some
mi-cro-spore
mi-cro-tome
mi-cro-waves
mic-tu-rate
mid-brain
mid-day
mid-dle-of-the-road-er
mid-dling
midge
midg-et
mid-i-ron
mid-land
mid-leg
mid-most
mid-night
mid-noon
mid-riff
mid-ship
midst
mid-stream
mid-way
mid-week
mid-wife
might-i-ly
mi-gnon
mi-graine
mi-grate
mil-dew
mile-age
mile-stone
mil-i-ar-i-a
mi-lieu
mil-i-tant
mil-i-tar-y
mil-i-tate

mi-li-tia
mi-li-tia-man
mil-i-um
mil-le-nar-i-an
mil-len-ni-um
mil-lo-pede
mil-le-pore
mill-er-ite
mil-les-i-mal
mil-let
mil-li-bar
mil-li-gram
mil-li-li-ter
mil-li-me-ter
mil-li-ner
mil-lion-aire
mil-lionth
mil-li-pede
mill-stone
milque-toast
mime
mi-me-sis
mi-met-ic
mim-e-tite
mim-ic
mic-ic-ry
mi-mo-sa
mi-na-cious
min-a-ret
min-a-to-ry
mince-meat
min-er (digger)
min-er-al
min-e-stro-ne
min-gle
min-i-a-ture
min-im
min-i-mum
min-ion
min-is-ter
min-i-track
min-i-um
min-i-ver
min-now
mi-nor (lesser)

mi-nor-i-ty
min-strel
mint-age
min-u-end
min-u-et
mi-nus-cule
min-ute-man
mi-nu-ti-a
minx
mir-a-cle
mi-rage
mir-ror
mirth-less
mis-ad-ven-ture
mis-ad-vise
mis-al-li-ance
mis-an-thrope
mis-ap-plied
mis-ap-pre-hend
mis-ap-pro-pri-ate
mis-ar-range
mis-be-got-ten
mis-be-have
mis-be-lief
mis-cal-cu-late
mis-car-riage
mis-ce-ge-na-tion
mis-cel-la-ny
mis-chance
mis-chief
mis-ci-ble
mis-col-or
mis-con-ceive
mis-con-duct
mis-con-struc-tion
mis-con-strue
mis-cre-ate
mis-cue
mis-date
mis-deal
mis-deed
mis-de-mean-or
mis-de-rive
mis-de-scribe
mis-di-rect

mis-doubt
mis-ease
mis-em-ploy
mis-er-a-ble
mis-er-i-cord
mis-er-i-cor-di-a
mi-ser-ly
mis-er-y
mis-es-teem
mis-es-ti-mate
mis-fea-sance
mis-fea-sor
mis-fire
mis-fit
mis-for-tune
mis-give
mis-gov-ern
mis-guide
mis-han-dle
mish-mash
mis-in-form
mis-in-ter-pret
mis-join-der
mis-judge
mis-lay
mis-lead
mis-man-age
mis-mar-riage
mis-match
mis-mate
mis-no-mer
mi-sog-a-my
    (hatred of marriage)
mi-sog-y-ny
    (hatred of women)
mi-sol-o-gy
    (hatred of reason)
mis-o-ne-ism
    (hatred of change)
mis-place
mis-plead
mis-print
mis-pri-sion
mis-pro-nounce
mis-quote

mis-read
mis-reck-on
mis-re-port
mis-rep-re-sent
mis-rule
mis-sal (prayer book)
mis-shape
mis-sile (weapon)
mis-sion
mis-sive
mis-speak
mis-spell
mis-spend
mis-step
mis-take
mis-teach
mis-tle-toe
mis-trans-late
mis-trust
mis-tress
mis-tri-al
mis-trust
mis-un-der-stand
mis-use
mis-val-ue
mis-word
mis-write
mi-ter
mit-i-gate
mi-tis
mi-to-sis
mi-tral
mit-ten
mit-ti-mus
mitz-vah
mix-ture
mix-up
miz-zen-mast
mob-cap
mo-bile
mob-oc-ra-cy
mob-ster
moc-ca-sin
mock-er-y
mock-ing-bird

mock-up
mode
mod-el
mod-er-a-tor
mod-ern-is-tic
mod-est
mod-i-fi-ca-tion
mo-dil-lion
mod-ish
mo-diste
mod-u-late
mod-ule
mo-hair
moire
mois-ture
mo-lar
mo-las-ses
mold-er
mol-e-cule
mole-hill
mole-skin
mo-lest
mol-li-fy
mol-ten
mo-lyb-date
mo-men-tar-y
mon-ad
mo-nan-dry
mon-arch
mon-as-ter-y
mon-a-tom-ic
mon-au-ral
mon-ax-i-al
mon-e-tar-y
mon-eyed
mon-ger
mon-gol-oid
mon-goose
mon-grel
mo-nil-i-form
mo-nism
mo-ni-tion
mon-i-tor
mon-key
mon-o-bas-ic

mon-o-carp
mon-o-chord
mon-o-chrome
mon-o-cle
mon-o-cline
mo-noc-ra-cy
mo-noc-u-lar
mon-o-cul-ture
mo-nod-ic
mon-o-dra-ma
mo-nog-a-my
mon-o-gen-e-sis
mon-o-gram
mon-o-graph
mo-nog-y-ny
mon-o-hy-dric
mon-o-lith
mon-o-logue
mon-o-ma-ni-a
mon-o-mer
mon-o-me-tal-lic
mo-no-mi-al
mon-o-mo-lec-u-lar
mon-o-mor-phic
mon-o-nu-cle-o-sis
mon-o-pho-bi-a
mon-o-plane
mon-o-pode
mo-nop-o-ly
mon-o-sper-mous
mon-o-stich
mon-o-stome
mo-nos-tro-phe
mon-o-syl-la-ble
mon-o-tone
mo-not-o-ny
mon-o-treme
mon-o-type
mon-o-va-lent
mon-ox-ide
mon-soon
mon-strance
mon-stros-i-ty
mon-tage
mon-tane

mon-teith
mon-te-ro
mon-ti-cule
mon-u-ment
moon-eye
moon-light
moon-lit
moon-rise
moon-shine
moon-stone
moon-struck
moor-age
mop-pet
mo-quette
mo-ra-ceous
mor-al (ethical)
mo-rale
    (mental condition)
mo-rass
mor-a-to-ri-um
mor-bid
mor-da-cious
mor-dant (sarcastic)
mor-dent
    (musical ornament)
mo-reen
mo-rel (mushroom)
more-o-ver
mor-gan-ite
morgue
morn-ing-glo-ry
mo-ron
mo-rose
mor-pheme
    (of linguistics)
mor-phine (narcotic)
mor-pho-gen-e-sis
mor-phol-o-gy
mor-row
mor-sel
mor-tal
mor-tar
mort-gage
mor-ti-cian
mor-ti-fi-ca-tion

mor-tise
mort-main
mor-tu-ar-y
mor-u-la
mo-sa-ic
mos-chate
mosque
mos-qui-to
mo-tel
moth-eat-en
moth-er-hood
moth-er-in-law
moth-er-land
moth-er-of-pearl
mo-tif
mo-tion
mo-tive
mot-ley
mo-tor-boat
mo-tor-cy-cle
mot-tle
mot-to
mou-lage
mould-board
mou-lin
moun-tain-eer
moun-te-bank
mourn-er
mousse
mous-tache
mouth-ful
mov-a-ble
move-ment
mov-ie
mown
moz-zet-ta
mu-cid
mu-ci-lage
mu-cin
muck-le
mu-co-pro-tein
mu-cous (like mucus)
mu-cus (secretion)
mud-cap
mud-cat

mud-dle
mud-guard
muf-fin
muf-fle
mug-ger
mu-lat-to
mul-ber-ry
mulch
mu-le-teer
mu-li-eb-ri-ty
mul-let
mul-li-gan
mul-lock
mul-ti-cel-lu-lar
mul-ti-coil
mul-ti-col-ored
mul-ti-cyl-in-der
mul-ti-den-tate
mul-ti-far-i-ous
mul-ti-fid
mul-ti-flo-rous
mul-ti-fold
mul-ti-form
mul-ti-lam-i-nate
mul-ti-lat-er-al
mul-ti-mil-lion-aire
mul-ti-mo-tored
mul-ti-nu-cle-ar
mul-tip-a-rous
mul-ti-par-tite
mul-ti-ped
mul-ti-phase
mul-ti-ple
mul-ti-plex
mul-ti-pli-cand
mul-ti-tude
mul-ture
mum-ble
mum-mer-y
mum-mi-fy
mun-dane
mu-nic-i-pal
mu-nif-i-cent
mu-ni-ment
mu-ni-tion

mu-ral
mur-der
mu-ri-ate
mu-rine
mur-mur
mur-rey
mu-sa-ceous
mus-ca-dine (grape)
mus-cat
mus-ca-tel (wine)
mus-cid
mus-cle (tissue)
mus-cle-bound
mus-cone
mus-co-va-do (sugar)
mus-co-vite (mica)
mus-cu-lar
mu-se-um
mush-room
mu-si-cal (melodious)
mu-si-cale (program)
mus-keg
mus-ket
musk-rat
mus-lin
mus-sel (mollusk)
mus-tache
mus-ta-chio
mus-tang
mus-tard
mus-tee (half-breed)
mus-te-line (weasel-like)
mus-ter
mus-ty (stale)
mu-ta-ro-ta-tion
mu-tate
mu-ti-late
mu-ti-ny
mut-ter
mut-ton
mu-tu-al
muz-zle
my-al-gi-a
my-as-the-ni-a
my-o-bac-te-ri-um

my-col-o-gy
my-o-sis
my-dri-a-sis
myd-ri-at-ic
my-e-len-ceph-a-lon
my-e-li-tis
my-na
my-o-car-di-o-graph
my-o-car-di-tis

my-o-graph
my-ol-o-gy
my-o-ma
my-o-pi-a
my-o-scope
my-o-so-tis
myr-i-ad
myr-i-a-pod

myrrh
myr-tle
mys-ta-gogue
mys-ter-y
mys-tic
myth
my-thol-o-gy
myth-o-ma-ni-a
myx-e-de-ma

N

na-celle
na-dir
na-ive
na-ive-te
name-a-ble
name-sake
nan-keen
nan-ny
na-palm
na-per-y
naph-tha
na-pi-form
nap-kin
na-prap-a-thy
nar-cis-sus
nar-co-lep-sy
nar-co-sis
nar-co-syn-the-sis
nar-cot-ic
nar-es
nar-rate
nar-row-mind-ed
na-sal
nase-berry
na-so-fron-tal
nas-tic
na-stur-tium
na-tal
na-ta-to-ri-al
na-tion-al-ism
na-tive-born
na-tiv-ism

nat-ty
nat-u-ral
naugh-ty
nau-se-a
nau-ti-cal
na-val (of ships)
nave
na-vel (pit in belly)
nav-i-cert
na-vic-u-lar
nav-i-gate
nav-i-ga-tor
neap
near-sight-ed
neb-u-la
nec-es-sar-y
ne-ces-si-ty
neck-er-chief
neck-lace
neck-tie
ne-crol-a-try
ne-crol-o-gy
nec-ro-man-cy
nec-ro-ma-ni-a
nec-ro-pho-bi-a
nec-rop-sy
ne-crose
nec-tar
nec-tar-ine
nee-dle
ne'er-do-well
ne-far-i-ous

ne-gate
neg-a-tive
neg-lect
neg-li-gee
neg-li-gence
neg-li-gi-ble
ne-go-ti-ate
ne-gro-phile
ne-gro-pho-bi-a
neigh
neigh-bor
nei-ther
nek-ton
ne-o-clas-sic
ne-o-im-pres-sion-ism
ne-ol-o-gy
ne-o-my-cin
ne-o-phyte
ne-o-plasm
ne-pen-the
neph-ew
neph-o-graph
ne-phrec-to-my
neph-rite
nep-o-tism
ne-rol
nerv-ate
neth-er
net-ting
net-tle
net-work
neu-ral

neu-ral-gia
neu-ras-the-ni-a
neu-ra-tion
neu-rec-to-my
neu-ri-lem-ma
neu-ri-tis
neu-ro-blast
neu-rol-o-gy
neu-ro-path
neu-ro-psy-chi-a-try
neu-ro-psy-cho-sis
neu-ro-sis
neu-ro-sur-ger-y
neu-rot-ic
neu-ter
neu-tral
neu-tron
nev-er-more
nev-er-the-less
new-born
new-com-er
new-el
new-fan-gled
new-fash-ioned
news-boy
news-pa-per
news-print
news-reel
news-stand
news-wor-thy
ni-a-cin
nib-ble
nic-o-lite
ni-ce-ty
niche
nick-el
nick-el-if-er-ous
nick-el-o-de-on
nick-nack
nick-name
nic-o-tine
nid-i-fy
niece
nif-ty
nig-gard-ly

night-cap
night-fall
night-gown
night-in-gale
night-mare
night-rid-er
night-shirt
ni-gres-cent
nig-ri-tude
ni-hil-ism
nim-ble
ni-mi-e-ty
nin-com-poop
nose-bleed
nose-gay
nose-piece
no-show
no-sog-ra-phy
nos-tal-gia
nos-tril
nos-trum
no-ta-ble
no-ta-ry
note-book
note-wor-thy
no-tice-a-ble
no-ti-fy
no-tion
no-to-ri-e-ty
no-trump
not-with-stand-ing
nou-gat
nour-ish
no-vac-u-lite
no-va-tion
nov-el
no-vel-la
nov-el-ty
no-ve-na
nov-ice
no-vi-ti-ate
no-vo-caine
now-a-day
no-way
no-where

nox-ious
noz-zle
nu-ance
nub-bin
nub-ble
nu-bi-a
nu-bile
nu-cle-ar
nu-cle-i
nudge
nu-di-branch
nu-di-ty
nu-ga-to-ry
nug-get
nui-sance
nul-li-fy
num-ber-less
nu-mer-a-ble
nu-mer-al
nu-mer-a-tor
nu-mis-mat-ic
nu-mis-ma-tol-o-gy
num-ma-ry
num-skull
nun-ci-o
nun-cu-pa-tive
nun-ner-y
nup-tial
nurse-maid
nurs-er-y-man
nur-ture
nu-ta-tion
nut-brown
nut-crack-er
nut-meg
nu-tri-ent
nu-tri-tion
nut-shell
nuz-zle
nyc-ta-lo-pi-a
ny-lon
nymph
nym-phae-a-ceous
nym-pho-lep-sy
nym-pho-ma-ni-a
nys-tag-mus

O

oared
oar-fish
oars-man
o-a-sis
oat-meal
ob-bli-ga-to
ob-cor-date
ob-du-rate
o-be-di-ence
o-bei-sance
ob-e-lisk
o-bese
ob-fus-cate
o-bit-u-ar-y
ob-ject
ob-jur-gate
ob-late
ob-li-gate
ob-lique
ob-lit-er-ate
ob-liv-i-on
ob-long
ob-nox-ious
o-boe
ob-scene
ob-scure
ob-se-crate
ob-se-qui-ous
ob-ser-va-tion
ob-serve
ob-sess
ob-so-les-cent
ob-so-lete
ob-sta-cle
ob-stet-ric
ob-ste-tri-cian
ob-sti-nate
ob-sti-pant
ob-strep-er-ous
ob-struct
ob-stru-ent
ob-tain
ob-tect-ed

ob-test
ob-trude
ob-tu-rate
ob-tuse
ob-verse
ob-vert
ob-vi-ate
ob-vo-lute
oc-ca-sion
oc-ci-den-tal
oc-cip-i-tal
oc-ci-put
oc-clude
oc-cult
oc-cu-pa-tion-al
oc-cu-py
oc-cur
oc-cur-rence
o-ce-a-nog-ra-phy
o-cel-lar
o-ce-lot
o-chre
o'-clock
oc-tad
oc-ta-gon
oc-tam-e-ter
oc-tane
oc-tan-gu-lar
oc-tant
oc-tave
oc-ten-ni-al
oc-til-lion
oc-to-ge-nar-i-an
oc-to-nar-y
oc-to-pus
oc-to-syl-la-ble
oc-tu-ple
oc-u-lar
odd-i-ty
o-de-um (hall)
o-di-ous
o-di-um (hatred)
o-do-graph

o-dom-e-ter
o-don-to-graph
o-don-tol-o-gy
o-dor-if-er-ous
o-dor-ous
oe-soph-a-gus
off-beat
off-cast
off-chance
off-col-or
of-fend
of-fer-to-ry
off-hand
of-fice
of-fi-cial
off-print
off-set
off-shore
off-side
off-stage
off-white
of-ten-times
o-give
o-gle
o-gre
ohm-age
ohm-me-ter
oil-cloth
oil-skin
oint-ment
o-kra
old-fash-ioned
old-fo-gy-ish
old-ster
old-time
old-wom-an-ish
o-le-a-ceous
o-le-an-der
o-le-as-ter
o-le-o-graph
o-le-o-mar-ga-rine
ol-fac-to-ry
ol-i-gu-ri-a

ol-i-va-ceous
ol-i-var-y
ol-ive green
o-me-ga
om-e-let
o-men-tum
om-i-nous
o-mis-sion
om-ni-bus
om-ni-far-i-ous
om-nip-o-tent
om-ni-pres-ent
om-nis-cient
om-niv-o-rous
o-mo-pha-gi-a
on-a-gra-ceous
on-col-o-gy
on-coming
on-do-gram
on-do-graph
on-dom-e-ter
o-nei-ro-crit-ic
on-er-ous
one-self
one-sid-ed
one-step
one-track
one-way
on-ion-skin
on-look-er
on-rush
on-set
on-shore
on-slaught
on-tog-e-ny
on-tol-o-gy
on-ward
on-yx
ooze
o-pac-i-ty
o-pal
o-pal-esce
o-paque
o-pen-and-shut
o-pen-eyed

o-pen-faced
o-pen-hand-ed
o-pen-heart-ed
o-pen-hearth
o-pen-mind-ed
op-er-a
op-er-ate
op-er-a-tor
o-per-cu-late
op-er-et-ta
op-er-ose
oph-thal-mi-a
oph-thal-mi-tis
oph-thal-mol-o-gy
o-pi-ate
o-pin-ion
o-pi-um
o-pos-sum
op-pi-late
op-po-ment
op-por-tune
op-pose
op-po-site
op-press
op-pro-bri-ous
op-pug-nant
op-ti-cal
op-ti-mism
op-ti-mum
op-tion
op-tom-e-ter
op-u-lent
o-pus-cule
or-a-cle
o-rac-u-lar
or-ange-ade
or-ange-wood
o-rang-u-tan
orator
or-bic-u-late
or-bi-tal
or-chard
or-ches-tra
or-chid
or-chi-da-ceous

or-dain
or-deal
or-der-ly
or-di-nal
or-di-nance (law)
or-di-nar-y
or-di-nate
ord-nance (artillery)
or-dure
o-rec-tic
o-reg-a-no
or-gan-ic
or-ga-nog-ra-phy
or-ga-nol-o-gy
or-ga-non
or-gasm
or-gi-as-tic
or-gy
o-ri-ent
o-ri-en-tate
or-i-fice
or-i-flamme
or-i-gin
o-rig-i-nal
o-rig-i-nate
o-ri-ole
or-i-son
or-na-ment
or-ner-y
or-ni-thol-o-gy
o-rog-e-ny
o-rog-ra-phy
o-ro-ide
o-rol-o-gy
or-phan-age
or-ris-root
or-tho-cen-ter
or-tho-ce-phal-ic
or-tho-chro-mat-ic
or-tho-don-tia
or-tho-dox
or-tho-gen-e-sis
or-thog-o-nal
or-thog-ra-phy
or-tho-pe-dic

or-tho-phos-phate	o-to-scope	out-reach
or-tho-psy-chi-a-try	ot-ter	out-ri-der
or-thop-ter-ous	ought	out-rig-ger
or-thop-tic	ounce	out-right
or-tho-trop-ic	our-self	out-run
os-cil-late	oust-er	out-side
os-cil-la-tor	out-board	out-spo-ken
os-cil-lo-graph	out-break	out-spread
os-cil-lo-scope	out-build-ing	out-stand-ing
os-ci-tant	out-burst	out-stretch
os-cu-late	out-cast	out-strip
os-mic	out-come	out-ward
os-mo-sis	out-cry	out-weigh
os-se-in	out-date	out-wit
os-si-cle	out-dis-tance	out-worn
os-sif-er-ous	out-do	o-val
os-si-fi-ca-tion	out-door	o-var-i-an
os-si-frage	out-er-di-rect-ed	o-var-i-ot-o-my
os-si-fy	out-er-most	o-va-ri-tis
os-su-ar-y	out-field	o-va-ry
os-te-i-tis	out-fit	o-vate
os-ten-si-ble	out-go	ov-en-bird
os-ten-ta-tious	out-group	o-ver-a-bun-dance
os-te-o-blast	out-grow	o-ver-act
os-te-oc-la-sis	out-guess	o-ver-age
os-te-o-clast	out-house	o-ver-all
os-te-o-gen-e-sis	out-land	o-ver-bal-ance
os-te-o-ma	out-last	o-ver-bear
os-te-o-my-e-li-tis	out-law	o-ver-blown
os-te-o-path	out-lay	o-ver-board
os-te-o-plas-tic	out-let	o-ver-bur-den
os-te-ot-o-my	out-line	o-ver-cap-i-tal-ize
os-ti-ar-y	out-live	o-ver-cast
os-ti-ole	out-ly-ing	o-ver-cer-ti-fy
os-to-sis	out-ma-neu-ver	o-ver-charge
os-tra-cize	out-most	o-ver-coat
os-trich	out-num-ber	o-ver-come
o-tal-gi-a	out-of-date	o-ver-com-pen-sa-tion
oth-er-di-rect-ed	out-of-doors	o-ver-con-fi-dent
oth-er-guess	out-of-the-way	o-ver-crit-i-cal
oth-er-wise	out-pa-tient	o-ver-de-vel-op
oth-er-world-ly	out-post	o-ver-do
o-ti-ose	out-pour-ing	o-ver-dose
o-to-lar-yn-gol-o-gy	out-put	o-ver-draft
o-tol-o-gy	out-rage	o-ver-draw

o-ver-dress
o-ver-drive
o-ver-es-ti-mate
o-ver-ex-cite
o-ver-ex-pose
o-ver-feed
o-ver-flow
o-ver-grow
o-ver-hang
o-ver-haul
o-ver-head
o-ver-hear
o-ver-in-dulge
o-ver-joy-ed
o-ver-land
o-ver-lap
o-ver-lay
o-ver-load
o-ver-match
o-ver-night
o-ver-pass
o-ver-pay
o-ver-per-suade
o-ver-pop-u-late
o-ver-pow-er-ing
o-ver-rate
o-ver-ride
o-ver-ripe

o-ver-rule
o-ver-run
o-ver-seas
o-ver-see
o-ver-shoe
o-ver-shot
o-ver-sight
o-ver-sized
o-ver-sleep
o-ver-spend
o-ver-spread
o-ver-stay
o-ver-strung
o-ver-stud-y
o-ver-stuffed
o-ver-sup-ply
o-vert
o-ver-take
o-ver-tax
o-ver-the-count-er
o-ver-throw
o-ver-time
o-vert-ly
o-ver-tone
o-ver-ture
o-ver-turn
o-ver-watch

o-ver-wea-ry
o-ver-weigh
o-ver-whelm
o-ver-work
o-ver-wrought
o-vi-form
o-vip-a-rous
o-vule
o-vum
ow-ing
owl-ish
own-er-ship
ox-a-late
ox-blood
ox-bow
ox-cart
ox-heart
ox-ide
ox-tail
ox-tongue
ox-y-ac-id
ox-y-da-tion
ox-y-gen
ox-y-hy-dro-gen
ox-y-salt
ox-y-sul-fide
oys-ter-man
o-zone

P

pace-set-ter
pach-y-derm
pac-i-fy
pack-age
pack-er
pack-et
pac-tion
pad-ding
pad-dle
pad-dock
pad-lock
pa-dre
pad-u-a-soy

pa-gan-ism
pag-eant
pag-i-nate
pa-go-da
pa-gu-ri-an
paid-in
pail-lette (spangle)
pain-ful
pains-tak-ing
paint-brush
pal-ace
pal-at-a-ble
pal-ate

pa-la-tial
pal-a-tine
pa-lav-er
pa-le-a
pa-le-o-ge-og-raph-y
pa-le-og-ra-phy
pa-le-o-lith-ic
pal-ette (tablet)
pal-in-drome
pal-in-gen-e-sis
pal-i-node
pal-i-sade
pal-ish

pal-lad-ic
pal-la-dous
pal-li-ate
pal-lor
pal-mate
palm-is-try
pal-mi-tate
pal-mi-tin
pal-my-ra
pal-pa-ble
pal-pate
pal-pe-bral
pal-pi-tate
pal-ter
pal-u-dism
pam-pas
pam-per
pam-phlet
pam-phlet-eer
pan-a-ce-a
pa-na-da
pan-cake
pan-chro-mat-ic
pan-cre-as
pan-da
pan-da-na-ceous
pan-dem-ic
pan-de-mo-ni-um
pan-der
pan-do-ra
pan-dow-dy
pan-du-rate
pan-el
pan-han-dle
pan-ic
pan-i-cle
pa-nic-u-late
pan-nier
pan-ni-kin
pa-no-cha
pan-op-tic
pan-o-ram-a
pan-sy
pan-ta-lets
pan-to-loon

pan-the-ism
pan-ther
pan-tile
pan-to-mime
pan-try
pa-pal
pa-pav-er-ine
pa-paw
pa-pa-ya
pa-per
pa-pier-ma-che
pa-pil-la
pa-pil-lon
pa-pist
pa-poose
pap-ri-ka
pap-ule
pa-py-rus
par-a-bi-o-sis
par-a-blast
par-a-ble
par-a-bol-ic
par-a-chute
pa-rade
par-a-dise
par-a-dos (fort)
par-a-dox
   (self-contradictory)
par-af-fin
par-a-gen-e-sis
par-a-go-ge
par-a-gon
par-a-graph
par-a-keet
par-al-lel
pa-ral-y-sis
par-a-lyze
par-a-mag-net
pa-ram-e-ter
par-a-mor-phism
par-a-mount
par-a-mour
par-a-noi-a
par-a-nymph
par-a-pet

par-a-pher-nal-ia
par-a-phrase
pa-raph-y-sis
par-a-ple-gi-a
par-a-psy-chol-o-gy
par-a-site
par-a-sol
par-a-syn-the-sis
par-a-thy-roid
par-a-troop
par-boil
par-buck-le
par-cel
par-chee-si
parch-ment
par-don
pare (cut away)
par-e-gor-ic
par-ent
pa-ren-the-sis
par-ent-hood
pa-re-sis
par-es-the-sia
pa-ret-ic
par-fait
pa-ri-e-tal
par-ish
pa-rish-ion-er
par-i-ty
par-ka
par-lance
par-lay (to bet)
par-ley (conference)
par-lia-ment
par-lor
pa-ro-chi-al
par-o-dy
pa-role
par-o-no-ma-si-a
par-o-nym
par-o-ti-tis
pa-ro-toid
par-ox-ysm
par-quet
par-rot

par-ry	pa-tel-la	pec-cant
par-si-mo-ny	pat-en	pec-ca-ry
pars-ley	pat-ent	pec-ti-nate
pars-nip	pa-ter-nal	pec-to-ral
par-son	pa-thet-ic	pec-u-late
par-take	path-less	pe-cu-li-ar-i-ty
par-the-no-gen-e-sis	path-o-gen-ic	pe-cu-li-um
par-tial	path-o-log-i-cal	pe-cu-ni-ar-y
par-ti-ble	path-way	ped-a-gogue
par-tic-i-pate	pa-tient	ped-al (foot lever)
par-ti-ci-ple	pat-i-na	ped-ant
par-ti-cle	pa-ti-o	ped-ate
par-ti-col-ored	pa-tri-arch	ped-dle (sell)
par-tic-u-lar	pat-ri-cide	ped-er-as-ty
par-ti-san	pat-ri-mo-ny	ped-es-tal
par-ti-tion	pa-tri-ot	pe-des-tri-an
part-ner-ship	pa-tris-tic	pe-di-a-tri-cian
par-took	pa-trol-man	ped-i-cel
par-tridge	pa-tron	pe-dic-u-lar
par-tu-ri-ent	pat-ro-nym-ic	ped-i-cure
par-ty	pat-ten	ped-i-gree
pa-rure	pat-ter	ped-i-ment
par-ve-nu	pat-tern	pe-dom-e-ter
pass-a-ble	pat-u-lous	pe-dun-cle
pas-sade	pau-ci-ty	peel (pare)
pas-sage	paunch	peer-age
pass-book	pau-per	pee-vish
pas-sen-ger	pause (delay)	peign-oir
pass-er-by	pave-ment	pe-jo-ra-tive
pas-sion	pa-vil-ion	pe-lag-ic
pas-sive	paws (feet)	pel-i-can
pass-key	pay-day	pe-lisse
pass-port	pay-off	pe-lite
pass-word	pay-o-la	pel-la-gra
pas-ta	peace (calm)	pel-let
pas-tel	pea-cock	pel-li-to-ry
pas-tern	peal (sound of bells)	pel-lu-cid
pas-teur-ize	pea-nut	pel-tate
pas-time	pearl	pelt-ry
pas-tor	peas-ant	pel-vis
pas-to-ral (of shepherds)	pea-vey	pe-nal
pas-to-rale (opera)	peb-ble	pen-ance
pas-tra-mi	pe-can	pen-chant
pas-try	pec-ca-ble	pen-cil
pas-ture	pec-ca-dil-lo	pend-ant

pen-drag-on
pen-du-lum
pen-e-trate
pen-guin
pen-i-cil-lin
pen-in-su-la
pe-nis
pen-i-tence
pen-i-ten-tia-ry
pen-man-ship
pen-nant
pen-nate
pen-ni-less
pe-nol-o-gy
pen-sion
pen-sive
pen-stock
pen-ta-cle
pen-ta-gon
pen-ta-gram
pen-tam-e-ter
pen-tar-chy
pen-ta-stick
pent-house
pen-tom-ic
pen-tose
pe-nul-ti-mate
pe-num-bra
pe-nu-ri-ous
pe-on-age
pep-lum
pep-per-idge
pep-per-mint
pep-sin
pep-tic
pep-tide
pep-tize
pep-tone
per-ad-ven-ture
per-am-bu-la-tor
per-bo-rate
per-cale
per-ca-line
per-ceive
per-cent

per-cep-ti-ble
per-chance
per-chlo-ride
per-cip-i-ent
per-co-late
per-cus-sion
per-di-tion
per-dur-a-ble
per-e-grine
per-emp-to-ry
per-en-ni-al
per-fect-i-ble
per-fer-vid
per-fi-dy
per-fo-li-ate
per-fo-rate
per-force
per-form
per-fume
per-func-to-ry
per-fuse
per-go-la
per-i-blem
per-i-car-di-al
per-i-carp
per-i-cy-cle
per-i-derm
per-il-ous
per-im-e-ter
per-i-neph-ri-um
per-i-ne-um
per-i-neu-ri-tis
pe-ri-od-ic
per-i-o-dide
per-i-os-ti-tis
per-i-o-tic
pe-riph-er-al
per-i-phras-tic
per-i-scope
per-ish-a-ble
per-i-stal-sis
per-i-stome
per-i-style
per-i-to-ni-tis
per-i-wig

per-i-win-kle
per-jure
per-lite
perm-al-loy
per-ma-nent
per-man-ga-nate
per-me-ate
per-mis-si-ble
per-mu-ta-tion
per-ni-cious
per-nick-et-y
per-o-ne-al
per-o-rate
per-ox-ide
per-pen-dic-u-lar
per-pet-u-al
per-pe-tu-i-ty
per-plex
per-qui-site
per se
per-se-cute
per-se-vere
per-si-flage
per-sim-mon
per-sist
per-son-al
per-son-i-fy
per-son-nel
per-sorp-tion
per-spec-tive
per-spi-cac-i-ty
per-spic-u-ous
per-spire
per-suade
per-sul-fate
per-tain
per-ti-nent
per-turb
per-tus-sis
pe-ruke
pe-ruse
per-vade
per-verse
per-vert
per-vi-ous

pes-ky
pes-si-mism
pes-ter
pest-i-cide
pes-tif-er-ous
pes-ti-lent
pes-tle
pet-al (of a flower)
pet-a-lo-dy
pe-tard
pet-i-ole
pe-ti-tion-ar-y
pet-rel
pet-ri-fy
pet-ro-chem-i-cal
pe-trog-ra-phy
pe-tro-le-um
pe-tro-sal
pet-ti-coat
pet-ti-fog
pet-tish
pet-u-lant
pe-tu-ni-a
pew-ter
pha-lanx
phal-lus
phan-ta-sy
phan-tom
phar-ma-ceu-tic
phar-ma-cy
phar-yn-gi-tis
pha-ryn-go-scope
phar-ynx
pheas-ant
phel-lo-derm
phe-na-caine
phe-nol
phe-nom-e-na
phe-nom-e-non
phe-no-type
phe-nox-ide
phi-lan-der
phi-lan-thro-py
phi-lat-e-ly
phil-har-mon-ic

phil-o-den-dron
phi-log-y-ny
phil-o-pe-na
phi-los-o-phy
phil-ter
phle-bi-tis
phle-bot-o-my
phlegm
phlog-o-pite
phlox
pho-bi-a
pho-net-ic
phon-ic
pho-no-gram
pho-no-graph
pho-nog-ra-phy
pho-no-lite
pho-nol-o-gy
pho-no-scope
pho-no-type
phos-ge-nite
phos-phate
phos-phide
phos-phite
phos-pho-pro-tein
phos-pho-rate
phos-pho-resce
phos-phor-ic
phos-phor-o-scope
phos-pho-rous
pho-to-cell
pho-to-chem-is-try
pho-to-chron-o-graph
pho-to-dra-ma
pho-to-dy-nam-ics
pho-to-e-lec-tric
pho-to-en-grav-ing
pho-to-gen-ic
pho-to-gram-me-try
pho-to-graph
pho-to-ki-ne-sis
pho-to-li-thog-ra-phy
pho-tol-y-sis
pho-tom-e-ter
pho-to-off-set

pho-to-pho-bi-a
pho-to-play
pho-to-sphere
pho-to-stat
pho-to-syn-the-sis
pho-to-tax-is
pho-to-ther-a-py
pho-to-ther-mic
pho-to-trop-ic
pho-to-tube
pho-to-type
phra-se-o-gram
phra-se-o-graph
phra-se-ol-o-gy
phre-net-ic
phren-ic
phre-nol-o-gy
phthis-ic
phy-col-o-gy
phy-co-my-ce-tous
phy-lac-ter-y
phyl-lite
phyl-lo-tax-is
phy-log-e-ny
phys-ic
phy-si-cian
phys-i-o-crat
phys-i-og-no-my
phys-i-og-ra-phy
phys-i-ol-o-gy
phys-i-o-ther-a-py
phy-sique
phy-to-gen-e-sis
phy-to-ge-og-ra-phy
phy-tog-ra-phy
phy-tol-o-gy
pi-ac-u-lar
piaffe
pi-ama-ter
pi-a-nis-si-mo
pi-an-ist
pi-an-o-for-te
pi-as-ter
pi-az-za
pi-ca (size of type)

pic-a-dor
pic-a-resque
pic-a-roon
pic-a-yune
pic-ca-lil-li
pic-co-lo
pic-e-ous
pick-a-nin-ny
pick-ax
pick-er-al
pick-et
pick-le
pick-up
pic-nic
pic-o-line
pi-cot
pic-o-tee
pic-rate
pic-tog-ra-phy
pic-to-ri-al
pic-tur-esque
pid-dle
pid-dock
pidg-in
piece (part)
pier
pierce
pi-e-ty
pi-e-zo-e-lec-tric-i-ty
pi-e-zom-e-ter
pif-fle
pi-geon
pig-let
pig-ment
pig-skin
pig-sty
pig-tail
pi-ka (type of mammal)
pi-las-ter
pi-lau
pil-chard
pi-le-ate
pil-fer
pil-fer-age
pil-grim

pi-lif-er-ous
pil-i-form
pil-lar
pil-low-case
pi-lo-car-pine
pi-lose
pi-lot
pil-u-lar
pi-men-to
pi-mien-to
pim-per-nel
pim-ple
pi-na-ceous
pin-a-fore
pi-nas-ter
pince-nez
pin-cers
pin-cush-ion
pin-dling
pin-e-al
pine-ap-ple
pi-nene
pin-er-y
ping-pong
pin-head
pin-hole
pin-ion
pin-nace
pin-na-cle
pin-nate
pin-ni-grade
pin-ni-ped
pin-nule
pi-noch-le
pi-no-le
pin-point
pin-tail
pin-tle
pin-to
pin-up
pin-wheel
pin-worm
pi-o-neer
pi-ous
pip-age

pi-per-i-dine
pip-er-ine
pi-per-o-nal
pip-kin
pip-pin
pi-quet
pi-rate
pi-rogue
pir-ou-ette
pis-ca-ry
pis-ci-cul-ture
pis-ci-na
pis-cine
pi-si-form
pi-so-lite
pis-ta-chi-o
pis-til
pis-til-late
pis-tol
pis-ton
pitch-er
pit-e-ous
pit-fall
pit-i-a-ble
pit-man
pit-saw
pit-tance
pi-tu-i-tar-y
pit-y-ri-a-sis
piv-ot
pix-i-lat-ed
piz-za
pla-cate
place-ment
pla-cen-ta
pla-cet
plac-id
plack-et
pla-fond
pla-gal
pla-gia-rism
plague
plaid
plains-man
plain-tiff

plain-tive
plait
pla-nar-i-an
planch-et
plan-er
plan-e-tar-i-um
plan-e-tes-i-mal
plan-et-struck
plan-gent
pla-nim-e-ter
plan-i-sphere
plank-ing
plank-ton
plan-ner
pla-no-con-cave
pla-no-con-vex
pla-nom-e-ter
plan-tain
plan-ti-grade
plaque
plash-y
plas-ma
plas-mo-di-um
plas-mol-y-sis
plas-mo-some
plas-ter
plas-tic
plas-tid
pla-teau
plate-ful
plate-let
plat-en
plat-form
plat-i-na
plat-ing
pla-tin-ic
plat-i-no-type
plat-i-nous
plat-i-num
plat-i-tude
pla-ton-ic
pla-toon
plat-ter
plat-y-pus
plau-si-ble

play-a-ble
play-back
play-boy
play-mate
play-off
play-pen
play-thing
pla-za
pleach
plead-a-ble
pleas-ant
pleas-ure
pleat
ple-be-ian
pleb-i-scite
plec-trum
pledge
ple-na-ry
ple-nip-o-tent
plen-i-po-ten-ti-ar-y
plen-te-ous
plen-ti-ful
ple-num
ple-o-nasm
ple-o-pod
pleth-o-ra
pleu-ri-sy
pleu-ro-dont
pleu-ro-pneu-mo-ni-a
plex-i-form
plex-i-glass
plex-im-e-ter
plex-or
pli-a-ble
pli-cate
pli-er
plight
plum-age
plum-ba-go
plumb-er
plum-bic
plum-bif-er-ous
plume
plum-met
plun-der

plung-er
plu-per-fect
plu-ral
plu-to-crat
plu-ton-ic
plu-vi-al
ply-wood
pneu-mat-ic
pneu-ma-tol-y-sis
pneu-ma-to-ther-a-py
pneu-mo-dy-nam-ics
pneu-mo-gas-tric
pneu-mo-nec-to-my
pneu-mo-ni-a
poach
po-chard
pock-et-book
pock-et-ful
pock-mark
po-co-cu-ran-te
po-dag-ra
po-di-a-try
po-di-um
pod-o-phyl-lin
po-et-as-ter
po-et-ry
po-go-ni-a
po-grom
poign-ant
poin-ci-a-na
poind
poin-set-ti-a
point-blank
poin-til-lism
poise
poi-son
po-lar-im-e-ter
po-lar-i-scope
po-lar-i-ty
po-lar-o-graph
pole-ax
pole-cat
po-lem-ic
po-len-ta
po-lice-man

pol-i-clin-ic
pol-i-o-my-e-li-tis
po-lit-i-cal
pol-ka
pol-lack
pol-lard
pol-len
pol-len-o-sis
pol-lex
pol-li-nate
pol-lin-i-um
pol-li-no-sis
pol-li-wog
poll-ster
pol-lute
po-lo-naise
po-lo-ni-um
pol-ter-geist
pol-troon
pol-y-an-dry
pol-y-bas-ic
pol-y-cha-si-um
pol-y-chrome
pol-y-clin-ic
pol-y-em-bry-o-ny
pol-y-eth-yl-ene
pol-y-foil
po-lyg-a-la
po-lyg-a-my
pol-y-ge-net-ic
pol-y-glot
pol-y-gon
pol-y-go-na-ceous
pol-y-graph
po-lyg-y-ny
pol-y-he-dron
pol-y-mer
po-lym-er-i-za-tion
pol-y-mor-phous
pol-y-no-mi-al
pol-y-nu-cle-ar
pol-yp
pol-y-pep-tide
pol-y-phase
pol-y-phon-ic

pol-y-phy-let-ic
pol-yp-tych
pol-y-sac-cha-ride
pol-y-sty-rene
pol-y-sul-fide
pol-y-syl-la-ble
pol-y-tech-nic
pol-y-the-ism
pol-y-thene
pol-y-to-nal-i-ty
pol-y-typ-ic
pol-y-va-lent
pom-ace
po-made
po-man-der
pome-gran-ate
pom-e-lo
po-mi-cul-ture
po-mif-er-ous
pom-mel
po-mol-o-gy
pom-pa-dour
pom-pa-no
pom-pom
pom-pos-i-ty
pon-cho
pon-der-a-ble
pon-gee
pon-iard
pon-ti-fex
pon-tiff
pon-tif-i-cate
pont-lev-is
pon-to-nier
pon-toon
po-ny-tail
pool-room
poor-spir-it-ed
pop-corn
pop-gun
pop-in-jay
pop-lar
pop-lin
pop-lit-e-al
pop-o-ver

pop-pet
pop-ple
pop-py-cock
pop-py-head
pop-u-lace
pop-u-lar
pop-u-late
por-ce-lain
por-cu-pine
po-rif-er-ous
po-ri-on
por-nog-ra-phy
po-ros-i-ty
por-phy-ry
por-poise
por-ridge
por-rin-ger
por-tage
por-tal
por-ta-men-to
por-ta-tive
port-cul-lis
por-tend
por-ter-house
port-fo-li-o
port-hole
por-ti-co
por-tiere
por-tion
por-trait
pos-it
pos-i-tive
pos-se
pos-sess
pos-si-ble
pos-sum
post-age
post-ax-i-al
post-date
pos-te-ri-or
pos-tern
post-fix
post-free
post-grad-u-ate
post-hu-mous

pos-tiche
pos-til-lion
post-lim-i-ny
post-lude
post-man
post-mark
post-mas-ter
post-me-rid-i-an
post-mil-len-ni-al
post-na-tal
post-o-bit
post-or-bit-al
post-pone
post-po-si-tion
post-script
pos-tu-late
pos-ture
post-war
po-ta-ble
po-tam-ic
pot-ash
po-tas-si-um
po-ta-tion
po-ta-to
pot-bel-ly
pot-boil-er
po-tent
po-ten-tate
po-ten-tial
po-ten-ti-om-e-ter
poth-er
pot-hole
pot-hook
pot-house
po-tiche
po-tion
pot-latch
pot-luck
pot-pie
pot-pour-ri
pot-tage
pot-ter-y
pouch
pou-lard
poul-tice

poul-try
pounce
pound-cake
pov-er-ty-strick-en
pow-der
pow-er-boat
pow-er-house
prac-tice
prac-ti-tion-er
prae-di-al
prae-to-ri-an
prag-mat-ic
prai-rie
praise-wor-thy
pra-line
prance
pran-di-al
prase
prate
prat-in-cole
pra-tique
prat-tle
prawn
prax-is
preach-ment
pre-ad-o-les-cent
pre-al-lot-ment
pre-am-ble
pre-am-pli-fi-er
pre-ap-point
pre-ar-range
pre-ax-i-al
pre-can-cel
pre-car-i-ous
prec-a-to-ry
pre-cau-tion-ar-y
pre-cede
pre-cen-tor
pre-cep-tor
pre-ces-sion-al
pre-cinct
pre-ci-os-i-ty
pre-cious
prec-i-pice
pre-cip-i-tate

pre-cise
pre-clin-i-cal
pre-clude
pre-co-cious
pre-con-ceive
pre-con-cep-tion
pre-con-cert
pre-con-demn
pre-con-tract
pre-crit-i-cal
pre-cur-so-ry
pre-da-cious
pre-date
pred-a-to-ry
pre-de-cease
pred-e-ces-sor
pre-des-ig-nate
pre-des-tine
pre-de-ter-mine
pre-di-al
pred-i-cate
pre-dict
pre-di-gest
pre-di-lec-tion
pre-dis-pose
pre-dom-i-nate
pre-em-i-nence
pre-empt
preen
pre-en-gage
pre-es-tab-lish
pre-ex-ist
pre-fab-ri-cate
pref-ace
pre-fect
pref-er-a-ble
pre-fig-ure
pre-fix
pre-form
preg-nant
pre-heat
pre-hen-sion
pre-his-tor-ic
pre-ig-ni-tion
pre-judge

prej-u-dice
prel-ate
pre-li-ba-tion
pre-lim-i-nar-y
pre-lit-er-ate
prel-ude
pre-ma-ture
pre-med-i-cal
pre-med-i-tate
pre-mier
pre-mil-le-nar-i-an
prem-ise
pre-mi-um
pre-mon-ish
pre-morse
pre-mun-dance
pre-na-tal
pre-nom-i-nate
pre-no-tion
pre-oc-cu-py
pre-or-dain
pre-par-a-to-ry
pre-pay
pre-pense
pre-pon-der-ate
pre-pos-i-tor
pre-pos-sess-ing
pre-pos-ter-ous
pre-po-ten-cy
pre-print
pre-req-ui-site
pre-rog-a-tive
pres-age
pres-by-o-pi-a
pres-by-te-ri-an
pre-school
pre-sci-ence
pre-scind
pre-scribe
pre-script
pres-ence
pre-sen-ta-tion
pres-ent-day
pre-sen-ti-ment
    (foreboding)

pre-sent-ment
    (presentation)
pre-serv-a-tive
pre-side
pres-i-dent-e-lect
pre-sid-ium
pre-sig-ni-fy
press-man
press-mark
pres-sure
pres-ti-dig-i-ta-tion
pres-tige
pres-tis-si-mo
pre-sum-a-ble
pre-sump-tive
pre-sup-pose
pre-sur-mise
pre-tense
pre-ten-tious
pre-ter-hu-man
pre-ter-mit
pre-ter-nat-u-ral
pre-text
pret-ti-fy
pret-zel
pre-vail
prev-a-lent
pre-var-i-cate
pre-ven-ient
pre-vent
pre-view
pre-vi-sion
pre-vo-ca-tion-al
prick-et
prick-le
prie-dieux
priest-hood
priest-rid-den
pri-ma-cy
pri-mage
pri-ma-ry
pri-me-val
pri-mi-ge-ni-al
prim-i-tive
pri-mo-gen-i-tor

pri-mor-di-al
prim-rose
prince-dom
prin-ci-pal (chief)
prin-ci-ple (rule)
print-er-y
pri-or-ate
pri-or-i-ty
prism
pris-mat-ic
pris-on-er
pris-tine
pri-vate
priv-i-lege
priv-i-ty
prob-a-ble
pro-bate
pro-bi-ty
prob-lem
pro-caine
pro-ca-the-dral
pro-ce-dure
pro-ceed-ing
proc-ess
pro-claim
pro-cliv-i-ty
pro-con-sul
pro-cras-ti-nate
pro-cre-ate
proc-tor
proc-to-scope
pro-cum-bent
pro-cur-a-ble
pro-cur-ance
proc-u-ra-tor
prod-i-gy
pro-drome
prod-uct
pro-em
pro-fane
pro-fess
pro-fes-sor-ship
prof-fer
pro-fi-cient
pro-file

prof-it-eer
prof-li-gate
prof-lu-ent
pro-found
pro-fun-di-ty
pro-fuse
pro-gen-i-tor
prog-e-ny
pro-ges-ter-one
prog-no-sis
prog-nos-ti-cate
pro-gram
prog-ress
pro-hib-it
pro-ject
pro-lac-tin
pro-lapse
pro-late
pro-lep-sis
pro-le-tar-y
pro-lif-ic
pro-line
pro-loc-u-tor
pro-logue
pro-lon-gate
pro-lu-sion
prom-e-nade
prom-i-nent
pro-mis-cu-ous
prom-ise
prom-on-to-ry
pro-mate
prompt-er
promp-ti-tude
pro-mul-gate
pro-nate
pro-na-tion
prone
pro-neph-ros
pro-nom-i-nal
pro-noun
pro-nu-cle-us
pro-nun-ci-a-tion
proof-read
prop-a-gan-da

prop-a-gate
pro-pane
pro-pel-lant
(propelling agent)
pro-pel-lent
(propelling)
pro-pel-ler
pro-pend
prop-er-ly
prop-er-ty
pro-phase
proph-et
pro-phy-lax-ic
pro-pin-qui-ty
pro-pi-o-nate
pro-pi-ti-ate
pro-po-nent
pro-por-tion
prop-o-si-tion
pro-pound
pro-pri-e-tor
pro-pri-o-cep-tive
prop-to-sis
pro-pul-sion
pro-pyl-ene
prop-y-lite
pro-rate
pro-sa-ic
pro-scribe
pro-sec-tor
pros-e-cu-tor
pros-e-lyte
pros-en-ceph-a-lon
pro-slav-er-y
pros-o-dy
pros-pect
pros-per-i-ty
pros-tate
pros-the-sis
pros-ti-tute
pros-trate
pro-style
pro-tag-o-nist
pro-ta-mine
prot-a-sis

pro-tec-tor-ate
pro-te-ge
pro-tein
pro-test
proth-e-sis
pro-thon-o-tar-y
pro-tho-rax
pro-throm-bin
pro-tist
pro-ti-um
pro-to-col
pro-to-lith-ic
pro-to-mar-tyr
pro-to-path-ic
pro-to-plasm
pro-to-type
pro-to-zo-an
pro-trac-tor
pro-trude
pro-tu-ber-ant
proust-ite
prov-e-nance
prov-en-der
prov-erb
prov-i-dence
prov-ince
pro-vi-sion
pro-vi-so-ry
pro-vi-ta-min
prov-o-ca-tion
pro-voke
pro-vost
prow-ess
prox-im-i-ty
prox-y
pru-dent
pru-ri-ent
pru-rig-i-nous
pru-ri-tus
prus-si-ate
psal-mo-dy
pseud-ax-is
pseu-do-a-quat-ic
pseu-do-carp
pseu-do-clas-sic

pseu-do-learn-ed
pseu-do-morph
pseu-do-nym
psit-ta-co-sis
pso-ri-a-sis
psy-che-del-ic
psy-chi-a-trist
psy-chic
psy-cho-a-nal-y-sis
psy-cho-an-a-lyze
psy-cho-bi-ol-o-gy
psy-cho-gen-ic
psy-cho-log-i-cal
psy-chol-o-gize
psy-cho-man-cy
psy-chom-e-try
psy-cho-neu-ro-sis
psy-cho-path-ic
psy-cho-phys-ics
psy-cho-sis
psy-cho-so-mat-ic
psy-cho-ther-a-peu-tics
psy-cho-ther-a-py
psy-chrom-e-ter
pto-maine
pty-a-lin
pu-ber-ty
pu-bic
pub-li-ca-tion
puck-er
pud-ding
pud-dle
pu-den-cy
pu-den-dum
peub-lo
pu-er-ile
puf-fin (bird)
pu-gil-ist
pug-na-cious
pul-ing
pul-let
pul-ley

pul-lu-late
pul-mo-nar-y
pul-pit
pul-sate
pul-sim-e-ter
pul-ver-ize
pul-vi-nate
pum-ice
pum-mel
pum-per-nick-el
pump-kin
pump-kin-seed
pun-cheon
punc-tate
punc-til-i-ous
punc-tu-ate
punc-ture
pun-gent
pun-ish-ment
pu-ni-tive
pu-pate
pu-pil-age
pu-pil-lar-y
pup-pet-ry
pur-chase
pure-bred
pur-ga-tive
pu-ri-tan-i-cal
pur-loin
pur-port
pur-pose
purs-er
pur-sue
pu-ru-lent
pur-vey
pur-view
pu-sil-la-nim-i-ty
puss-y-foot
pus-tule
pu-ta-tive
put-out

pu-tre-fy
pu-tres-ci-ble
pu-trid
put-tee (leg cover)
put-ty (cement)
put-up
puz-zle
pyc-nom-e-ter
py-e-li-tis
py-e-lo-gram
py-e-mi-a
py-jam-as
py-lon
py-lo-rec-to-my
py-o-gen-ic
py-or-rhe-a
pyr-a-mid
py-rar-gy-rite
pyre
py-rene
pyr-e-tol-o-gy
py-rex
py-rite
py-ro-chem-i-cal
py-ro-clas-tic
py-ro-crys-tal-line
py-ro-e-lec-tric
py-ro-gen-ic
py-rog-nos-tics
py-rog-ra-phy
py-rol-y-sis
py-ro-mag-net-ics
py-ro-ma-ni-a
py-rom-e-ter
py-ro-mor-phite
py-ro-sis
py-ro-sul-fate
py-ro-tox-in
pyr-rho-tite
py-thon
pyx-ie
pyx-is

Q

quack-er-y   quad-ran-gle   quad-ren-ni-al

quad-ri-cen-ten-ni-al	quar-tet	qui-e-tude
quad-ri-ceps	quar-to	quill
quad-ri-cy-cle	quartz	quilt
quad-ri-fid	qua-sar	qui-na-ry
quad-ri-lat-er-al	quash	quince
quad-ri-lin-gual	qua-si	quin-cunx
qua-drille	qua-si-ju-di-cial	quin-dec-a-gon
quad-ri-no-mi-al	quass	quin-de-cen-ni-al
quad-ri-syl-la-ble	qua-ter-na-ry	quin-i-dine
quad-ri-va-lent	qua-ter-ni-on	qui-nine
quad-riv-i-al	qua-tre	quin-o-line
quad-roon	quat-re-foil	quin-qua-ge-nar-i-an
quad-ru-ped	qua-ver	quin-que-fo-li-o-ate
quad-ru-ple	quay	quin-quen-ni-al
quad-ru-plex	quea-sy	quin-que-va-lent
quad-ru-pli-cate	queen-hood	quin-sy
quag-mire	queer	quint
qua-hog	quell	quin-tal
quail	quench-less	quin-tan
quaint	quer-ce-tin	quin-tes-sence
quak-er	quer-cine	quin-tet
qual-i-fy	quer-cit-ron	quin-til-lion
qual-i-ty	quer-u-lous	quin-tu-plet
qualm-ish	que-ry	quip-ster
quan-da-ry	quest	quis-ling
quar-an-tine	ques-tion	quit-claim
quar-rel-some	ques-tion-naire	quit-rent
quar-ry	ques-tor	quit-tance
quar-tan	queue	quiv-er
quar-ter-back	quib-ble	quix-ot-ic
quar-ter-deck	quick-sand	quiz-zi-cal
quar-ter-hour	quick-tem-pered	quoit
quar-ter-mas-ter	quick-wit-ted	quo-rum
quar-ter-phase	quid-di-ty	quo-ta
quar-ter-saw	qui-es-cent	quo-tient

R

rab-bet (groove)	rack-et-eer	rad-dle (to paint with red)
rab-bin-i-cal	rack-rent	ra-di-al
rab-ble	rack-work	ra-di-ate
rab-id	rac-on-teur	ra-di-a-tor
rac-coon	ra-coon	rad-i-cal (extremist)
ra-cial	ra-dar-scope	rad-i-cle (primary root)

ra-di-o-ac-tive
ra-di-o-as-tron-o-my
ra-di-o-broad-cast
ra-di-o-car-bon
ra-di-o-chem-is-try
ra-di-o-fre-quen-cy
ra-di-o-gram
radi-o-graph
ra-di-ol-o-gy
ra-di-om-e-ter
ra-di-o-paque
ra-di-o-phone
ra-di-os-co-py
ra-di-o-tel-e-gram
ra-di-o-tel-e-graph
ra-di-o-tel-e-phone
ra-di-o-ther-a-py
ra-di-o-ther-my
rad-ish
ra-di-um
ra-di-um-ther-a-py
ra-di-us
ra-dix
ra-don
raff-ish
raf-fle
rafts-man
rag-a-muf-fin
rag-ged
rag-lan
rag-man
ra-gout
rag-time
rail-road
rail-way
rai-ment
rain-bow
rain-coat
rain-drop
rain-fall
rain-storm
rai-sin
ra-jah
rak-ish
ral-line

ral-ly
ram-ble
ram-bunc-tious
ram-bu-tan
ram-e-kin
ram-i-fi-ca-tion
ram-jet
ram-page
ram-pa-geous
ramp-an-cy
ramp-ant
ram-part
ram-rod
ram-shack-le
ram-son
ram-u-lose
ra-mus
ranch-er
ran-che-ro
ranch-man
ran-cho
ran-cid
ran-cor-ous
ran-dom
rang-er
rang-y
ran-kle
ran-sack
ran-som
ra-pa-cious
rap-id-fire
ra-pi-er
rap-pee
rap-port
rap-proche-ment
rap-scal-lion
rap-to-ri-al
rap-ture
rar-e-fac-tion
ras-cal-i-ty
ra-so-ri-al
rasp-ber-ry
rasp-ing
rat-al
ra-tan

ratch-et
rate-a-ble
raths-kel-ler
rat-i-fy
ra-ti-ne
ra-tio
ra-ti-o-ci-nate
ra-tion-al (reasonable)
ra-tion-a-le (reasons)
rat-ite
rat-line
ra-toon
rat-tan
rat-tle (clatter)
rat-tle-snake
rat-tle-trap
rat-trap
rau-cous
rav-age
rave-lin (type of fort)
rav-el-ing (drawn thread)
rav-en-ous
ra-vine
ra-vi-o-li
rav-ish
raw-hide
ray-on
raze
ra-zor
ra-zor-back
razz
re-ac-tor
read-a-ble
read-i-ness
re-ad-just
read-y-made
read-y-to-wear
re-a-gent
re-al-is-tic
re-al-ize
realm
re-al-tor (broker)
re-al-ty (property)
ream-er
re-an-i-mate

reap-er
rea-son-a-ble
re-as-sure
reave
re-bate
re-bel-lion
re-birth
reb-o-ant
re-born
re-bound
re-broad-cast
re-buff
re-buke
re-but-tal
re-cal-ci-trant
re-ca-lesce
re-cant
re-cap-i-tal-ize
re-ca-pit-u-late
re-cap-ture
re-cast
re-cede
re-ceipt
re-ceiv-a-ble
re-ceiv-er-ship
re-cen-sion
re-cep-ta-cle
re-cep-tor
re-ces-sion-al
re-cid-i-vism
rec-i-pe
re-cip-i-ent
re-cip-ro-cal
re-cip-ro-cate
rec-i-proc-i-ty
re-ci-sion
re-cit-al
reck-on
re-claim
rec-la-ma-tion
re-cline
rec-luse
rec-og-ni-tion
re-cog-ni-zance
re-coil

re-col-lect
rec-om-mend
re-com-mit
rec-om-pense
re-com-pose
rec-on-cil-a-ble
rec-on-cil-i-a-to-ry
rec-on-dite
re-con-nais-sance
re-con-noi-ter
re-con-sid-er
re-con-sign-ment
re-con-sti-tute
re-con-struct
re-con-vey
re-cord-er
re-count
re-coup
re-course
re-cov-er
rec-re-ate
re-crim-i-nate
re-cru-desce
re-cruit
rec-tal
rec-tan-gle
rec-ti-fi-er
rec-ti-lin-e-ar
rec-ti-tude
rec-to
rec-to-cele
rec-tor
rec-tum
re-cum-bent
re-cu-per-ate
re-cu-per-a-tive
re-cu-per-a-tor
re-cur
re-cur-rence
re-cur-rent
re-cur-vate
re-curve
rec-u-san-cy
rec-u-sant
re-cuse

re-dact
red-blood-ed
redd
red-den
red-dish
re-deem
re-deem-a-ble
re-deem-er
re-de-liv-er
re-de-mand
re-demp-tion
Re-demp-tor-ist
re-de-vel-op
red-hand-ed
red-head-ed
red-hot
red-in-te-grate
re-di-rect
re-dis-count
re-dis-trict
red-o-lent
re-dou-ble
re-doubt-a-ble
re-dound
re-draft
re-dress
re-duce
re-duc-tor
re-dun-dant
re-du-pli-cate
red-wood
reed (stalk)
re-ed-u-cate
reef-er
reek
reel
re-en-force
re-en-ter
reeve
re-ex-am-ine
re-ex-port
re-face
re-fec-to-ry
ref-er-ee
ref-er-ent

re-fi-nance
re-fined
re-flec-tor
re-flet
re-flex
ref-lu-ent
re-flux
re-for-est
re-form-a-to-ry
re-fract
re-frac-tom-e-ter
re-frac-tor
re-frain
re-fran-gi-ble
re-fresh-er
re-frig-er-a-tor
re-frin-gent
re-fu-el
ref-uge (shelter)
ref-u-gee
 (one who flees)
re-ful-gent
re-fund
re-fur-bish
re-fus-al
re-fute
re-gain
re-gal (royal)
re-gale (to entertain)
re-ga-li-a (rights of king)
re-gard
re-ge-late
 (freeze together)
re-gen-er-a-tor
re-gent
reg-i-cide
re-gime (form of rule)
reg-i-men
 (therapeutic system)
reg-i-ment
re-gion-al
reg-is-ter
reg-is-trar
reg-let
reg-nant

re-gorge
re-grate
re-gress
re-gret-ful
reg-u-lar-ize
reg-u-late (control)
reg-u-la-tor
re-gur-gi-tate
re-ha-bil-i-tate
re-hash
re-hearse
re-i-fy
reign (royal rule)
re-im-burse
re-im-port
re-im-pres-sion
rein (thin strap)
re-in-car-nate
rein-deer
re-in-force
re-in-state
re-in-sure
re-it-er-ate
re-ject
re-joice
re-ju-ve-nate
re-lapse
re-late
re-la-tion-al
rel-a-tive
re-la-tor
re-lax-a-tion
re-lay
re-lease
rel-e-gate
re-lent-less
rel-e-vant
re-li-a-ble
rel-ic
re-lieve
re-li-gion
re-lin-quish
rel-ish
re-luc-tance
re-lume

re-main-der
re-mand
re-mark-a-ble
re-marque (engraving)
re-me-di-al
re-mem-brance
re-mind-ful
rem-i-nisce
re-mise (give up claim)
re-miss (negligent)
re-mis-sion (pardon)
re-mit-tance
 (money sent)
re-mit-ter
 (holds property)
re-mit-tor
 (sends money)
rem-nant
re-mod-el
re-mo-lade
re-mon-e-tize
re-mon-strate
re-mon-tant
re-morse-ful
re-mote
re-mount
re-mov-a-ble
re-mu-ner-ate
ren-ais-sance
 (a new birth)
re-nal
re-nas-cence (rebirth)
ren-count-er
ren-der
ren-dez-vous
ren-di-tion
ren-e-gade
re-nege
re-new-al
re-ni-tent
ren-net
re-nounce
ren-o-vate
re-nown
re-nun-ci-a-tion

re-or-der
re-or-gan-ize
re-paint
re-pair-man
re-pand
rep-a-ra-ble
rep-ar-tee
re-par-ti-tion
re-pass (pass back)
re-past (food)
re-pa-tri-ate
re-peal
re-peat-er
re-pel-lent
re-pent-ant
re-peo-ple
re-per-cus-sion
rep-er-toire
rep-e-tend
rep-e-ti-tious
re-phrase
re-pine
re-place
re-plead-er
re-plen-ish
re-plate
re-plev-i-sa-ble
rep-li-ca
re-port-er
rep-or-to-ri-al
re-pos-al
re-pos-i-tor-y
re-pos-sess
rep-re-hend
rep-re-sent
re-pres-sion
re-prieve
rep-ri-mand
re-print
re-pris-al
re-proach-ful
rep-ro-bate
re-proc-essed
re-pro-duce
re-prove

rep-tant
rep-tile
re-pub-lic
re-pu-di-ate
re-pug-nant
re-pulse
re-pur-chase
rep-u-ta-ble
rep-u-ta-tion
re-quest
re-qui-es-cat
re-quire
req-ui-site
re-quite
re-ra-di-a-tion
re-scind
re-sist-i-ble
re-scis-so-ry
re-script
res-cue
re-search
re-seat
re-sect
res-e-da-ceous
re-sem-blance
re-sem-ble
re-send
re-sent-ful
re-sent-ment
res-er-pine
res-er-va-tion
re-served
re-serv-ist
res-er-voir
re-set
re-shape
re-ship
re-side
res-i-dence
res-i-dent
res-i-due
re-sign
re-sil-i-ent
res-in (solid from plant)
re-sist-ance

res-o-lute
re-sol-vent
res-o-nate
re-sorb
re-sort
re-sound
re-source
re-spect-a-ble
res-pi-ra-tor
re-spire
res-pite
re-splend-ence
re-spond-ence
re-spon-si-ble
re-state
res-tau-rant
res-tau-ra-teur
res-ti-tu-tion
res-to-ra-tion
re-strain
re-stric-tion
re-sult-ant
re-sume (go on)
re-su-me (summary)
re-sump-tion
re-su-pine
re-sur-face
re-sur-gent
res-ur-rect
re-sus-ci-tate
re-ta-ble
re-tail
re-tain-er
re-tal-i-ate
re-tard
retch
re-ten-tion
ret-i-cent
ret-i-cle
re-tic-u-late
ret-i-cule
re-ti-form
ret-i-na
ret-i-ni-tis
ret-i-nol

ret-i-nos-co-py
ret-i-nue
re-tire-ment
re-tort
re-touch
re-trace
re-tract
re-tread
re-treat
re-trench-ment
ret-ri-bu-tion
re-trieve
ret-ro-ac-tive
ret-ro-cede
ret-ro-flex
ret-ro-gress
re-trorse
ret-ro-spect
ret-ro-ver-sion
re-turn-a-ble
re-tuse
re-u-nite
re-used
re-val-ue
re-vamp
re-veal-ment
re-veg-e-tate
rev-eil-le
rev-e-la-tor
rev-e-nant
re-venge
rev-e-nue
re-ver-ber-ate
re-verse
rev-er-ie
re-vers (as a lapel)
re-vers-i-ble
re-vert
re-vest
re-vet-ment
re-view
re-vile
re-vise
re-vive
rev-i-vis-cence

rev-o-ca-ble
re-voice
re-voke
re-volt
rev-o-lu-tion-ar-y
re-volve
re-vul-sion
re-word
re-wire
re-ward
re-write
rhap-so-dy
rhe-mat-ic
rhe-nic
rhe-ol-o-gy
rhe-om-e-ter
rhe-o-scope
rhe-o-stat
rhe-o-tax-is
rhe-ot-ro-pism
rhet-o-ric
rheu-mat-ic
rhi-nen-ceph-a-lon
rhine-stone
rhi-ni-tis
rhi-noc-er-os
rhi-nol-o-gy
rhi-no-plas-ty
rhi-no-scope
rhi-zo-car-pous
rhi-zo-ceph-a-lous
rhi-zot-o-my
rho-di-um
rho-do-den-dron
rho-do-lite
rhom-ben-ceph-a-lon
rhom-boid
rhu-barb
rhyme-ster
rhythm
rhyth-mi-cal
ri-al-to
ri-ant
rib-ald
rib-band

rib-bon-fish
ri-bo-fla-vin
rick-ets
rick-rack
rick-shaw
ric-o-chet
rid-a-ble
rid-dance
rid-dle
ri-dent
ridge-ling
rid-i-cule
rif-fle
riff-raff
ri-fle
rig-a-doon
rig-ger
right-eous
right-hand-ed
right-ist
rig-id
rig-ma-role
rig-or-ous
rill-et
ri-mose
rin-der-pest
ring-let
ring-side
rinse
ri-ot-ous
ri-par-i-an
rip-en
rip-ple
rip-rap
rip-roar-ing
rip-saw
rip-tide
ris-i-ble
ri-sot-to
ris-que
ri-tar-dan-do
rit-u-al
riv-age
ri-val-ry
riv-en

riv-er-side
riv-et
ri-viere (necklace)
riv-u-let
roach
road-block
road-way
roam
roar-ing
roast-er
rob-ber
robe
rob-in
ro-ble
rob-o-rant
ro-bust
roch-et
rock-a-way
rock-bound
rock-et
rock-fish
ro-co-co
ro-dent
ro-de-o
rod-man
rod-o-mon-tade
roent-gen-ol-o-gy
roent-gen-o-ther-a-py
rog-a-to-ry
ro-guer-y
roist-er
rol-lick-ing
ro-ly-po-ly
ro-maine
ro-mance
ro-man-esque
romp-ers
ron-del
ron-do
ron-dure
rook-ie
room-mate
roost-er
roque (croquet)
roq-ue-laure

ro-quet (strike a ball)
ro-sa-ceous
ros-an-i-line
ro-sa-ry
ro-se-ate
rose-bud
ro-se-o-la
ro-sette
ros-in (brittle resin)
ros-in-weed
ros-tel-late
ros-ter
ros-trum
ro-ta-ry
ro-tate
ro-ti-fer
ro-tis-ser-ie
ro-tor
rot-ten-stone
ro-tun-da
rouge
rough-age
rough-house
rough-neck
rough-rid-er
rou-lade
rou-lette
round-a-bout
roun-del
roun-de-lay
round-up
roup-y
roust-a-bout
rout (disperse)
route (road)
rou-tine
rove-o-ver
row-boat
row-dy
row-el
roy-al
ru-basse
ru-ba-to
rub-ber-neck
rub-bish

rub-ble
rub-down
ru-be-fa-cient
ru-bel-la
ru-bel-lite
ru-be-o-la
ru-bes-cent
ru-bi-a-ceous
ru-big-i-nous
ru-bric
ruche
ruck-sack
ruc-tion
rud-der-post
rud-dle
ru-di-ment
rue-ful
ru-fes-cent
ruf-fi-an
ruf-fle
ru-gate
ru-in-a-tion
rum-ba
rum-ble
ru-men
ru-mi-nate
rum-mage
ru-mor
rum-ple
rum-pus
run-a-round
run-a-way
run-ci-nate
run-dle
run-down
run-in
run-nel
run-ner-up
run-off
run-on
run-way
rup-ture
ru-ral
rus-set
rust-col-ored

rus-tic
rus-tle
rust-proof

ru-ta-ba-ga
ru-then-ic
ruth-less

ru-ti-lant
rye
rynd

S

sab-bat-i-cal
sa-ber
sa-ber-toothed
sa-ble
sa-bot
sab-o-tage
sab-o-teur
sa-bre-tache
sab-u-lous
sac-cha-rin
   (crystalline compound)
sac-cha-rine
   (nature of sugar)
sac-cha-roze
sac-cule
sac-er-do-tal
sa-chem
sa-cral
sac-ra-ment
sa-crar-i-um
sa-cred
sac-ri-lege
sac-ris-tan
sac-ris-ty
sa-cro-il-i-ac
sac-ro-sanct
sa-cro-sci-at-ic
sa-crum
sad-dle
sad-ism
sad-ness
sa-fa-ri
safe-keep-ing
safe-ty
saf-flow-er
saf-fron
sa-gac-i-ty
sag-a-more

sage-brush
sag-gar
sag-it-tal
sa-go
sa-gua-ro
sa-hib
sail-er (vessel)
sail-or (mariner)
saint-hood
sa-laam
sal-a-ble
sa-la-cious
sal-ad
sal-a-man-der
sa-la-mi
sal-a-ry
sale-a-ble
sal-e-ra-tus
sal-i-ca-ceous
sal-i-cyl-ate
sa-lif-er-ous
sa-li-na (salt marsh)
sa-line (salty)
sal-li-va
sal-low
sal-ly
sal-ma-gun-di
sal-mi
salm-on
salm-on-ber-ry
sa-lon (drawing room)
sa-loon (bar)
sa-loop
sal-pa
sal-si-fy
sal-tant
salt-cel-lar
salt-ern

sal-ti-grade
sal-tire
sa-lu-bri-ous
sal-u-tar-y
sa-lu-ta-to-ri-an
sa-lute
sal-vage
sal-ver
sal-vi-a
sal-vo
sam-a-ra
sa-mar-i-um
sa-mar-skite
sam-i-sen
sam-o-var
sam-pan
sam-u-rai
san-a-tive
san-a-to-ry (curative)
sanc-ti-fy
sanc-ti-mo-ny
sanc-tion
sanc-tu-ar-y
san-dal
san-dal-wood
san-da-rac
sand-bag
sand-blast
sand-box
sand-er-ling
sand-man
sand-pa-per
sand-pi-per
sand-wich
san-for-ize
san-ga-ree
san-guif-er-ous
san-guine

san-i-cle
sa-ni-ous
san-i-tar-i-an
san-i-tar-i-um
san-i-tar-y
(free from germs)
san-tal
san-tir
san-ton-i-ca
san-to-nin
sa-pi-ent
sap-in-da-ceous
sap-o-dil-la
sa-pon-i-fy
sa-por
sap-phire
sap-phism
sa-pre-mi-a
sap-ro-gen-ic
sap-ro-phyte
sap-so-go
sap-suck-er
sa-ran
sar-casm
sarce-net
sar-co-carp
sar-co-ma
sar-coph-a-gus
sar-cous
sar-dine
sar-di-us
sar-don-ic
sar-do-nyx
sa-ri
sar-men-tose
sa-rong
sar-sa-pa-ril-la
sar-to-ri-al
sa-shay
sas-sa-fras
sa-tan-ic
satch-el
sa-teen
sat-el-lite
sa-ti-ate

sat-in
sat-in-pod
sat-ire (sarcasm)
sat-is-fac-tion
sat-is-fy
sat-u-rate
sat-ur-nine
sat-yr (diety)
sau-cer
sau-er-kraut
sau-ger
saun-ter
sau-ral
sau-ry
sau-sage
sau-te
sau-terne
sav-age
sa-van-na
sa-vant
sav-in
sav-ior
sa-vor
sa-vor-y
sav-vy
saw-dust
saw-horse
saw-mill
saw-yer
sax-horn
sax-o-phone
scab-bard
scab-ble
sca-bies
scab-land
scaf-fold
scagl-io-la
scal-a-ble
sca-lar
scal-a-wag
sca-lene
scal-lion
scal-lop
scal-pel
scam-per

scan-dal
scan-dal-mon-ger
scan-dent
scan-di-a
scan-sion
scan-so-ri-al
scant-ling
scape-goat
scaph-oid
scap-u-lar
scar-ab
scarce
scare-crow
scare-mon-ger
scarf
scar-i-fy
scar-i-ous
scar-la-ti-na
scar-let
scarp
scarves
scath-ing
sca-tol-o-gy
scat-ter-brain
scav-enge
sce-nar-i-o
scend
scene (view)
sce-nog-ra-phy
scent (odor)
scep-ter
scep-tic
sched-ule
sche-mat-ic
scheme
scher-zo
schil-ler
schip-per-ke
schism
schis-mat-ic
schist (rocks)
schis-to-some
schiz-o-carp
schiz-o-gen-e-sis
schiz-oid

schiz-o-my-co-sis	scope	scruff
schiz-o-phre-nia	sco-pol-a-mine	scrump-tious
schiz-o-pod	sco-po-line	scrunch
schnap-per (fish)	scop-u-late	scru-ple
schnapps (liquor)	scorch	scru-pu-lous
schnau-zer	score	scru-ta-ble
sch-nor-kle	scorn-ful	scru-ti-ny
schol-ar	scor-pi-on	scu-ba
schol-ar-ship	scotch	scud
school-boy	sco-ter	scuf-fle
school-girl	scot-free	scull (oar)
school-house	scoun-dre	scul-pin
school-mas-ter	scourge	sculp-tor
school-teach-er	scout-mas-ter	sculp-tur-esque
school-yard	scow (barge)	scum-ble
schoon-er	scowl (angry frown)	scup-per
schot-tische	scrab-ble	scurf
sci-am-a-chy	scrag-gly	scur-ril-ous
sci-at-ic	scram-ble	scur-ry
sci-ence	scrap-book	scur-vy
sci-en-tif-ic	scrap-er	scu-tate
scil-i-cet	scrap-ple	scu-tel-late
scil-la	scratch	scut-tle
scim-i-tar	scrawl	scut-tle-butt
scin-coid	scraw-ny	scy-phi-form
scin-til-late	screak	scythe
sci-o-lism	scream	sea-board
sci-on	screech	sea-coast
scir-rhus	screed	sea-far-er
scis-sile	screen	sea-girt
scis-sion	screw	sea-go-ing
scis-sor	scrib-ble	sea is-land
sci-u-rine	scribe	seal-skin
sclaff	scrim-mage	sea-maid
scle-ra	scrim-shaw	sea-man
scler-o-der-ma	scrip (receipt)	sea-mark
scle-rom-e-ter	script (handwriting)	seam-stress
scle-ro-sis	scrip-tur-al	se-ance
scle-rot-o-my	scro-bic-u-late	sea-plane
sco-li-o-sis	scrof-u-la	sea-quake
scol-lop	scroll	sear (burn)
scom-broid	scroop	search-light
sconce	scro-tum	sea-scope
scoop	scrouge (squeeze)	sea-shore
scoot-er	scrounge (forage)	sea-sick

sea-side
sea-son
sea-ward
sea-way
sea-wor-thy
se-ba-ceous
seb-or-rhe-a
se-cant
se-cede
se-ces-sion
se-clude
sec-ond-hand
se-con-do
sec-ond-rate
se-cre-cy
sec-re-tar-y
se-crete
se-cre-tin (hormone)
se-cre-tion (separation)
sec-tar-i-an
sec-tile
sec-tion-al
sec-tor
sec-u-lar
se-cund
se-cure
se-dan
se-date
sed-en-tar-y
sedged
se-di-le
sed-i-ment
se-di-tion
se-duce
sed-u-lous
see-catch
seed-ling
seep-age
seer (prophet)
seer-suck-er (fabric)
see-saw
seethe
seg-ment
seg-re-gate
se-gui-dil-la

seis-mic
seis-mo-gram
seis-mo-graph
seis-mog-ra-phy
seis-mol-o-gy
seis-mom-e-ter
sei-zure
se-lec-tive
se-lect-man
se-le-ni-um
sel-e-nog-ra-phy
self-a-buse
self-act-ing
self-ad-dressed
self-as-ser-tion
self-as-sur-ance
self-cen-tered
self-com-mand
self-com-pla-cent
self-con-ceit
self-con-fi-dence
self-con-scious
self-con-sist-ent
self-con-tained
self-con-tent
self-con-trol
self-de-cep-tion
self-de-fense
self-de-ni-al
self-de-struc-tion
self-de-ter-mi-na-tion
self-dis-ci-pline
self-ed-u-ca-ted
self-es-teem
self-ex-am-i-na-tion
self-ex-ist-ent
self-ex-plan-a-to-ry
self-ex-pres-sion
self-gov-erned
self-help
self-i-den-ti-ty
self-im-por-tant
self-im-posed
self-im-prove-ment
self-in-duced

self-in-dul-gent
self-in-sur-ance
self-in-ter-est
self-liq-ui-dat-ing
self-load-ing
self-made
self-pit-y
self-pos-sessed
self-pres-er-va-tion
self-pro-pelled
self-pro-tec-tion
self-re-al-i-za-tion
self-re-cord-ing
self-re-gard
self-re-li-ance
self-re-spect
self-re-straint
self-right-eous
self-sac-ri-fice
self-sat-is-fied
self-serv-ice
self-styled
self-suf-fi-cient
self-sup-port
self-taught
sel-vage
se-man-tic (of meaning)
sem-a-phore
se-mat-ic (danger sign)
sem-blance
se-mes-ter
sem-i-an-nu-al
sem-i-au-to-mat-ic
sem-i-cen-ten-ni-al
sem-i-cir-cle
sem-i-co-lon
sem-i-con-duc-tor
sem-i-con-scious
sem-i-de-tached
sem-i-fi-nal-ist
sem-i-month-ly
sem-i-nal
sem-i-nar-y
sem-i-of-fi-cial
se-mi-ol-o-gy

sem-i-plas-tic
sem-i-por-ce-lain
sem-i-pre-cious
sem-i-pub-lic
sem-i-tone
sem-i-trans-par-ent
sem-o-li-na
sem-pli-ce
sen-a-ry
sen-a-tor
send-off
se-nes-cent
se-nile
sen-ior
sen-nit
sen-sate
sen-sa-tion-al
sen-si-ble
sen-si-tive
sen-si-tom-e-ter
sen-so-ry
sen-su-al
sen-tence
sen-ten-tious
    (magisterial)
sen-tient (conscious)
sen-ti-men-tal
sen-ti-nel
sen-try
sep-a-rate
sep-a-ra-tor
se-pi-a
sep-sis
sep-tal
sep-tar-i-um
sep-tate
sep-tem-par-tite
sep-te-nar-y
sep-ten-ni-al
sep-ten-tri-o-nal
sep-tet
sep-tic
sep-til-lion
sep-tine
sep-tu-a-ge-nar-i-an

sep-tum
sep-tu-ple
sep-ul-cher
sep-ul-ture
se-qua-cious
se-quel
se-que-la
se-quence
se-quen-tial
se-ques-ter
se-ques-trec-to-my
se-quin
se-quoi-a
se-ra-pe
ser-aph
se-rein
ser-e-nade
ser-e-na-ta
ser-en-dip-i-ty
se-ren-i-ty
serf (slave)
serge (fabric)
ser-geant
se-ri-al
se-ri-ceous
ser-i-cin
ser-i-cul-ture
se-ries
se-ri-o-com-ic
se-ri-ous
ser-mon-ize
se-rol-o-gy
ser-o-tine (bat)
ser-o-to-nin (amine)
se-rous
ser-pen-tine
ser-pi-go
ser-rate
ser-ri-form
ser-ru-late
se-rum
serv-ant
serv-ice
ser-vo-con-trol
ser-vo-mech-an-ism

ses-a-me
ses-qui-ox-ide
ses-qui-pe-da-li-an
ses-site
ses-sion
ses-tet
se-ta-ceous
set-back
se-ti-form
se-tig-er-ous
set-off
se-ton
se-tose
set-screw
set-tee
set-tle
set-up
sev-en-fold
sev-enth-day
sev-en-up
sev-er
sev-er-al
sev-er-ance
se-vere
sew-age (waste matter)
sew-er
sew-er-age
    (sewer system)
sex-a-ge-nar-i-an
sex-cen-te-nar-y
sex-en-ni-al
sex-tan (of a fever)
sex-tant (instrument)
sex-tet
sex-tile
sex-til-lion
sex-ton
sex-tu-ple
sex-u-al
shab-by
shack-le
shad-ber-ry
shad-bush
shad-dock
shad-ow

sha-green
shal-loon (fabric)
shal-lop (boat)
shal-lot (onion)
shal-low
sha-man
sham-ble
shame-ful
sham-mer
sham-poo
sham-rock
shan-ty
share-hold-er
shark-skin
sharp-set
sharp-shoot-er
sharp-sight-ed
shat-ter
shav-er
shawl
sheaf
shear (cut)
sheath
sheave
sheen
sheep-herd-er
sheep-shank
sheeps-head
sheep-shear-ing
sheep-skin
sheer (transparent)
shel-lac
shell-fire
shell-fish
shel-ter
shelve
she-nan-i-gan
shep-herd
sher-bet
sher-iff
sher-ry
shib-bo-leth
shied
shield
shift-less

shil-le-lagh
shil-ly-shal-ly
shim-mer
shin-bone
shin-gles
shin-ing
shin-ny
shin-plas-ter
ship-own-er
ship-per
ship-shape
ship-wreck
ship-yard
shirk
shirt-ing
shirt-waist
shiv-a-ree
shiv-er
shoal
shoat
shock-head-ed
shod-dy
shoe-mak-er
shoe-string
shop-keep-er
shop-lift-er
shop-worn
shore-line
short-age
short-bread
short-cake
short-hand-ed
short-lived
short-sight-ed
short-tem-pered
short-term
shot-ten
shoul-der
shov-el-board
show-boat
show-case
show-down
show-off
show-room
shrank

shrap-nel
shrewd
shriek
shrimp
shrine
shrink
shriv-el
shroud
shrove
shrub-ber-y
shuck
shud-der
shuf-fler
shut-down
shut-in
shut-off
shut-out
shut-tle-cock
shy-ster
si-al-a-gogue
sib-i-lant
sib-ling
sib-yl
sic-ca-tive
sick-le
sid-dur
side-board
side-burns
side-car
side-hill
side-kick
side-long
side-piece
si-de-re-al
sid-er-ite
sid-er-o-sis
side-sad-dle
side-slip
side-step
side-swipe
side-track
side-walk
side-wall
side-ways
side-wind-er

si-dle
siege
si-en-na
si-er-ra
si-es-ta
sieve
sight (vision)
sight-see-ing
sig-ma
sig-moid
sig-nal-man
sig-na-ture
sig-net
sig-nif-i-cant
sign-post
si-lage
si-le-na-ceous
si-lence
si-lent
si-lex
sil-hou-ette
sil-i-cate
si-li-cious
sil-i-cide
si-lic-i-fy
sil-i-cle
sil-i-con
   (nonmetallic element)
sil-i-cone
   (silicon compound)
sil-i-co-sis
si-lic-u-lose
silk-screen
silk-stock-ing
silk-worm
si-lo
si-lur-id
sil-ver-sides
sil-ver-smith
sil-ver-ware
sil-ver-weed
sil-vi-cul-ture
sim-i-lar
sim-i-le
si-mil-i-tude

sim-mer
si-mo-ni-ac
si-mo-nize
sim-per
sim-ple
sim-plex
sim-plic-i-ty
sim-u-lar
sim-u-late
si-mul-ta-ne-ous
sin-a-pism
sin-cere
sin-ci-put
si-ne-cure
sin-ew
singe
sin-gle-breast-ed
sin-gle-hand-ed
sin-glet
sing-song
sin-gu-lar
sin-is-ter
sin-is-tral
sin-ter
sin-u-ate
sin-u-ous
si-nus-i-tis
si-phon
sip-id
sip-pet
si-ren
sir-loin
si-roc-co
sis-ter-hood
sis-ter-in-law
sis-troid
site (position)
si-to-ma-ni-a
si-to-pho-bi-a
sit-u-ate
si-tus
sixth
six-ti-eth
siz-a-ble
siz-zle

skat-er
ske-dad-dle
skeet
skein
skel-e-ton
skep-tic
sketch-a-ble
skew-er
ski-a-scope
skid-doo
ski-er
skiff
skil-let
skill-ful
skim-mer
skin-ner
skin-tight
skip-knot
skirl
skir-mish
skit-ter
skit-tle
skiv-er
skoal
skul-dug-ger-y
skulk
skull-cap
sky-line
sky-rock-et
sky-scrap-er
sky-writ-ing
slab-sid-ed
slain
slake
slan-der
slant-wise
slap-jack
slap-stick
slat-tern
slaugh-ter
slaugh-ter-house
slave-hold-er
slea-zy
sledge-ham-mer
sleep-walk-ing

sleet
sleeve
sleigh
sleight
slen-der
sleuth
slick-en-side
slight-ing
sling-shot
slip-knot
slip-on
slip-o-ver
slip-per-y
slip-slop
slip-up
slith-er
sliv-er
slob-ber
sloe-eyed
slo-gan
sloth-ful
slough
slov-en
slow-down
slow-mo-tion
slow-wit-ted
sludge
slug-gard
sluice
slum-ber
slum-lord
small-pox
smart-weed
smash-up
smat-ter
smelt-er
smi-la-ca-ceous
smi-lax
smith-er-eens
smith-son-ite
smit-ten
smock-ing
smoke-stack
smol-der
smudge

smug-gle
snaf-fle
snag-gle-tooth
snail-paced
snap-drag-on
snap-shot
snare
sneak-ing
sneer
sneeze
snick-er
snif-fle
snig-ger
snig-gle
snip-pet
sniv-el
snob-bish
snor-kel
snow-ball
snow-bound
snow-fall
snow-flake
snow-man
snow-shoe
snow-storm
snow-suit
snow-white
snuff-box
snuf-fle
snug-gle
soap-bark
soap-box
soap-stone
soap-suds
soar (fly)
so-be-it
so-ber-mind-ed
so-bri-e-ty
so-called
soc-cer (game)
so-cia-ble
so-cial-is-tic
so-ci-e-ty
so-ci-om-e-try
sock-et

so-dal-i-ty
sod-den
so-di-um
sod-o-my
so-ev-er
so-fa
sof-fit
soft-ball
soft-heart-ed
soft-spo-ken
soil-age
soi-ree
so-journ
sol-ace
sol-a-na-ceous
so-lar
sol-der
sol-dier
sol-e-cism
sol-emn
sol-le-noid
sol-fa-ta-ra
sol-feg-gio
so-lic-it
sol-i-dar-i-ty
so-lid-i-fy
sol-i-fid-i-an
so-lil-o-quy
sol-ip-sism
sol-i-taire
sol-i-tar-y
sol-i-tude
sol-ler-et
sol-mi-za-tion
so-lo-ist
sol-stice
sol-u-ble
so-lu-tion
solv-a-ble
sol-vent
so-mat-ic
so-ma-tol-o-gy
som-ber
som-bre-ro
some-bod-y

some-day
some-how
some-one
som-er-sault
some-thing
some-time
some-what
some-where
some-while
so-mite
som-nam-bu-late
som-nif-er-ous
som-nil-o-quy
som-no-lent
so-nant
so-na-ta
son-der-class
song-bird
son-ic
so-nif-er-ous
son-in-law
son-net
so-no-rous
soothe
sooth-say-er
so-phis-ti-cat-ed
soph-ist-ry
soph-o-more
sop-o-rif-ic
so-pran-o
sor-cer-er
sor-did
sore (painful)
sore-head
sor-ghum
sor-i-cine
so-ri-tes
so-ro-rate
so-ror-i-ty
so-ro-sis
sorp-tion
sor-rel
sor-row
sor-tie
sor-ti-lege

sos-te-nu-to
so-te-ri-ol-o-gy
sot-tish
sou-bise
sou-brette
souf-fle
sough
sought
soul-ful
sound-proof
soup
sour-dough
sour-sop
sou-sa-phone
sou-tache
sou-tane
south-east
sou-ve-nir
sov-er-eign
so-vi-et
spa-cious
spade-fish
spa-di-ceous
spa-dix
spa-ghet-ti
spa-gyr-ic
span-drel
span-gle
span-iel
spar-a-ble
spare-rib
spar-kle
spar-row
spas-mod-ic
spastic
spa-tha-ceous
spathe
spa-tial
spat-ter
spat-u-la
spav-in
spear-mint
spe-cial
spe-cies
spec-i-fy

spec-i-men
spe-ci-os-i-ty
spe-cious
speck-le
spec-ta-cle
spec-ta-tor
spec-ter
spec-tro-bo-lom-e-ter
spec-tro-gram
spec-tro-graph
spec-tro-he-li-o-gram
spec-trom-e-ter
spec-tro-scope
spec-trum
spec-u-late
speech-i-fy
speed-om-e-ter
speed-up
speed-way
spe-le-ol-o-gy
spell-bound
spel-ter
spend-thrift
sper-ma-ce-ti
sper-mat-o-cyte
sper-mat-o-gen-e-sis
sper-mat-o-go-ni-um
sper-mat-o-phore
sper-mat-o-phyte
sper-mat-or-rhe-a
sper-mat-o-zo-id
sper-mat-o-zo-on
sper-mo-phile
sper-ry
sphac-e-lus
sphag-num
sphal-er-ite
sphe-noid
spher-i-cal
sphe-roid
sphinc-ter
sphinx
sphra-gis-tic
sphyg-mic
sphyg-mo-na-nom-e-ter

spi-ca
spi-cate
spice-ber-ry
spice-bush
spic-and-span
spic-ule
spi-der-wort
spie-gel-ei-sen
spig-ot
spike-let
spi-na-ceous
spin-ach
spi-nal (of backbone)
spin-dle-legs
spin-drift
spi-nel (mineral)
spin-et
spi-nif-er-ous
spin-ner-et
spin-ster
spi-nule
spi-ra-cle
spi-rae-a
spi-ral
spi-rant
spir-it-u-al
spi-ro-chete
spi-ro-graph
spi-roid
spi-rom-e-ter
spir-u-la
spitch-cock
spite-ful
spit-fire
spit-tle
spit-toon
splat-ter
splay-foot
spleen
splen-did
splen-dor
sple-nec-to-my
sple-net-ic
splen-ic
splin-ter

split-lev-el
splurge
splut-ter
spoils-man
spokes-man
spo-li-a-tion
spon-da-ic
spon-dle
spon-dy-li-tis
sponge
spon-sion (promise)
spon-son
     (ship platform)
spon-sor
spon-ta-ne-i-ty
spoon-fed
spoor (track)
spo-rad-ic
spore (germ cell)
spo-rif-er-ous
spo-ro-carp
spo-ro-cyst
spo-ro-phore
spo-ro-phyll
spo-ro-phyte
spo-ro-tri-cho-sis
spor-ran
sports-man
spor-u-late
spot-light
spouse
sprawl
spread
spright-ly
sprin-kle
sprock-et
spu-mes-cent
spu-ri-ous
spurt
sput-ter
spu-tum
squab-ble
squad-ron
squal-id
squall

squan-der
square-rigged
squar-rose
squaw-fish
squaw-root
squeal
squeam-ish
squee-gee
sque-teague
squint-eyed
squire-ar-chy
squirm
squir-rel
sta-bil-i-ty
sta-bi-liz-er
sta-ble-boy
stac-ca-to
sta-di-um
stage-coach
stage-craft
stage-hand
stage-struck
stag-ger
stag-hound
stag-nate
staid
stair (steps)
stair-case
stair-head
stair-way
stair-well
stake-hold-er
sta-lac-tite
sta-lag-mite
stale-mate
stalk-ing-horse
stall-feed
stal-lion
stal-wart
sta-men
stam-i-na
stam-mer
stam-pede
stan-chion
stand-ard-bearer

stand-by
stand-in
stand-off
stand-out
stand-pat
stand-pipe
stand-point
stand-still
stand-up
stan-hope
stan-nic
stan-za
sta-pes
staph-y-lo-coc-cus
sta-ple
star-board
star-dom
stare (gaze)
star-fish
star-gaze
star-let
star-light
star-tle
star-va-tion
starve-ling
state-hood
state-side
states-man
stat-ic
sta-tion-ar-y (fixed)
sta-tion-er-y
(writing paper)
stat-ism
sta-tis-ti-cal
stat-is-ti-cian
stat-o-cyst
sta-tor
stat-o-scope
stat-ue
stat-u-esque
sta-tus
stat-u-ta-ble
stat-ute
stat-u-to-ry
stau-ro-lite

stau-ro-scope
stead-fast
stealth
steam-ship
ste-a-rate
ste-a-rin
ste-a-tite
steel-head
steel-works
steel-yard
steel-work
stee-ple
steers-man
steeve
stein
stel-lar
stel-la-ra-tor
stem-mer
sten-cil
sten-o-graph
ste-nog-ra-pher
sten-o-type
sten-to-ri-an
steph-an-ite
step-in
step-lad-der
ster-e-o-bate
ster-e-o-chrome
ster-e-o-gram
ster-e-o-graph
ster-e-o-phon-ic
ster-e-op-ti-con
ster-e-o-scope
ster-e-o-type
ster-ile
ster-nal
ster-nu-ta-tor
stern-way
ster-oid
ster-ol
ster-tor
ste-thom-e-ter
steth-o-scope
ste-ve-dore
stew-ard

sthen-ic
stiac-cia-to
sti-chom-e-try
stick-le
stick-up
sti-fle
stig-ma
sti-let-to
stil-i-form
still-ness
stim-u-late
sting-ray
sti-pend
sti-pen-di-ar-y
stip-i-tate
stip-i-ti-form
stip-ple
stip-u-late
stir-rup
sti-ver
stock-ade
stock-bro-ker
stock-fish
stock-hold-er
stock-i-net
stock-room
stock-yard
sto-gy
sto-i-cal
stol-id
stom-ach
sto-ma-ti-tis
stom-a-to-plas-ty
stone-blind
stone-broke
stone-chat
stone-crop
stone-cut-ter
stone-deaf
stone-ma-son
stop-o-ver
stop-ple
stor-age
store-keep-er
store-room

sto-ried
sto-ri-ette
storm-bound
storm-proof
sto-ry-tell-er
stow-a-way
stra-bot-o-my
strad-dle
strafe
strag-gle
straight-arm
straight-a-way
straight-edge
straight-en
straight-for-ward
straight-line
straight-out
straight-way
strait-en (hamper)
strait-laced
strake
stra-min-e-ous
strange
stran-gle
stran-gu-late
strap-pa-do
strap-per
strat-a-gem
strat-e-gy
strat-i-fy
stra-tig-ra-phy
strat-o-cruis-er
stra-to-cu-mu-lus
strat-o-sphere
strat-o-vi-sion
straw-ber-ry
stream-line
strength-en
stren-u-ous
strep-to-coc-cus
strep-to-my-cin
stretch-out
stret-ta
stret-to
stri-ate

strick-en
strick-le
stric-ture
stri-dent
stri-dor
strid-u-late
strife
stri-gose
strike-break-er
string-board
string-course
strin-gent
string-halt
string-piece
strip-ling
strob-ile
strob-o-scope
stro-ma
struc-ture
stru-del
strug-gle
stru-ma
strum-pet
stru-thi-ous
strych-nine
stub-ble
stub-born
stuc-co
stud-ding
stu-dent
stud-horse
stu-di-o
stul-ti-fy
stum-ble
stump-age
stu-pe-fa-cient
stu-pe-fy
stu-pen-dous
stu-pid-i-ty
stu-por
stur-geon
stut-ter
sty-lar
style-book
sty-li-form

sty-lis-tic
sty-lo-bate
sty-lo-graph
sty-loid
sty-mie
styp-tic
sty-rene
su-a-ble
suave
sub-ac-id
sub-a-gent
sub-al-pine
sub-al-tern
sub-a-que-ous
sub-au-ric-u-lar
sub-ax-il-la-ry
sub-base-ment
sub-cal-i-ber
sub-cat-e-go-ry
sub-cla-vi-an
sub-com-mit-tee
sub-con-scious
sub-con-trac-tor
sub-dea-con
sub-due
su-ber-ic
sub-hu-man
sub-ja-cent
sub-jec-tive
sub-junc-tive
sub-lease
sub-lime
sub-lin-gual
sub-mar-gin-al
sub-ma-rine
sub-me-di-ant
sub-merge
sub-mit
sub-mon-tane
sub-mul-ti-ple
sub-or-di-nate
sub-ox-ide
sub-poe-na
sub-prin-ci-pal
sub-ro-gate

sub-scribe
sub-script
sub-se-quence
sub-ser-vi-ent
sub-sid-i-ar-y
sub-sist-ence
sub-stance
sub-stand-ard
sub-stan-tial
sub-stit-u-ent
sub-sti-tute
sub-strate
sub-ter-fuge
sub-tle
sub-tract
sub-tra-hend
sub-type
su-bu-late
sub-ur-ban
sub-ver-sive
sub-way
suc-ceed
suc-ces-sor
suc-cinct
suc-cor
suc-co-tash
suc-cu-lent
suc-cumb
suc-cur-sal
suc-cuss
suck-le
suc-tion
suc-to-ri-al
su-dar-i-um
su-da-to-ry
su-dor
suf-fer-ance
suf-fice
suf-fi-cient
suf-fix
suf-flate
suf-fo-cate
suf-fra-gan
suf-fu-mi-gate
suf-fuse

sug-gest-i-ble
su-i-cide
suit (garmets)
suit-case
suite (a set)
suit-or
su-ki-ya-ki
sul-cate
sul-fa-di-a-zene
sul-fa-nil-a-mide
sul-fa-pyr-i-dine
sulf-ars-phen-a-mine
sul-fate
sul-fa-thi-a-zole
sul-fa-tize
sul-fide
sul-fo-nate
sul-fon-ic
sul-fur
sul-len
sul-ly
sul-phide
sul-phon-ic
sul-phu-rate
sul-tan
su-mac
sum-ma-ry (abstract)
sum-mer-y
   (like summer)
sum-mit
sum-mon
sump-tu-ar-y
sump-tu-ous
sun-beam
sun-bird
sun-bonnet
sun-bow
sun-burst
sun-date
sun-der-ance
sun-di-al
sun-flow-er
sun-light
sun-lit
sun-rise

sun-set
sun-shine
sun-stroke
su-per-a-ble
su-per-a-bun-dant
su-per-an-nu-ate
su-perb
su-per-car-go
su-per-charg-er
su-per-cil-i-ar-y
su-per-con-duc-tiv-i-ty
su-per-ego
su-per-fi-cial
su-per-flu-ous
su-per-fuse
su-pe-ri-or
su-per-la-tive
su-per-lu-na-ry
su-per-man
su-per-mar-ket
su-per-nat-u-ral
su-per-scribe
su-per-sede
su-per-sen-so-ry
su-per-son-ic
su-per-sti-tious
su-per-vene
su-per-vise
su-pine
sup-plant
sup-ple-ment
sup-ple-tive
sup-ple-to-ry
sup-pli-ant
sup-pli-cate
sup-port-er
sup-posed
sup-po-si-tion
sup-press
sup-pu-rate
su-preme
su-ral
sur-base
sur-cease
sur-charge

sur-cu-lose
sure-ty
surf (sea swell)
sur-face
surf-board
sur-feit
surge (rush)
sur-gi-cal
sur-mise
sur-mount
sur-name
sur-pass-ing
sur-plice (vestment)
sur-plus (excess)
sur-print
sur-prise
sur-re-al-ism
sur-ren-der
sur-rep-ti-tious
sur-ro-gate
sur-round
sur-tax
sur-veil-lance
sur-vey-or
sur-vi-vor
sus-cep-ti-ble
sus-pect
sus-pense
sus-pi-cion
sus-pire
sus-tain
sus-te-nance
sus-ten-tac-u-lar
sus-ten-tion

su-sur-rant
su-sur-ra-tion
sut-ler
su-ture
swad-dle
swag-ger
swal-low-tail
swamp-land
swan's-down
sward
swas-ti-ka
swathe
sweat-band
sweat-shop
sweep-stakes
sweet-bread
sweet-heart
sweet-meat
sweet-sop
swel-ter
swerve
swift-foot-ed
swin-dle
swiv-el
swiz-zle
sword-bill
sword-fish
sword-play
swords-man
sword-tail
syc-a-more
syc-o-phant
sy-co-sis (hair disease)

sy-e-nite
syl-la-ble
syl-van
sym-bi-o-sis
sym-bol-ic
sym-me-try
sym-pa-thy
sym-pho-ny
symp-tom
syn-a-gogue
syn-carp
syn-chro-nize
syn-chro-tron
syn-clas-tic
syn-co-pate
syn-cre-tize
syn-di-cate
syn-drome
syn-e-col-o-gy
syn-er-gy
syn-od
syn-o-nym
syn-on-y-my
syn-op-sis
syn-tac-ti-cal
syn-tax
syn-the-sis
syn-thet-ic
syph-i-lis
syr-inge
syr-up
sys-tal-lic
sys-tem-at-ic

T

tab-er-nac-le
tab-leau
ta-ble-cloth
ta-ble-spoon
tab-loid
ta-boo
ta-bor

tab-o-ret
tab-u-late
tach-o-graph
ta-chom-e-ter
tac-it
tac-i-turn
tack-le

tac-o-nite
tact-ful
tac-tic
tad-pole
taf-fe-ta
tai-lor
take-off

tal-ent	tar-iff	tee-to-tal-er
tale-tell-er	tar-la-tan	teg-men
tal-i-grade	tar-nish	teg-u-lar
tal-i-on	tar-pau-lin	tel-a-mon
tal-i-ped	tar-pon	tel-e-cast
tal-is-man	tar-ra-gon	te-leg-o-ny
tal-low	tar-so-met-a-tar-sus	tel-e-gram
tam-a-ble	tar-tan	tel-e-graph
ta-ma-le	tar-tar	tel-e-graph-o-scope
tam-a-rack	ta-sim-e-ter	tel-e-kin-e-sis
tam-a-rau	task-mas-ter	tel-e-me-ter
tam-a-rin	tas-sel	tel-e-motor
tam-a-rind	tat-ter-sall	tel-en-ceph-a-lon
tam-a-risk	tat-tle-tale	te-le-ol-o-gy
tam-bou-rine	tat-too	te-lep-a-thy
tam-per	taupe	tel-e-phone
tam-pi-on (gun plug)	tau-rine	tel-e-pho-to
tam-pon (cloth plug)	tau-tol-o-gize	tel-e-pho-to-graph
tan-a-ger	tav-ern	tel-e-scope
tan-dem	taw-dry	tel-e-ster-e-o-scope
tan-gent	taw-ny	tel-e-ther-mom-e-ter
tan-ge-rine	tax-a-tion	tel-e-type
tan-gi-ble	tax-ex-empt	tel-e-view
tan-gle	tax-i-cab	tel-e-vi-sion
tan-go	tax-i-der-my	tel-har-mo-ni-um
tan-ner	tax-i-me-ter	te-li-al-stage
tan-ta-lize	tax-on-o-my	te-li-o-spore
tan-ta-mount	tax-pay-er	te-li-um
tan-trum	tea-ber-ry	tell-tale
ta-per	tea-cart	tel-lu-rate
(reduce gradually)	tea-ket-tle	tel-lu-ric
tape-re-cord-er	team-ster	tel-lu-ride
tap-es-try	tea-pot	tel-o-dy-nam-ic
ta-pe-tum	tear-drop	tel-o-phase
tape-worm	tea-spoon-ful	tel-pher-age
tap-i-o-ca	tech-ne-ti-um	te-mer-i-ty
ta-pir (animal)	tech-ni-cal	tem-per-a-ment
tap-is (tapestry)	tech-ni-col-or	tem-per-ance
tap-room	tech-nique	tem-per-a-ture
tap-root	tech-noc-ra-cy	tem-pes-tu-ous
tar-an-tel-la (dance)	tech-nog-ra-phy	tem-plate
tar-ant-ism	tech-no-lith-ic	tem-ple
ta-ran-tu-la (spider)	tech-nol-o-gy	tem-po
tar-di-grade	tec-ton-ic	tem-po-ral
tar-get	te-di-ous	tem-po-rar-y

tem-po-rize
temp-ta-tion
ten-a-ble
te-nac-i-ty
ten-ant
tend-ance
tend-en-cy
ten-den-tious
ten-der-heart-ed
ten-der-loin
ten-don
ten-dril
ten-e-ment
te-nes-mus
ten-et
ten-fold
te-nique
ten-nant-ite
ten-nis
ten-o-ni-tis
ten-or
te-nor-rha-phy
ten-si-om-e-ter
ten-sion
ten-ta-cle
ten-ta-tive
ten-u-ous
ten-ure
te-nu-to
te-pee
tep-e-fy
teph-rite
tep-id
ter-a-tol-o-gy
ter-bi-a
ter-cen-te-nar-y
ter-cet
ter-e-bin-thic
te-re-do
te-rete
ter-gi-ver-sate
ter-gum
ter-ma-gant
ter-mi-na-ble
ter-mi-nal

ter-mi-na-tor
ter-mi-nol-o-gy
ter-mi-nus
ter-mite
term-or
ter-nate
ter-rate
ter-rain
ter-ra-pin
ter-raz-zo
ter-res-tri-al
ter-ri-ble
ter-ri-er
ter-ri-fy
ter-ri-to-ry
ter-ror-ize
ter-tial
ter-tian
ter-va-lent
tes-sel-late
tes-ta-ment
tes-tate
tes-ta-tor
tes-ti-cle
tes-ti-fy
tes-ti-mo-ni-al
tes-tos-ter-one
te-tan-ic
tet-a-nus
teth-er
tet-ra-bas-ic
te-trac-id
tet-ra-gon
tet-ra-gram
tet-ra-he-dron
te-tram-er-ous
te-tram-e-ter
tet-ra-pet-al-ous
te-trap-ter-ous
te-trarch
tet-ra-spore
te-tras-ti-chous
tet-ra-syl-la-ble
tet-ra-tom-ic
tet-ra-va-lent

tet-rode
te-trox-ide
tet-ter
tex-tile
tex-ture
tha-las-sic
thal-li-um
than-a-top-sis
thanks-giv-ing
thau-ma-trope
thau-ma-tur-gy
the-a-ceous
the-an-throp-ic
the-ar-chy
the-a-ter
the-at-ri-cal
the-ine
the-mat-ic
the-o-crat
the-od-i-cy
the-ol-o-gy
the-op-a-thy
the-o-rem
the-o-ret-i-cal
the-o-ry
ther-a-peu-tic
ther-a-py
ther-e-min
ther-mal
therm-an-es-the-si-a
therm-i-on-ic
therm-is-tor
ther-mit
ther-mo-bar-o-graph
ther-mo-dy-nam-ics
ther-mo-graph
ther-mo-nu-cle-ar
ther-mo-plas-tic
ther-mo-scope
ther-mo-stat
ther-mo-ther-a-py
the-roid
ther-sit-i-cal
the-sau-rus
the-sis

the-ur-gy
thi-a-mine
thi-a-zine
thick-et
thick-set
thieve
thim-ble-weed
thi-o-al-de-hyde
thi-o-cy-a-nate
thi-on-ic
thi-o-sul-fate
this-tle
thix-ot-ro-phy
tho-rac-ic
tho-rax
thor-ough-bred
thor-ough-fare
thrash-er
thread-bare
three-col-or
three-deck-er
three-di-men-sion-al
three-fold
three-quar-ter
three-score
threm-ma-tol-o-gy
thren-o-dy
thre-o-nine
thresh-old
throat-latch
throm-bin
throm-bo-sis
throt-tle
through-out
throw-a-way
throw-back
thu-li-um
thumb-nail
thumb-screw
thumb-tack
thump
thun-der-bolt
thun-der-clap
thun-der-cloud
thun-der-head

thun-der-show-er
thun-der-storm
thun-der-struck
thy-mol
thy-mus
thy-roid
thy-roid-ec-to-my
thy-rox-ine
thy-self
ti-ar-a
tib-i-a
tick-et
tick-le
tid-al
tid-bit
tide-wa-ter
tie-up
tif-fin
ti-ger's-eye
tight-fist-ed
tight-lipped
tight-rope
tight-wad
ti-gress
til-de
tile-fish
til-i-a-ceous
till-age
til-land-si-a
tim-bal
tim-ber (wood)
tim-ber-head
tim-ber-land
tim-bre (sound quality)
tim-brel
time-card
time-hon-ored
time-keep-er
time-piece
time-sav-ing
time-ta-ble
time-worn
tim-id
ti-moc-ra-cy
tim-or-ous

tim-pa-ni
tin-cal
tinc-to-ri-al
tinc-ture
tin-der
tin-der-box
tin-e-a
tin-gle
tink-er
tins-man
tin-sel
tin-smith
tin-stone
tin-tin-nab-u-lar
tin-type
tin-work
tip-cart
tip-cat
tip-off
tip-pet
tip-ple
tip-staff
tip-toe
tip-top
ti-rade
tire-less
tis-sue
ti-tan-ate
ti-ta-ni-um
ti-ter
tit-il-late
tit-i-vate
tit-lark
ti-tle
tit-mouse
ti-trate
tit-ter
tit-tle
tit-u-ba-tion
tit-u-lar
toad-fish
toad-stone
toad-stool
toast-mas-ter
to-bac-co

to-bog-gan
to-col-o-gy
to-coph-er-ol
toc-sin
tod-dle
toe-dance
toe-nail
toe-shoe
tof-fee
to-geth-er
tog-ger-y
tog-gle
toile (linen)
toi-let
to-ken
tol-i-dine
toll-booth
toll-gate
toll-house
toll-keep-er
tol-u-ate
tol-u-ene
tol-u-ide
tom-a-hawk
to-ma-to
tom-boy
tomb-stone
tom-cat
to-men-tose
tom-fool-er-y
to-mog-ra-phy
to-mor-row
tom-tom
to-nal-i-ty
tongue-tied
ton-ic
to-night
ton-nage
ton-neau
to-nom-e-ter
ton-sil-lec-to-my
ton-so-ri-al
ton-sure
tooth-ache
tooth-brush

tooth-paste
tooth-pick
too-tle
to-paz
top-coat
top-flight
top-heavy
to-phus
to-pi-ar-y
top-i-cal
top-notch
to-pog-ra-pher
to-pol-o-gy
top-o-nym
top-ple
top-sail
top-side
top-soil
top-sy-tur-vy
toque
torch-light
tor-e-a-dor
tor-ic
tor-men-tor
tor-na-do
to-roid
to-rose
tor-pe-do
tor-pid
tor-por
tor-quate
torque
tor-re-fy
tor-rent
tor-rid
tor-sade
tor-si-bil-i-ty
tor-sion
tor-so
tor-tile
tor-til-la
tor-toise
tor-tu-ous
tor-ture
to-rus

to-tal-i-tar-i-an
to-tal-iz-er
to-tem
toth-er
to-ti-pal-mate
tot-ter
touch-down
tough-en
tou-pee
tour-ist
tour-ma-line
tour-na-ment
tour-ni-quet
tou-sle
tow-age
to-ward
tow-el-ing
tow-er-ing
tow-head
tow-line
town-ship
towns-man
towns-peo-ple
tow-rope
tox-e-mi-a
tox-ic
tox-i-pho-bia
tox-o-plas-mo-sis
tra-be-at-ed
trac-er
tra-che-a
tra-che-ot-o-my
tra-cho-ma
trac-ing
trac-ta-ble
trac-tate
trac-tile
trac-tor
trade-in
trades-man
tra-di-tion
trad-i-tive
tra-duce
tra-du-cian-ism
traf-fic

trag-e-dy

trag-ic

trag-i-com-e-dy

trag-i-on

tra-gus

trail-er

train-man

traipse

trai-tor

tra-jec-to-ry

tram-mel

tram-ple

tram-po-line

tram-rod

tram-way

tran-quil-iz-er

tran-quil-li-ty

trans-act

trans-at-lan-tic

trans-ca-lent

tran-scend

trans-con-ti-nen-tal

tran-scribe

tran-script

trans-cur-rent

trans-duc-er

tran-sect

tran-sept

trans-e-unt

trans-fer

trans-fer-or (law, one
    who makes a transfer)

trans-fer-rer
    (one who transfers)

trans-fig-ure

trans-fix

trans-flu-ent

trans-flux

trans-form

trans-fuse

trans-gress

tran-ship

trans-hu-mance

tran-sient

tran-sil-i-ent

trans-il-lu-mi-nate

tran-sis-tor

trans-it

trans-late

trans-lit-er-ate

trans-lo-cate

trans-lu-cent

trans-lu-nar-y

trans-mis-sion

trans-mit

trans-mog-ri-fy

trans-mon-tane

trans-mun-dane

trans-mute

trans-nep-tu-ni-an

trans-nor-ma

trans-o-ce-an-ic

tran-som

tran-son-ic

trans-par-ent

tran-spire

trans-plant

trans-po-lar

trans-port

trans-pose

tran-sude

trans-verse

tra-peze

trap-e-zoid

trau-ma

trav-ail

trav-el-er

trav-e-logue

trav-erse

trav-er-tine

trav-es-ty

trawl-er

treach-er-y

trea-dle

tread-mill

trea-son

treas-ure

trea-tise

treat-ment

tre-ble

tre-cen-to

tree-top

tre-foil

trel-lis

trem-ble

tre-men-dous

trem-o-lant

trem-or

trem-u-lous

trench-ant

trench-er

tre-pan

trep-i-da-tion

tres-pass

tres-sure

tres-tle

tri-a-ble

tri-ac-id

tri-ad

tri-al

tri-an-gle

tri-ar-chy

tri-a-tom-ic

tri-ax-i-al

tri-a-zine

trib-al

tri-bas-ic

trib-u-la-tion

trib-une

trib-u-tar-y

trib-ute

tri-cen-ten-ni-al

tri-ceps

tri-chi-na

trich-i-no-sis

trich-o-cept

tri-chol-o-gy

tri-chro-mat-ic

tri-cot

tri-cus-pid

tri-cy-cle

tri-dent

tri-di-men-sion-al

tri-en-ni-al

tri-er-arch

tri-fle
tri-fo-li-ate
tri-form
tri-fur-cate
trig-ger
tri-gon
trig-o-nom-e-try
tri-graph
tri-he-dral
tri-ju-gate
tri-lat-er-al
tri-lin-e-ar
tril-lion
tril-li-um
tri-loc-u-lar
tril-o-gy
trim-er-ous
tri-mes-ter
trim-e-ter
tri-mor-phism
tri-na-ry
trin-ket
tri-no-mi-al
tri-ode
tri-o-let
tri-ox-ide
trip
triph-thong
tri-ple
tri-plic-i-ty
tri-pod
trip-per
trip-pet
trip-ter-ous
trip-tych
tri-que-trous
tri-ra-di-ate
tri-sac-cha-ride
tri-sect
tri-sep-al-ous
tri-se-ri-al
tris-mus
tris-oc-ta-he-dron
tri-some
tri-sper-mous

tris-tich-ous
tri-sty-lous
tri-syl-la-ble
tri-the-ism
trit-i-um
tri-tone
trit-u-rate
tri-umph
tri-um-vir
tri-une
tri-u-ni-tar-i-an
tri-va-lent
triv-et
triv-i-a
tro-car
tro-chal
tro-che
troch-i-lus
trod-den
trog-lo-dyte
tro-gon
trol-ley
trol-lop
trom-bi-di-a-sis
trom-bone
trom-mel
trompe
troop-er
trope
troph-o-blast
troph-o-plasm
tro-phy
trop-ic
trop-i-cal
tro-pine
tro-pol-o-gy
trop-o-pause
tro-poph-i-lous
trop-o-sphere
trou-ba-dour
trou-ble-some
troup-er
trou-sers
trous-eau
tro-ver

trow-el
tru-ant
truck-le
truc-u-lent
truf-fle
tru-ism
trum-pet-er
trun-cate
trun-cheon
trun-dle
trun-nion
truss-ing
trus-tee
trust-wor-thy
truth
try-out
tryp-a-no-some
tryp-sin
tryp-to-phan
tryst
tu-bate
tu-ber
tu-ber-cle
tu-ber-cu-lo-sis
tu-ber-ous
tu-bu-lar
tu-bu-li-flo-rous
tu-bu-lous
tuck-a-hoe
tuft
tu-i-tion
tu-la-re-mi-a
tu-lip
tulle
tul-li-bee
tum-ble
tum-ble-down
tum-ble-weed
tum-brel
tu-me-fac-tion
tu-mor
tu-mu-lar
tu-mult
tu-mu-lus
tun-a-ble

tun-dra
tune-up
tung-sten
tu-ni-cate
tu-ni-cle
tun-nel
tun-ny
tu-pe-lo
tur-ban
tur-ba-ry
tur-bel-lar-i-an
tur-bid
tur-bi-nate
tur-bine
tur-bo-jet
tur-bo-prop
tur-bu-lent
tur-di-form
tu-reen
turt-nan
tur-ges-cent
tur-gid
tur-gor
tur-key
tur-mer-ic
tur-moil
turn-a-bout
turn-buck-le
turn-coat
turn-down

turn-er-y
turn-key
turn-out
turn-o-ver
turn-pike
turn-spit
turn-stile
turn-stone
turn-up
tur-pi-tude
tur-quoise
tur-ret
tur-ri-cal
tur-tle-back
tur-tle-dove
tur-tle-head
tus-sis
tus-sle
tus-sock
tu-te-lage
tu-tor
tu-to-ri-al
tut-ti
tux-e-do
tu-yere
twad-dle
tway-blade
tweet-er
tweez-ers
twice-laid

twice-told
twid-dle
twi-light
twin-ber-ry
twin-flow-er
twi-night
twin-kle
twin-leaf
twin-screw
twit-ter
two-some
two-way
ty-coon
tym-pan
type-script
type-set-ter
type-writ-er
typh-li-tis
typh-lol-o-gy
ty-pho-gen-ic
ty-phoid
ty-phoon
ty-phus
typ-i-cal
typ-ist
ty-pog-ra-pher
ty-pol-o-gy
tyr-an-ny
ty-rant
ty-ro-sine

U

u-biq-ui-ty
U-boat
ud-der
ug-li-fy
u-ku-le-le
ul-cer-ous
ul-lage
u-lot-ri-chous
ul-te-ri-or
ul-ti-mate
ul-ti-mo-gen-i-ture

ul-tra-ism
ul-tra-ma-rine
ul-tra-mi-cro-scope
ul-tra-mon-tane
ul-tra-mun-dane
ul-tra-son-ic
ul-tra-vi-o-let
ul-u-late
um-bel-late
um-ber
um-bil-i-cal

um-bil-i-cus
um-bo-nal
um-bra
um-brage
um-brel-la
um-brette
um-brif-er-ous
um-pire
un-ac-cus-tomed
u-nan-i-mous
un-at-tached

un-a-ware
un-bear-a-ble
un-bro-ken
un-cer-tain
un-com-fort-a-ble
un-com-mon
un-con-cerned
un-con-di-tion-al
un-con-scious
un-con-sti-tu-tion-al
un-con-ven-tion-al
un-couth
un-cov-er
unc-tion
un-de-cid-ed
un-der-age
un-der-es-ti-mate
un-der-gar-ment
un-der-go
un-der-ground
un-der-line
un-der-neath
un-der-priv-i-leged
un-der-rate
un-der-stand
un-der-state
un-der-stud-y
un-der-take
un-der-wa-ter
un-der-wear
un-der-weight
un-der-write
un-de-sir-a-ble
un-do-ing
un-dress
un-du-late
un-du-ly
un-dy-ing
un-earth-ly
un-eas-y
un-ed-u-cat-ed
un-em-ployed
un-e-qual
un-e-quiv-o-cal
un-e-vent-ful

un-ex-pect-ed
un-fail-ing
un-fair
un-faith-ful
un-fa-mil-iar
un-fa-vor-a-ble
un-se-cured
un-self-ish
un-set-tle
un-sight-ly
un-skilled
un-snap
un-so-cia-ble
un-so-phis-ti-cat-ed
un-speak-a-ble
un-sta-ble
un-stead-y
un-strung
un-suc-cess-ful
un-suit-a-ble
un-sus-pect-ed
un-tan-gle
un-thank-ful
un-think-a-ble
un-ti-dy
un-time-ly
un-touch-a-ble
un-truth-ful
un-u-su-al
un-veil
un-whole-some
un-will-ing
un-world-ly
un-wor-thy
un-wrap
un-writ-ten
up-braid
up-bring-ing
up-date
up-grade
up-heav-al
up-hol-ster
up-keep
up-lift
up-per-case

up-per-class
up-ris-ing
up-roar-i-ous
up-set
up-stairs
up-stand-ing
up-start
up-state
up-stream
up-town
up-turned
up-ward
u-ran-i-nite
u-ra-ni-um
u-ra-nog-ra-phy
u-rate
ur-ban (of a city)
ur-bane (courteous)
ur-ce-o-late
ur-chin
u-re-ase
u-re-ter
u-re-thra
u-re-thro-scope
ur-gent
u-ri-nal-y-sis
u-ri-nate
u-ro-chord
u-ro-chrome
u-ro-gen-i-tal
u-ro-lith
u-rol-o-gy
u-ros-co-py
ur-ti-cate
us-age
us-ance
use-a-ble
ush-er
us-tu-late
u-su-fruct
u-su-rer
u-surp
u-ten-sil
u-ter-ine
u-til-i-ty

ut-most
u-tri-cle
ut-ter-ance

ut-ter-ly
ut-ter-most
u-va-rov-ite

u-ve-a
u-ve-i-tis
u-vu-la
ux-o-ri-al

V

va-can-cy
va-cate
vac-cine
vac-cin-i-a-ceous
vac-il-late
va-cu-i-ty
vac-u-o-late
vac-u-um
vag-a-bond
va-gar-y
va-gi-na
va-grant
vague
vain (worthless)
val-ance (short curtain)
val-e-dic-to-ri-an
va-lence (atomic)
val-en-tine
va-ler-ic
val-et
val-e-tu-di-nar-i-an
val-iant
val-id
val-i-date
va-lise
val-la-tion
val-lec-u-late
val-ley
val-or
val-u-a-ble
val-vu-lar
va-moose
vam-pire
van-a-date
va-na-di-um
van-dal
vane
   (blade moved by air)

van-guard
va-nil-la
van-ish
van-i-ty
van-quish
van-tage
vap-id
va-por-es-cence
va-por-ize
var-i-a-ble
var-i-cel-la
var-i-col-ored
var-i-cose
var-i-e-gate
va-ri-e-ty
var-i-form
var-i-o-late
var-i-om-e-ter
var-i-ous
var-mint
var-nish
var-si-ty
vas-cu-lar
vas-ec-to-my
vas-e-line
vas-o-di-la-tor
vas-sal-age
vas-ti-tude
vaude-ville
vault-ed
vec-tor
veg-e-ta-ble
ve-he-ment
ve-hi-cle
veil-ing
vein (tube)
ve-lar-ize
ve-late

vel-le-i-ty
vel-li-cate
vel-lum
ve-lo-ce
ve-loc-i-pede
ve-loc-i-ty
ve-lum
ve-lure
ve-lu-ti-nous
vel-vet
ve-nal
vend-ee
ven-det-ta
vend-i-ble
ven-di-tion
ven-dor
ven-due
ve-neer
ven-er-ate
ve-ne-re-al
venge-ance
ve-ni-al
ven-i-punc-ture
ven-i-son
ven-om-ous
ve-nous
vent-age
ven-tail
ven-ter
ven-ti-duct
ven-ti-late
ven-tral
ven-tri-cle
ven-tril-o-quism
ven-ture-some
ven-ue
ven-u-lose
ve-ra-cious

ve-ran-da	ver-tex	vice ver-sa
ve-rat-ri-dine	ver-ti-cal	vi-chy-ssoise
ver-a-trine	ver-ti-cil-las-ter	vi-cin-i-ty
ver-bal-ize	ver-tic-il-late	vi-cious
ver-ba-tim	ver-ti-go	vi-cis-si-tude
ver-be-na	ves-i-ca	vic-tim-ize
ver-bi-age	ves-i-cle	vic-to-ry
ver-bid	ves-per	vic-tress
ver-bose	ves-per-til-i-o-nine	vict-ual
ver-bo-ten	ves-per-tine	vi-cu-na
ver-dant	ves-pi-ary	vi-de-li-cet
ver-dict	ves-sel	vid-e-o
ver-di-gris	ves-tal	view-point
ver-din	ves-ti-ar-y	vi-ges-i-mal
ver-di-ter	ves-ti-bule	vig-il
ver-dure	ves-tige	vig-i-lan-te
ve-rid-i-cal	ves-tig-i-al	vi-gnette
ver-i-est	vet-er-an	vig-or
ver-i-fi-ca-tion	vet-er-i-nar-i-an	vi-go-ro-so
ver-i-sim-i-lar	vet-i-ver	vil-i-fy
ver-sion	ve-to	vil-i-pend
ver-i-ta-ble	vex-a-tious	vil-lage
ver-juice	vi-a-ble	vil-lain
ver-meil	vi-a-duct	vil-la-nelle
ver-mi-cel-li	vi-al	vil-lat-ic
ver-mi-cide	vi-and	vil-li-form
ver-mic-u-late	vi-at-ic	vil-los-i-ty
ver-mi-form	vi-at-i-cum	vi-men
ver-mi-fuge	vi-a-tor	vi-min-e-ous
ver-mil-ion	vi-brate	vi-na-ceous
ver-mouth	vi-bra-tile	vin-ai-grette
ver-nac-u-lar	vi-bra-to	vi-nasse
ver-nal-ize	vib-ri-o	vin-ci-ble
ver-na-tion	vi-bur-num	vin-cu-lum
ver-ni-er	vic-ar	vin-di-cate
ve-ron-i-ca	vi-car-i-al	vin-e-gar
ver-ru-cose	vice-ad-mi-ral	vine-yard
ver-sa-tile	vice-chan-cel-lor	vin-i-cul-ture
ver-si-cle	vice-con-sul	vin-i-fi-ca-tor
ver-si-col-or	vice-ge-rent	vin-om-e-ter
ver-si-fy	vic-e-nar-y	vin-tage
ver-sion	vi-cen-ni-al	vi-nyl
ver-so	vice-pres-i-dent	vi-nyl-ite
ver-sus	vice-re-gent	vi-o-la
ver-te-bra	vice-roy	vi-o-late

vi-o-lent
vi-o-les-cent
vi-o-let
vi-o-lin
vi-os-ter-ol
vi-per-ish
vi-ra-go
vir-e-o
vi-res-cent
vir-ga
vir-gate
vir-gin-i-ty
vir-gu-late
vir-gule
vir-i-des-cent
vi-rid-i-an
vir-ile
vir-tue
vir-tu-o-so
vir-u-lent
vi-rus
vi-sa
vis-age
vis-ca-cha
vis-cer-a
vis-cid
vis-cos-i-ty
vis-count
vis-cous
vis-i-ble
vi-sion-al
vis-i-tor
vi-sor
vis-ta
vis-u-al
vi-ta-ceous
vi-tal
vi-ta-min

vi-ta-scope
vi-tel-lin
vi-ti-ate
vit-i-cul-ture
vit-i-li-go
vit-re-ous
vi-tres-cent
vit-ri-fy
vit-ri-ol-ic
vit-ta
vi-tu-per-ate
vi-va-ceous
vi-var-i-um
vi-ver-rine
viv-id
viv-i-fy
vi-vip-a-ra
viv-i-sect
vix-en
viz-ard
vo-cab-u-lar-y
vo-cal
vo-ca-tion
vo-cif-er-ous
vod-ka
vogue
void-a-ble
voile
vo-lant
vo-lar
vol-a-tile
vo-la-tion
vol-can-ic
vol-i-tant
vo-li-tion
vol-ley-ball
vol-plane
vol-ta

volt-age
vol-tam-e-ter
volt-am-me-ter
volt-am-pere
volte-face
vol-u-ble
vol-ume
vo-lu-me-ter
vol-un-tar-y
vol-un-teer
vo-lup-tu-ous
vo-lute
vol-va
vol-vu-lus
vo-mer
vom-i-ca
vom-it
voo-doo-ism
vo-ra-cious
vor-tex
vor-ti-cal
vor-ti-cel-la
vo-ta-ry
vouch-er
vouge
vow-el
voy-age
vo-yeur
vul-can-ism
vul-can-ite
vul-gar
vul-ner-a-ble
vul-ner-ar-y
vul-pec-u-la
vul-pine
vul-ture
vul-va
vy-ing

W

wab-ble
wad-dle
wa-fer

waf-fle
wa-ger
wag-gle

wag-on-er
wain-scot-ing
waist-line

waiv-er
wake-up
walk-out
walk-up
wal-la-by
wal-let
wal-lop
wal-low
wal-nut
wal-rus
waltz
wam-ble
wam-pum
wan-der-lust
wan-gle
wan-ton
war-ble
ward-en
ward-robe
ward-room
ward-ship
ware-house
ware-house-man
ware-room
war-fare
war-head
war-i-ly
war-i-son
war-like
war-lock
warm-blood-ed
warm-heart-ed
war-mong-er
warn-ing
war-path
war-plane
war-rant
war-ran-tee (one who
gets a warranty)
war-ran-tor
war-ran-ty (assurance)
war-ren
war-ri-or
war-saw
war-ship

war-time
wash-a-ble
wash-board
wash-cloth
wash-day
washed-out
washed-up
wash-er-man
wash-out
wash-rag
wash-room
wash-stand
wash-tub
wasp-ish
was-sail
wast-age
watch-case
watch-dog
watch-maker
watch-man
watch-tow-er
watch-word
wa-ter-borne
wa-ter-brain
wa-ter-buck
wa-ter-cool
wa-ter-course
wa-ter-craft
wa-ter-fall
wa-ter-find-er
wa-ter-fowl
wa-ter-jack-et
wa-ter-logged
wa-ter-man
wa-ter-man-ship
wa-ter-mark
wa-ter-mel-on
wa-ter-proof
wa-ter-re-pel-lent
wa-ter-scope
wa-ter-shed
wa-ter-sick
wa-ter-soak
wa-ter-sol-u-ble
wa-ter-spout

wa-ter-tight
wa-ter-wave
wa-ter-way
wa-ter-weed
wa-ter-works
wa-ter-worn
watt-age
watt-hour
watt-me-ter
wave-let
wa-ver
wax-ber-ry
wax-bill
wax-plant
wax-weed
wax-wing
way-bill
way-far-er
way-go-ing
way-lay
way-worn
weak-fish
weak-kneed
weak-mind-ed
wean-ling
weap-on
wear-a-ble
wea-ri-some
wea-sel
weath-er-beat-en
weath-er-board
weath-er-cock
weath-er-glass
weath-er-man
weath-er-proof
weath-er-strip
weath-er-wise
weath-er-worn
weav-er-bird
web-toed
web-worm
wed-lock
week-day
week-end
wee-vil

wei-ge-la
weigh (measure)
weight (heaviness)
wel-come
wel-fare
well-bal-anced
well-be-haved
well-be-ing
well-born
well-bred
well-con-tent
well-dis-posed
well-do-er
well-fav-ored
well-fed
well-found-ed
well-groomed
well-head
well-in-formed
well-known
well-man-nered
well-mean-ing
well-nigh
well-off
well-point
well-pre-served
well-read
well-spo-ken
well-spring
well-timed
well-to-do
well-wish-er
well-worn
wel-ter-weight
wen-tle-trap
were-wolf
wer-ner-ite
west-ern-most
wet-back
wet-blan-ket
wet-nurse
whale-back
whale-boat
whale-bone
whale-man

wharf (pier)
wharve (flywheel)
what-not
what-so-ev-er
wheat-ear
wheat-worm
whee-dle
wheel-bar-row
wheel-base
wheel-man
wheel-work
wheel-wright
wheeze
whelm
whelp
when-ev-er
when-so-ev-er
where-a-bouts
where-as
where-at
where-by
where-fore
where-from
where-in
where-of
where-on
where-so-ev-er
where-through
where-up-on
where-with
wheth-er
whet-stone
which-ev-er
which-so-ev-er
whif-fle-tree
whig-ger-y
whim-per
whim-si-cal
whine (pevish sound)
whin-stone
whip-cord
whip-lash
whip-per-snap-per
whip-pet
whip-poor-will

whip-saw
whip-stock
whip-worm
whirl-a-bout
whirl-i-gig
whirl-pool
whirl-wind
whirl-y-bird
whisk-er
whis-key
whis-per
whis-tle
white-beard
white-cap
white-col-lar
white-eye
white-faced
white-fish
white-head-ed
white-liv-ered
white-tailed-deer
white-throat
white-wash
white-wood
whit-low
whit-tle
whiz-bang
whole-heart-ed
whole-sale
whole-some
whole-souled
whole-wheat
whoop-ing
whop-per
whore
whore-mon-ger
whore-son
whor-tle-ber-ry
wick-ed-ness
wick-er-work
wick-et (door)
wick-i-up
wic-o-py
wide-an-gle
wide-a-wake

wide-o-pen
wide-spread
widg-eon
wid-ow-hood
width-wise
wield
wie-ner
wig-gle
wig-wam
wild-cat
wil-de-beest
wil-der-ness
wild-eyed
wild-fire
wild-wood
wild-ing
will-a-ble
will-ful
will-o-the-wisp
wil-low
wi-ly
wim-ble
wim-ple
wind-bag
wind-blown
wind-borne
wind-break
wind-fall
wind-flow-er
wind-hov-er
wind-jam-mer
wind-lass
wind-mill
win-dow-pane
wind-pipe
wind-row
wind-shak-en
wind-shield
wind-swept
wind-tight
wind-up
wind-way
wine-bib-ber
wine-glass
wine-grow-er

wine-shop
wine-skin
wing-foot-ed
wing-spread
win-now
win-some
win-ter-ber-ry
win-ter-bourne
win-ter-feed
win-ter-green
win-ter-kill
win-ter-time
wire-draw
wire-hair
wire-pho-to
wire-pull-er
wire-spun
wire-work
wire-worm
wise-a-cre
wise-crack
wish-bone
wish-y-wash-y
wisp-y
wis-te-ri-a
wist-ful
witch-craft
witch-es'-broom
with-draw
with-er
with-er-ite
with-hold
with-in
with-out
with-stand
wit-ness
wit-ti-cism
wi-vern
wiz-ard
wiz-ened
wob-ble
woe-be-gone
wolf-ber-ry
wolf-hound
wolf-ram

wolf-ra-mi-um
wol-las-ton-ite
wol-ver-ine
wom-an-kind
wom-an-like
wom-bat
wom-en-folk
won-der-land
won-der-strick-en
won-drous
wood-bin
wood-chat
wood-chuck
wood-cock
wood-craft
wood-cut-ter
wood-en-head
wood-en-ware
wood-house
wood-land
wood-lark
wood-man
wood-peck-er
wood-ruff
wood-shed
woods-man
wood-work
wood-worm
woof-er
wool-fell
wool-gath-er-ing
wool-grow-er
wool-pack
wool-sack
wooz-y
word-blind
word-book
work-bag
work-bench
work-book
work-box
work-day
worked-up
work-folk
work-horse

work-house
work-ing-man
work-ing-day
work-man-ship
work-out
work-room
work-shop
work-ta-ble
work-up
work-wom-an
world-ly-mind-ed
word-ly-wise
world-wea-ry
world-wide
worm-eat-en

worm-hole
worm-seed
worm-wood
worn-out
wor-ri-some
wor-ship
wor-sted
worth-while
wo-ven
wrack (wreckage)
wraith
wran-gle
wrap-per
wrasse
wrath-ful

wreck-age
wres-tle
wretch-ed
wrig-gle
wright
wring-er
wrin-kle
write-in
write-up
writh-en
wrong-do-er
wrong-head-ed
wrought-up
wry-neck
wy-vern

X

xe-ni-a
xen-o-lith
xen-o-mor-phic
xe-non

xen-o-pho-bi-a
xe-rog-ra-phy
Xe-rox

x-ray
xy-lo-graph
xy-lo-phone
xys-ter

Y

yachts-man
yam-mer
yan-kee
Yar-bor-ough
yard-arm
yard-stick
yarn-dyed
year-book
year-long
yearn-ing
yel-low-bird

yel-low-green
yel-low-ham-mer
yel-low-legs
yel-low-tail
yel-low-throat
yel-low-wood
yeo-man
yes-ter-day
yes-ter-year
yield-ing
yo-del

yo-gurt
yoke-fel-low
yo-kel
young-ber-ry
young-eyed
youth-ful
yt-ter-bi-a
yt-ter-bite
yt-tri-a
yt-tri-um
yule-tide

Z

za-mi-a
za-ny
zeal-ot

zeal-ous
ze-bra-wood
zech-chi-no

ze-nith
zeph-yr
zest-ful

zeug-ma	zith-er	zwit-ter-i-on
zib-el-ine	zo-di-ac	zyg-a-poph-y-sis
zig-zag	zom-bie	zy-go-dac-tyl
zinc-ate	zon-ate	zy-go-ma
zin-co-graph	zo-o-chem-is-try	zy-go-mor-phic
zin-ken-ite	zo-og-ra-phy	zy-go-phyte
zin-ni-a	zo-o-log-i-cal	zy-mase
zip-per	zo-om-e-try	zy-mo-gen
zir-con	zo-o-plas-ty	zy-mol-o-gy
zir-co-ni-um	zo-o-sperm	zy-mot-ic
zir-co-nyl	zwie-back	zy-mur-gy

The
ABC's
of
Spelling

In English, no spelling rules cover all words. Happily, however, six basic spelling rules, together with general rules for plurals, possessives, verbs, adjectives, and adverbs cover the great majority of words you are likely to use. In this section, several examples are given to illustrate each rule and any exceptions are noted.

The Six Basic Rules

Rule 1. Words ending with a silent **e** usually drop the **e** before a suffix beginning with a vowel.

like	likable	opportune	opportunate
sense	sensible	continue	continual
provide	providing	guide	guidance
seduce	seducible	define	defining

Exceptions:
(a) Retain the **e** in a word that might be mistaken for another word if the rule is applied.

singe	singeing	shoe	shoeing
swinge	swingeing	toe	toeing
dye	dyeing	tinge	tingeing

(b) To keep a **c** or **g** from being pronounced with a hard sound, words ending in **ce** or **ge** retain the **e** before suffixes beginning with **a** or **o**.

outrage	outrageous	force	forceable
courage	courageous	trace	traceable
advantage	advantageous	notice	noticeable

(c) Retain the **e** before the suffix **age**.

| mile | mileage | acre | acreage |
| line | lineage | | |

(d) To keep two **i**'s from occurring together when words ends in **ie** and the suffix begins with **i**, drop the **e**, change the **i** to **y**, and add the suffix.

lie	lying	die	dying
tie	tying	hie	hying
vie	vying		

Rule 2. Words ending with a silent **e** usually retain the **e** before a suffix beginning with a consonant.

rope	ropelike	manage	management
issue	issueless	false	falseness
shape	shapely	subtle	subtlety
winsome	winsomely	encourage	encouragement

Exceptions:

acknowledge	acknowledgment	true	truly
argue	argument	wise	wisdom
awe	awful	whole	wholly
nine	ninth	judge	judgment

Rule 3. Words of one syllable ending in a single consonant preceded by a single vowel usually double the final consonant before a suffix beginning with a vowel.

club	clubbed	plan	planned
bag	baggage	hot	hotter
fit	fitting	fat	fattest
wrap	wrapped	net	netting

Note: Rule 3 does not apply when (a) a word ends in two or more consonants, or (b) the final consonant is preceded by two vowels.

tact	tactful	scream	screamed
fact	factor	tread	treading
yard	yardage	read	reader
arc	arcing	daub	daubed

Rule 4. Words of two or more syllables accented on the final syllable and ending in a single consonant preceded by a single vowel usually double the consonant if the suffix starts with a vowel.

infer	inferred	incur	incurrable
rebel	rebellious	deter	deterrable
patrol	patroller	extol	extolled
propel	propellant	control	controlling

Exceptions:
The word **transferable**.

Note: Rule 4 does not apply when:
   (a) the accent is not on the last syllable.

| revel | reveler | profit | profiting |
| catalog | cataloged | differ | difference |

(b) the word ends in two consonants.

| perform | performance | benign | benignly |
| assign | assigned | receipt | receiptor |

(c) the final consonant is preceded by two vowels.

| repeat | repeater | proceed | proceeding |
| conceal | concealable | period | periodic |

(d) the accent shifts to the first syllable when the suffix is added.

| prefer | preferable | refer | reference |
| defer | deference | infer | inference |

Rule 5. To make correct use of the vowel combinations **ei** and **ie**, proceed as follows:

(a) use **e** before **i** when the combination follows the letter **c** and is pronounced long **e**.

receipt	conceive
ceiling	perceive
deceit	receiver
conceit	ceilometer

(b) use **e** before **i** when the combination is pronounced long **a**.

rein	neighbor
weight	deign
vein	feign
veil	feint

(c) use **i** before **e** in most other cases.

alien	reprieve
besiege	sieve
convenience	hierarchy
obedient	chandelier

Exceptions:

ancient	forfeit
either	height
foreign	sovereign
seize	leisure

Rule 6. When adding suffixes to words ending in **y**, proceed as follows:
(a) retain the **y** when the suffix begins with **i**.

forty	fortyish	pity	pitying
accompany	accompanying	deify	deifying
magnify	magnifying	gray	grayish

(b) retain the **y** when it is preceded by a vowel.

spray	sprayed	buoy	buoys
pray	prayer	assay	assayer
key	keyed	journey	journeying
obey	obeying	buy	buys

(c) in most other cases, change the **y** to **i** and add the suffix.

modify	modifiable	company	companies
pity	pitiable	deny	denies
mercy	merciless	satisfy	satisfies
beauty	beautiful	crazy	crazier

Exceptions:

shy	shyness	plenty	plenteous
wry	wryness	bounty	bounteous
lady	ladylike	dry	dryness
baby	babyhood		

Plurals of Nouns

1. The plurals of nouns are most often formed by adding **s** to the singular word. Notice that the addition of the **s** does not form a separate syllable.

bath	baths	saucer	saucers
specialist	specialists	chair	chairs
book	books	text	texts
valley	valleys	boat	boats

2. When nouns end in **ch, sh, ss, s, x,** or **z,** the plurals are formed by adding **es** to the singular word. Notice that the addition of **es** forms a separate syllable. Words ending in silent **e** form a separate syllable with **s.**

box	boxes	church	churches
gas	gases	maze	mazes
dish	dishes	piece	pieces
dress	dresses	bus	buses

3. When nouns end in **y** preceded either by a consonant or by **u** pronounced as a consonant, the plural is formed by changing the **y** to **i** and adding **es.**

baby	babies	soliloquy	soliloquies
cherry	cherries	charity	charities
boundary	boundaries	agency	agencies
glossary	glossaries	party	parties

4. The plurals of nouns ending in **o** are formed as follows:
(a) when the **o** is preceded by a vowel, add **s** to the singular.

ratio	ratios	studio	studios
cameo	cameos	portfolio	portfolios

(b) add **s** to the singular of proper nouns and musical terms.

Eskimo	Eskimos	piano	pianos
Filipino	Filipinos	soprano	sopranos
Romeo	Romeos	allegro	allegros

(c) add **es** to the singular of frequently used nouns when the **o** is preceded by a consonant.

echo	echoes	potato	potatoes
hero	heroes	tornado	tornadoes
go	goes	veto	vetoes
negro	negroes	embargo	embargoes

(d) infrequently used, very long, or foreign-sounding nouns ending in **o** preceded by a consonant most often use **s** to form the plural.

crescendo	crescendos	pueblo	pueblos
medico	medicos	albino	albinos
poncho	ponchos	embryo	embryos
dynamo	dynamos	credo	credos

(e) some nouns ending in **o** preceded by a consonant form the plural by adding either **s** or **es** to the singular word. In dictionaries, the preferred form is given first.

halos	haloes	buffaloes	buffalos
tobaccos	tobaccoes	volcanoes	volcanos
mementos	mementoes	desperadoes	desperados
zeros	zeroes	mosquitoes	mosquitos

5. Nouns ending in **i** form the plural by adding **s** to the singular word.

alibi	alibis	rabbi	rabbis
safari	safaris	venturi	venturis

6. Nouns ending in **f, fe,** or **ff** usually form the plural by adding **s** to the singular form. A few, however, change the **f** or **fe** to **v** and add **es**.

roof	roofs	leaf	leaves
safe	safes	knife	knives
cuff	cuffs	calf	calves
sheriff	sheriffs	thief	thieves

7. Some nouns form the plural by a change in internal vowels.

foot	feet	man	men
woman	women	tooth	teeth
goose	geese		

8. A few nouns form the plural by a major change in spelling.

child	children	ox	oxen
louse	lice	mouse	mice
die	dice		

9. Some nouns have the same form in the plural as in the singular.

deer	moose	sheep
fish	corps	athletics

10. Certain foreign nouns retain their foreign plurals.

datum	data	alga	algae
phenomenon	phenomena	antenna	antennae
alumna	alumnae	alumnus	alumni

11. The plurals of compound nouns are formed as follows:

(a) add **s** to the most essential part of the compound.

sergeants-at-arms	sons-in-law
bills-of-fare	forget-me-nots

(b) compounds ending in **ful** form the plural by adding **s** to the end of the compound.

spoonfuls	pocketfuls

(c) if the compound contains no important word or words of equal importance, pluralize the last part of the compound.

toothbrushes	charwomen

12. Plurals of letters, symbols, and numbers are usually formed by adding an apostrophe and an **s**.

A's	B's	4's

When no ambiguity is likely, however, the plural of letters, symbols, and numbers may be formed simply by adding an **s**.

Rs	δs	8s

Possessives

1. When either a singular or plural noun does not end in **s**, form the possessive by adding an apostrophe and **s**.

child	child's	women	women's
church	church's	men	men's
teacher	teacher's	children	children's
lady	lady's	oxen	oxen's

2. If a singular noun ends in **s**, add an apostrophe and **s**.

class	class's	boss	boss's
James	James's	bus	bus's

3. If a plural noun ends in **s**, add only an apostrophe.

manufacturers	manufacturers'	potatoes	potatoes'
wives	wives'	studios	studios'

4. No apostrophe is used in the possessive personal pronouns.

he	his	it	its
your	yours	who	whose
her	hers	my	mine
their	theirs	we	ours

5. An apostrophe and **s** are used with indefinite pronouns.

anybody's	everybody's	someone's	somebody's

6. The possessive of either singular or plural compound words is formed by adding an apostrophe and **s** at the end of the compound.

commander in chief's	editors in chief's
brothers-in-law's	charwomen's

Verbs

1. The past tense or perfect tense of a verb is usually formed by adding **ed** to the present tense; add just a **d** when the present tense ends in **e**.

jump	jumped	gauge	gauged
shout	shouted	erase	erased
press	pressed	close	closed
gaze	gazed	praise	praised

2. The past or perfect tense of verbs ending in **y** is formed by changing the **y** to **i** and adding **ed**.

carry	carried	imply	implied
cry	cried	signify	signified

3. Distinctly different forms are used in the past and perfect tenses of irregular verbs.

take	took	taken	grow	grew	grown
ride	rode	ridden	tread	trod	trodden

4. The present participles of verbs are formed as follows:
(a) if the present tense ends in **e**, drop the **e** and add **ing**.

bake	baking	make	making
rake	raking	close	closing

Note: Rule 4 (a) does not apply if dropping the e causes confusion with another word.

dye	dyeing	shoe	shoeing
singe	singeing	tinge	tingeing

(b) if the present tense does not end in e, add **ing**.

sleep	sleeping	bang	banging
send	sending	drift	drifting

(c) if the verb ends in **ie**, change the **ie** to y and add **ing**.

belie	belying	vie	vying
die	dying	hie	hying

Adjectives

1. The comparative and superlative degrees of comparison in adjectives of one syllable are usually formed by adding **er** and **est** to the positive degree.

long	longer	longest	bright	brighter	brightest
warm	warmer	warmest	hot	hotter	hottest
cold	colder	coldest	short	shorter	shortest
sharp	sharper	sharpest	near	nearer	nearest

2. Adjectives of two or more syllables that end in y are usually compared by changing the **y** to **i** and adding **er** and **est**.

crazy	crazier	craziest	clammy	clammier	clammiest
dusty	dustier	dustiest	healthy	healthier	healthiest

Note: There are no rules to follow for making exceptions to Rules 1 and 2. Preference is given to the form of comparison that sounds best. It sounds better to say *bald, balder, baldest,* than to say *bald, more bald, most bald.* It also sounds better to say *eager, more eager, most eager,* than to say *eager, eagerer, eagerest.*

3. Adjectives of two or more syllables that do not end in y are usually compared by prefixing the words *more* and *most* to the simple form of the adjective.

famous	more famous	most famous
beautiful	more beautiful	most beautiful
harmful	more harmful	most harmful

4. Some adjectives are compared irregularly.

much	more	most
many	more	most
little	less	least
good	better	best
far	farther	farthest
far	further	furthest
bad	worse	worst
out	outer	outermost

5. When the simple form of an adjective expresses a quality to the highest possible degree, it is not compared.

unique	eternal
round	infinite
full	mortal
empty	final

Adverbs

1. Many adverbs are formed by adding **ly** to the adjective form. When the adjective ends in **y**, change the **y** to **i**, and add **ly**.

surprising	surprisingly	necessary	necessarily
extreme	extremely	funny	funnily
severe	severely	merry	merrily
usual	usually	fuzzy	fuzzily

2. To compare adverbs, prefix *more* (comparative) and *most* (superlative) to the word itself.

rapidly	more rapidly	most rapidly
strictly	more strictly	most strictly
swiftly	more swiftly	most swiftly
suddenly	more suddenly	most suddenly

The
ABC's
of
Punctuation

Improper use or omission of punctuation marks is the major reason why written messages are all too often misunderstood. Surprisingly, mastery of just a few simple principles will help you to punctuate properly.

When to Use the Period

Rule 1. The period is used to end a declarative sentence.
I shall come.
You will operate the motor controls.
Congress approved the new legislation on emission control.

Rule 2. The period is used to end an imperative sentence.
Close the window.
Signal the supporting troops immediately.
Proceed to the next checkpoint and wait there for further orders.

Rule 3. The period is used after an indirect question.
She asked if I would come.
They asked if we agreed with their conclusions.

Rule 4. The period is used after an abbreviation. (But see Rule 1 in the section on "When Not to Use the Period.")

Mr.	C.O.D.
Assn.	F.O.B.
Dr.	C.P.A.

Rule 5. The period is used after a number or letter in an outline.
 I. Features of this publication
   A. Football
   B. Basketball
   C. Soccer
     1. Tennis
     2. Baseball
     3. Swimming

Rule 6. The period is used in groups of three (called *ellipses*) to show:
(a) the omission of words within a quoted passage.

"It is the mark of an instructed mind to rest satisfied with that degree of precision ... the subject admits, and not to seek exactness where only an approximation ... is possible." *Aristotle*

(b) A pause, hesitation, or the like in dialogue and interrupted narrative.

She was shocked . . . continued screaming . . . . Then she ran out of the house.

Rule 7. The period is used in groups of four to indicate the omission of words at the end of a quoted passage.

"The congruent and harmonious fitting of parts in a sentence hath almost the fastning and force of knitting . . . . " *Ben Johnson*

Rule 8. The period is used after a nonsentence, for instance:
(a) a salutation: Good night.
(b) an answer to a question: Who am I? John.

When Not to Use the Period

Rule 1. The period is not used after the letters of an acronym (a word formed from the initial letters of other words) used to designate either national or international agencies or labor unions.

FCC	SEATO	AFL
UNESCO	FDA	CIO
NATO	OAS	IBEW

Rule 2. The period is not used after the call letters used to identify radio, television, or similar stations.

WARM	WRCA-TV
KLAC	KMPC-TV

Rule 3. The period is not used after ordinal numbers.

5th	Henry VIII
2nd	George III

Rule 4. The period is not used after the title of a composition.

The ABC's of Punctuation

Rule 5. The period is not used after either an exclamation mark or a question mark.

"Halt!" the guard shouted.
"What is your name?" he said.

When to Use the Comma

Rule 1. Use the comma to set off independent clauses (complete sentences) when they are joined by the coordinate conjunctions *and, but, or, nor, for, so,* and *yet.*

The descent looked like it would be easy, but ice under the snow made our footing precarious.
Baltimore is a major seaport, and it is rich in history.

Rule 2. Use the comma after an adverbial clause at the beginning of a sentence.

After he had completed his speech, the political candidate asked for questions from the audience.
From his perch atop the cliff, the eagle screeched his displeasure.

Rule 3. Use the comma after a participial phrase at the beginning of a sentence.

Knowing his colonel was angry, Captain Brown quickly left the room.

Rule 4. Use the comma after an infinitive phrase at the beginning of a sentence.

To be successful, you must work hard.

Rule 5. Use the comma to set off each word, phrase, or clause in a series of three or more.

Classical education stresses reading, writing, and arithmetic.
She opened the closet, took out a dress, and tried it on.
I write, I edit, and I teach.

Rule 6. Use the comma before *etc.* at the end of a series.

Meat, potatoes, fruit, etc. are common items in our diet.

Rule 7. Use the comma to set off a nonrestrictive adjective clause (one *not* needed to complete the meaning of a sentence) beginning with *who, which, whose,* and the like.

Paul Jones, who graduated from New York University, is a marketing consultant.
Mary Smith, whose father is a carpenter, is an excellent accountant.

Rule 8. Use the comma to set off a nonrestrictive phrase.

Bill Martin, winning the last round, won the golf tournament.

Rule 9. Use the comma to set off most parenthetical words, phrases, or clauses. (See Rule 14 under "When Not to Use the Comma.")

Moreover, the conclusion is not supported by sufficient data.
It was, in short, a disappointing performance.
There are, I think, sufficient reasons to reject the proposal.

Rule 10. Use the comma to set off nonrestrictive appositives, that is, two nouns, the second defining or identifying the first.

Shawn-Marie, our oldest daughter, is a lovely child.
George Washington, our first President, was a capable man.

Rule 11. Use the comma between coordinate adjectives of equal importance that modify the same noun.

Lovely, serene children marched in the procession.
Rugged, towering mountains filled the horizon.

Rule 12. Use the comma to set off words or phrases expressing contrast.

His inherent ability, not his formal schooling, made him successful.
She is a woman of sincere belief, not a hypocrite.

Rule 13. Use the comma to avoid an incorrect grouping of words.

Outside, the wind was howling.
After lunch, we returned to work.

Rule 14. Use the comma to separate duplicate words, *when and only when* the use of the comma clarifies the meaning.

The world that is, is the world in which we must live.
He who is truly humble, humble he will remain.

Rule 15. Use the comma to set off words in direct address.

We are happy to tell you, Miss Wilson, that you have won the talent contest.
Pick up the shovel, Henry.

Rule 16. Use the comma to set off geographical names and addresses.

Scranton, Pennsylvania, is my home.
Her address is 5 Elm Street, Danvers, Massachusetts 01923.

Rule 17. Use the comma to set off dates.

Tammy was born on January 27, 1969.
On November 11, 1918, World War I ended.

Rule 18. Use the comma to set off a *mild* expression of emotion.

Dear me, what shall I do?
He was, well, rather overbearing.

Rule 19. Use the comma to set off short direct quotations. (See also Rule 2 under "When to Use Double Quotations.")

The public relations representative asked, "What percentage of your employees contributed to the United Fund drive?"

Rule 20. Use the comma to show the inverted order of a person's name.

Doyle, John   Gouin, Rita

Rule 21. Use the comma to separate a declarative clause from an interrogative clause (confirmatory question) that immediately follows.

Tomorrow is a day off from work, isn't it?
We will get an increase in pay starting Monday, will we not?

Rule 22. Use the comma to separate a phrase from the rest of a sentence when the phrase is out of its natural order.

Like Churchill, Montgomery argued for invasion of the Balkans.
In spite of his many promises, he did not abstain from drinking.

Rule 23. Use the comma to indicate the omission of a word or words understood.

Nancy attended Marywood College; Pat, Pennsylvania State University; Bob, the University of Scranton.

Rule 24. Use the comma to set off a proper name when it is followed by an academic degree or honorary title and to separate two or more degrees or titles.

Joseph P. Elliott, B.S., M.A., P.E., consultant in electronics

Rule 25. Use the comma after the complimentary close in a letter.

Very truly yours,
Cordially,
As always,

Rule 26. Use the comma before *such as* and *especially*.

There are many different kinds of wood, such as birch, oak, and pine.
My wife enjoys reading, especially historical novels.

Rule 27. Use the comma after *yes* and *no*.

Yes, I am available for the job.
No, it cannot be as you say.

When Not to Use the Comma

Rule 1. The comma is not used to separate a subject and verb.

Right: Boys and girls danced on the stage.
Wrong: Boys and girls, danced on the stage.

Rule 2. The comma is not used to separate a verb and object.

Right: The government approved whatever money was needed by the army.
Wrong: The government approved, whatever money was needed by the army.

Rule 3. The comma is not used to join two complete sentences when *and, but, for, or,* or *nor* are not used between the sentences.

Right: The whistle sounded and the game started.
Wrong: The whistle sounded, the game started.
Alternate: When the whistle sounded, the game started.
Alternate: The whistle sounded; the game started.

Rule 4. The comma is not used to separate the parts of a compound verb.

Right: He writes and paints.
Wrong: He writes, and paints.

Rule 5. The comma is not used to separate a conjunction from the clause it introduces.

Right: He said he would serve, but I do not believe him.
Wrong: He said he would serve but, I do not believe him.

Rule 6. The comma is not used to separate very short independent clauses.

Right: He will win and you will lose.
Wrong: He will win, and you will lose.

Rule 7. The comma is not used to set off an adverb clause when it comes last in a sentence.

Right: We went home after the game was over.
Wrong: We went home, after the game was over.

Rule 8. The comma is not used to set off short introductory phrases.

Right: At three o'clock school ended.
Wrong: At three o'clock, school ended.

Rule 9. The comma is not used when *and* is used in a series of three or more items.

Right: The boys liked bowling and ice skating and swimming.
Wrong: The boys liked bowling, and ice skating, and swimming.

Rule 10. The comma is not used when only two words or phrases are used in a series.

Right: We enjoy movies and picnics.
Wrong: We enjoy movies, and picnics.

Rule 11. The comma is not used to set off a restrictive clause, that is, one essential to the meaning of the sentence.

Right: Most people who work will be eligible for Social Security benefits.
Wrong: Most people, who work, will be eligible for Social Security benefits.
Right: Any mathematics which does not have practical application should be omitted from most textbooks.
Wrong: Any mathematics, which does not have practical application, should be omitted from most textbooks.

Rule 12. The comma is not used to set off a restrictive phrase.

Right: The man living at 100 Orchard Street was injured in the accident.
Wrong: The man, living at 100 Orchard Street, was injured in the accident.

Rule 13. The comma is not used to set off a restrictive appositive.

Right: The composer Duke Ellington was honored.
Wrong: The composer, Duke Ellington, was honored.

Rule 14. The comma is not always used to set off such parenthetical expressions as *likewise*, *perhaps*, *too*, *also*, *at least*, and *indeed*. This is a matter of judgment.

When they too arrive, we will leave.
To make sure the indicated solution is indeed correct, rework the problem.

Rule 15. The comma is not used when an indirect quotation is employed.

He said that the work must be completed before we leave.

Rule 16. The comma is not used when a quotation contains either an exclamation point or a question mark.

"Do you want more ice cream?" she asked.
"We won the game!" they shouted.

Rule 17. The comma is not used when a quoted sentence is very short.

She screamed "Stop the car!"

Rule 18. The comma is not used when a quotation is merely a sentence fragment.

He sincerely believes that geometry is "a basic disciplinary study."

Handling the Semicolon

The semicolon is used to show a greater break in thought than the comma but less of a break than the period. Because its use tends to produce involved sentence patterns, use the semicolon sparingly.

Rule 1. Use the semicolon to separate two or more independent clauses or complete sentences *not* separated by a coordinate conjunction. (See Rule 1 under "When to Use the Comma.")

The football team practices daily; the band practices only twice each week.
The president did not like the proposed budget; he demanded major cutbacks in advertising expense; he suggested other drastic changes.

Rule 2. Use the semicolon between independent clauses joined by a coordinate conjunction if one or both clauses contain internal commas.

The policeman, a twenty-year veteran on the force, would not resign; nor would his accomplice, a rookie.
Shawn-Marie, our oldest daughter, likes to read; but Michaelanne, her sister, does not.

Rule 3. Use the semicolon between two independent clauses joined by a conjunctive adverb that connects parallel clauses but at the same time modifies within the clause.

He did not complete the prescribed studies; therefore, he did not graduate.
The plan of attack was executed poorly; consequently, the campaign failed.

Rule 4. Use the semicolon to group items with internal commas in a series.

Players cited for outstanding performance were Mary Smith, the pensive Lilly; George Pendleton, the audacious Mr. Williams; and Margaret Osborne, the enchanting Ruth.

Rule 5. Use the semicolon before such words as *for instance, that is, for example*, and *namely* when they introduce a second independent clause or complete sentence.

Automobiles are available in a wide variety of styles; for example, convertibles, sedans, and coupes.
Three persons were found guilty in traffic court; namely, Joseph Martin, George Mahoney, and Irene Dubowski.

Use of the Colon

The colon is used to indicate the strongest possible break within a sentence; it functions primarily to *introduce* remaining portions of the sentence.

Rule 1. Use the colon after the salutation of a business letter. (In a friendly letter, however, the comma may be used in place of the colon.)

Dear Mr. Jones:
Gentlemen:

Rule 2. Use the colon to introduce a list.

Please send me the following articles: scissors, comb, brush, and mirror. Arrange the items as follows: cover letter, membership card, warranty card, and instruction manual.

Notes: (a) When a list is in column form, capitalize the first letter of each item. An electronics technician must be proficient in the use of the following instruments:

1. Oscilloscope
2. Multimeter
3. Signal generators

(b) When a list is in sentence form, *do not* capitalize the first letter of each item.

An electronics technician must be proficient in the use of the following instruments: oscilloscope, multimeter, and signal generators.

Rule 3. Use the colon to introduce a formal quotation.

As children, we were all taught these familiar words: "I pledge allegiance to the flag . . . ."

Note: When the material following a colon is a formal quotation, it begins with a capital; otherwise, the colon may be followed by either a capital or a small letter.

Rule 4. Use the colon to introduce a "formal" question.

The question is: how much can we afford to spend?

Rule 5. Use the colon to introduce a subordinate clause that explains the first main clause.

His goal in life is clearly defined: he intends to become a professional musician.

Rule 6. Use the colon to introduce additional material after a word or phrase.

Warning: The Surgeon General has determined that cigarette smoking is dangerous to your health.

Rule 7. Use the colon before an appositive phrase or clause.

The store has this policy: no refund without a sales slip.

Rule 8. Use the colon to separate parts of titles, references, and numerals.

Title: Automotive Mechanics: Basic Principles and Practices.
Reference: Chapter 8: Section 10
Numerals: 8:20 A.M.

Rule 9. Use the colon in dialogue.

Ann: "Where were you last night?"
Mary: "I went to the movies."

When to Use the Question Mark

Rule 1. Use the question mark after a direct question.

Where are you going?
Are you looking in the correct file?

Note: (a) The question mark may be used after a declarative sentence.
You are going to win?
(b) Do not use a comma or period with the question mark.
Right: "Do you feel well?" he asked.
Wrong: "Do you feel well?," he asked.
Right: He asked, "Do you feel well?"
Wrong: He asked, "Do you feel well?."

Rule 2. Use the question mark after each separate part of a sentence containing more than one question.

What do you know about his family? his friends? his personal habits?

Note: When the question is not complete until the end of the sentence, place a single question mark at the end.
Will they play poker, bridge, or pinochle?

Rule 3. The question mark is used in various ways when only part of the sentence is a question. In such sentences the question is generally introduced by a comma, colon, semicolon, or dash.

I ask you again, where are we going?
Here is the problem: How can we best cross the river without boats?
The player was expelled from the game; however, do you think we should appeal that ruling?
I was told—did I hear correctly?—that you have resigned.

Rule 4. Use the question mark within parentheses to indicate uncertainty.

The book was written in 1960 (?) but did not become popular until 1970.

When To Use the Apostrophe

(See also the section on "Plurals of Nouns" in Section 2, *The ABC's of Spelling.*)

Rule 1. Use the apostrophe to form the possessive case of singular nouns.

a child's toy	John's home
a woman's coat	Lincoln's address
a robin's nest	the bride's gown

Exceptions:

Add only the apostrophe to form the possessive case of singular nouns ending in s when an added s makes pronunciation difficult.

Jones' automobile   Moses' tribe

Rule 2. Use only the apostrophe to form the possessive case of plural nouns when the plural ends in s.

five days' work	the Smiths' home
three girls' books	the bridesmaids' gowns

Rule 3. Use the apostrophe with s to form the possessive case of plural nouns which do not end in s.

children's toys	people's court
women's clothing	

Rule 4. Use the apostrophe to show omissions in words or numerals.

isn't (is not)   vintage of '53 (1953)

Rule 5. Use the apostrophe with an s to form the plurals of letters, symbols, and numbers.

A's   +'s   1980's

Note: Where no ambiguity is likely, the apostrophe may be omitted.

Bs   +s   1980s

When to Use the Exclamation Mark

Rule 1. Use the exclamation point after an emphatic word, phrase, clause, or sentence.

Hurrah!
What an upset!
Your accusation is incredible!
She called him a cad!

Rule 2. Use the exclamation point sparingly to add emphasis.

The time to act is now!

When to Use Double Quotation Marks

Rule 1. Use double quotation marks to enclose an uninterrupted direct quotation.

Patrick Henry said, "Give me liberty or give me death."

Note: Capitalize the first word of uninterrupted direct quotations.

Rule 2. Use double quotation marks to set off the quoted words of an interrupted quotation.

"Give me liberty," said Patrick Henry, "or give me death."

Note: Do not capitalize the first word in the second part of an interrupted quotation unless the second part starts a new sentence.

Rule 3. Use double quotation marks at the beginning of the first sentence and at the end of the last in a single quotation of several sentences.

The secretary said, "Please be patient. The director is at a staff meeting. He will see you in 20 minutes."

Rule 4. Use double quotation marks to enclose a quotation of several paragraphs. Place the double quotation marks at the beginning of each paragraph, but at the end of only the last paragraph. It is also proper to indent long quotations rather than use quotation marks.

Rule 5. Use double quotation marks, *but without a comma*, to enclose a short quotation or a quotation that is only a part of a sentence.

She screamed "Stop!" and fainted.
He referred to a humorous definition as a "daffynition."

Rule 6. Use closing double quotation marks *before* a question mark or exclamation point when it refers to the quoted material and *after* when it refers to the entire sentence.

Mr. Wilson asked, "When will the final report be ready?"
Did Mr. Wilson say, "The final report must be ready before the end of this month"?

Rule 7. Use double quotation marks around quoted dialogue and indent paragraphs to show each change of speaker.

"What type of work do you do?" John asked the girl.
"I teach in an elementary school," she replied.

Rule 8. Use double quotation marks to set off the title of any article, chapter title, short story, and the like in a printed publication.

Chapter: "Nonlinear Waveshaping" is a chapter in Doyle's *Pulse Fundamentals.*
Song: We all joined in singing "Auld Lang Syne."
Article: I read an article, "Blue-Collar Harvard," in this week's *Topics*.

Rule 9. Use double quotation marks to enclose the definition of a word.

The dictionary defines the word *precipitation* as meaning "a headlong rush or fall."

When to Use Single Quotation Marks

Rule 1. Use single quotation marks to enclose a quotation within a quotation.

The speaker said, "I keep telling myself, 'If others can learn mathematics, I, too, can do so.' "

When to Use Parentheses

Rule 1. Use parentheses to set off words, phrases, clauses, or sentences that provide explanation, translation, or comment.

His promotion (which will be announced soon) will come as no surprise to his co-workers.
A United States five-cent piece carries the motto "E Pluribus Unum" (in God we trust).
What (if you don't mind my asking) are your plans for the coming week?

Rule 2. Use parentheses to enclose letters, figures, references, and directions.

The purposes of the controls are as follows: (a) safety, (b) convenience, and (c) comfort.
The index (pages 318-325) will help you.
Here is the order of events: (1) breakfast, (2) lecture, (3) coffee break, (4) lecture, and (5) lunch.

Rule 3. Use parentheses to enclose a question mark which is intended to show uncertainty.

He is 50 (?) years old.

Rule 4. Use parentheses to enclose numbers that repeat spelled-out amounts.

There are fifty (50) states in the United States.

Notes: Use parentheses with other punctuation marks as follows:
(a) When parentheses set off material in a sentence, place the comma, semicolon, or period after the second (closing) parenthesis.

If my daughter wins the scholarship (we are still not sure), she will go abroad to continue her studies.
She had not graduated (we thought she had); therefore, she was not eligible for the prize.
Some people still believe former President Truman the best (but I am still a Kennedy fan).

(b) When parentheses enclose enumerations, the comma, semicolon, or colon may precede the first parenthesis.

He is not authorized to do the following: (1) issue company checks; (2) approve payment of bills exceeding $100; (3) directly purchase items costing more than $25.
He is an outstanding salesman because: (1) He does all work on schedule; he does not procrastinate. (2) He calls on all prospects in his territory; he does not avoid smaller companies. (3) He is always honest; he never cheats a customer.

(c) When parentheses are used to enclose a parenthetical element, and the question mark or exclamation point belongs to that element, place the punctuation inside the parenthesis; otherwise, outside.

When to Use the Dash

Rule 1. The dash may be used to indicate an abrupt change of thought in a sentence.

> The defendant—indeed, every one in the courtroom—breathlessly awaited the jury's verdict.

Rule 2. The dash may be used to set off a word or phrase repeated for emphasis.

> There was time for one play—one play only—before the game was over.

Rule 3. The dash may be used to indicate an afterthought or a summarizing thought added to the end of a sentence.

> The kit included wood, glue, paint—in fact, everything needed to make a model airplane.

Rule 4. The dash may be used to express an incomplete thought.

> Well, if that is my only choice—

Rule 5. The dash may be used to emphasize an appositive.

> She has only one interest—men.

Note: In general, the dash should be used sparingly.

Capitalization

When to Use Capital Letters

Rule 1. Capitalize the first word of every sentence (including quoted sentences).

We were nearing the end of our journey.
He said, "The show is over."

Rule 2. Capitalize single words or the first words of phrases used as sentences.

Should we strike? Yes!
She has decided to join us. All right?

Rule 3. Capitalize the first word of every line of poetry.

Grow old along with me!
The best is yet to be,
The last of life, for which the first was made.
                                       Browning, "Rabbi Ben Ezra"

Note: Some modern poets do not follow this rule. If you quote such a poet, follow his style on capitalization.

Rule 4. In general, capitalize the first word of a formal question or statement following a colon.

The policeman asked several questions: What is your name? How old are you? Where do you live?
The speaker offered this advice: For good health you must eat properly and get adequate rest.

Rule 5. Capitalize the first word and every important word in titles of books, articles, speeches, plays, and the like.

For Whom the Bell Tolls (book)
"How to Repair Plastics" (article)
Roosevelt's "Fireside Chat" (speech)
The Sound of Music (play)

Note: Capitals are not used for the unimportant words—i.e., articles, conjunctions, and short prepositions—in such titles.

Rule 6. Capitalize the first and last word in a letter salutation and the first word of a complimentary close.

My dear Julian:
Very truly yours,

Rule 7. Capitalize the first word of each item in an outline.

1. How to live to a ripe old age
   a. Proper diet
   b. Work habits
   c. Recreation
   d. Sleep

Rule 8. Capitalize all proper nouns and adjectives:
   (a) Persons, places, and their derivatives.

William J. Bryant	Baltimore	Pennsylvania
Mr. Smith	Baltimorean	Pennsylvanian

   (b) Tribes, nationalities, and languages.

Cherokee	Spanish
French	Indian

   (c) Geographic names, such as continents, countries, cities, states, rivers, lakes, and the like.

Europe	New York Harbor	Lake Huron
Italy	Blue Ridge Mountains	Maryland
Nile River	Niagara Falls	Shenandoah Valley

   (d) Definite regions, localities, and political divisions.

the Republic of China	Fifteenth Ward
Antarctica	United States
the Great Lakes	the Great Circle

   (e) Buildings, monuments, forts, streets, and so forth.

Empire State Building	Wyoming Avenue
Washington Monument	Statue of Liberty
Fort Apache	United Nations Building

   (f) Historic events, periods, and documents.

World War II	Alaskan Purchase
the Emancipation Proclamation	Yalta Agreement
Battle of Vicksburg	Bill of Rights

(g) Government units.

Department of Labor   United States Congress
Federal Aviation Agency   Federal Communications Commission

(h) Political parties, companies, institutions, and business and fraternal organizations.

University of Scranton   Chamber of Commerce
Democratic Party   United Mine Workers
General Motors Corporation   Rotarians

(i) Days of the week, months, and holidays.

Tuesday   Easter Sunday
February   Labor Day
Fourth of July   Yom Kippur

(j) Religious terms.

Heavenly Father   Allah   Talmud
Holy Ghost   Jehovah   Koran

(k) Titles of rank when they are joined to a person's name.

President Ford   King Hussein
Professor A.T. Powers   Prime Minister Wilson
Colonel William Cody   Secretary of State Kissinger

(l) Names of flags, emblems, and school colors.

Old Glory   the Orange and Black
the Silver Star   the Stars and Stripes

(m) Names of seasons, but only when personalized.

Wrong: Winter
Right: Winter's cold winds

(n) Compass points, but only when they refer to sections of the country.

the Northeast   The sun rises in the east.
the Southwest   Many immigrants moved westward.

(o) Names of stars and planets.

Milky Way   the North Star
Mars   Venus

Note: No capital is used with *earth*, *moon*, and *sun* unless personified.

Wrong: The atmosphere of earth permits human life.
Right: Earth's livable atmosphere

(p) Adjectives derived from proper nouns.

a Pullman car   Havannah cigar
English tweeds   Manila hemp

(q) School subjects, but only when listed as names of specific courses.

Wrong: Economics
Right: economics
Wrong: economics 101
Right: Economics 101

(r) Words that show family relationships when used with a person's name.

Uncle Tom   Grandfather Bill

Note: The words *mother* and *father* are not capitalized when they are preceded
by a pronoun. When referring to one's own parent, capitalization is optional.

(s) Trade names or registered trademarks.

Chromacolor   Underwriters' Laboratories, Inc.
Xerox   Quick Comp

How
To
Divide
Words

In reading typewritten materials, one frequently encounters words that are improperly divided. Errors of this type can be avoided by following the few easy-to-master guidelines given below.

Do Not Divide

1. At the end of the first line.
2. At the end of any line unless unusual length creates an unusually "rough" appearance in the right margin.
3. The last word in a paragraph.
4. The last word on a page.

When Word Division is Permitted

With the exceptions listed below, divide only between syllables.
Rule 1. Never separate a single-letter syllable from the rest of the word.

Right: agent	Wrong: a-gent
Right: elec-tion	Wrong: e-lection
Right: obe-dient	Wrong: o-bedient

Rule 2. Never divide a word either before or after a two-letter syllable.

Right: van-ity	Wrong: vani-ty
Right: effusion	Wrong: effu-sion
Right: or-ificial	Wrong: ori-ficial

Rule 3. Never divide words containing five or fewer letters; to do so violates either Rule 1 or Rule 2.

Right: alter	Wrong: al-ter
Right: begin	Wrong: be-gin
Right: odium	Wrong: odi-um

Rule 4. Although it should be obvious, never divide a word containing one syllable. When in doubt, consult the word listing in Section 1.

Right: retch	Wrong: ret-ch
Right: shunned	Wrong: shun-ned
Right: lapsed	Wrong: laps-ed

Rule 5. Where a final consonant is doubled and precedes a suffix, place the added consonant with the suffix when dividing a word. If, however, the root word ends in a double consonant, divide after the double consonant.

Right: slot-ted   Wrong: slott-ed
Right: bag-ging   Wrong: bagg-ing
Right: press-ing   Wrong: pres-sing
Right: roll-ing   Wrong: rol-ling

Working
with
Abbreviations

The rules presented here should be considered merely as guides for the use of abbreviations. There are no specific rules that apply to all situations.

When to Abbreviate

Rule 1. In business, use only those abbreviations that are common and easily recognized.

Mr.	Co.	Inc.	B.C.
Mrs.	Corp.	F.O.B.	A.D.

Rule 2. In *informal* writing, titles may be abbreviated when they appear with the full proper name following:

Prof. Robert A. Walker   Rev. Daniel C. Smith
Pres. Harry S. Truman   Gov. Thomas A. Dewey

Note: In *formal* writing, titles should be spelled out.

Rule 3. Academic titles may be abbreviated after a proper noun.

Ph.D.   LL.D.   D.D.

Rule 4. In letter writing, commonly used units of measurement that are accompanied by figures may be abbreviated.

192 lbs.   500 gals.   100 yds.

Rule 5. In *informal* writing, certain phrases may be abbreviated.

i.e. (that is)   e.g. (for example)
viz. (namely)   cf. (compare)
vs. (versus)   etc. (and so forth)

Note: Phrases such as the above should be spelled out in *formal* writing.

Rule 6. Government agencies may be abbreviated, usually without periods.

FBI   FHA   CAB

When Not to Abbreviate

Rule 1. Do not abbreviate titles when they precede the last name only.

Professor Walker   Reverend Smith
President Truman   Governor Dewey

Rule 2. Do not abbreviate a title when it appears in a sentence without a proper name.

The doctor listened to his patient.

Rule 3. Do not abbreviate words such as avenue, street, or the name of the state when they are used in addresses.

Wyoming Avenue   Broad Street   Alabama

Rule 4. In *formal* writing, do not abbreviate a title even when it appears with the full proper name following.

President Harry S. Truman   Governor Thomas A. Dewey

Compounding
Words

A compound is two or more words joined either with or without a hyphen. A compound frequently, but not always, expresses a thought more clearly than if the words were not joined. The purpose of the hyphen is to separate the parts of a compound for improved readability, understanding, and pronunciation.

Rule 1. Unless the compound aids readability, understanding, or pronunciation, do not join two or more words. This happens frequently when the words appear in regular order and the first word is used as an adjective to describe the second.

boarding school	night worker	market value
iron gate	real estate	back talk

Rule 2. Many nouns are joined simply because, through common usage, they have become one word.

northeast	torchbearer	football
serviceman	raincoat	sailboat

Rule 3. Verbs and adverbs are often combined to express either a literal or figurative thought.

holdup	runaround	downfall
overestimate	uproar	stronghold

Rule 4. Use a hyphen for most three-word combinations where the meaning might otherwise be confused.

mother-in-law	out-of-doors	free-for-all
ne'er-do-well	right-of-way	out-of-date

Rule 5. Use a hyphen to avoid doubling vowels or tripling consonants.

fire-escape	double-edged	doll-like
well-looking	cross-stitch	eagle-eyed

Rule 6. Write compound personal pronouns as one word.

myself	ourselves	yourselves
oneself	themselves	herself

Rule 7. When words are combined to form a unit modifier, they should be hyphenated when they precede the word modified, particularly if one element is a present or past participle.

long-term loan	easy-pay loan

ill-famed person   far-off space
part-time job   common-law marriage

Exceptions:

(a) When the meaning is clear and the use of a hyphen does not aid readability, the hyphen is *usually* avoided in a unit modifier that precedes a noun.

life insurance policy   income tax return
electric power plant   real estate tax

(b) When the first word of a unit modifier is an adverb ending in *ly*, omit the hyphen.

unusually short play   somberly discussed plan
happily involved children   realistically calculated cost

(c) When a unit modifier is a predicate adjective, omit the hyphen.

The peasants were debt ridden.
The singer is well known.

(d) If the first word of a unit modifier is a comparative or superlative, omit the hyphen.

higher priced food   lowest scoring team
most hated man   best acted play

(e) When a foreign phrase is used as a unit modifier, omit the hyphen.

prima facie evidence   bona fide agreement
ad hoc committee   ad lib performance

Rule 8. When a common word is omitted in all except the last term of a series of compounds, hyphenate as though the common word were not omitted.

low- and high-priced merchandise
short- and long-term loans

Rule 9. Hyphenate compound numbers from twenty-one to ninety-nine and all fractions.

thirty-three   eighty-six
four-fifths   nine-thousandths

Note: Hyphenate a compound adjective containing numbers.

a twelve-year-old boy
a forty-hour week

Rule 10. Use the hyphen to avoid ambiguity.

She re-covered the couch.
Along came six foot-soldiers.

Rule 11. Use a hyphen with the prefixes *ex*, *self*, and *all*.

ex-President Nixon
self-confidence
all-American

Rule 12. Use a hyphen with the suffix *elect*.

Governor-elect Jones

Rule 13. Hyphenate the prefix *semi* only with words beginning with *i* or with a proper noun.

semi-intellect
semi-American
semicolon